LIFE: A BOWL OF CHERRIES

AFC Bournemouth Who's Who

Leigh Edwards

A *SoccerData* Publication

Published in Great Britain by Tony Brown,
4 Adrian Close, Toton, Nottingham NG9 6FL.
Telephone 0115 973 6086.
E-mail soccer@innotts.co.uk
www.soccerdata.com

First published 2015

© Leigh Edwards 2015

All rights reserved. No part of this publication may be reproduced, stored in a retrieval system, or transmitted in any form, or by any means, electronic, mechanical, photocopying, recording or otherwise without the prior permission in writing of the Copyright holders, nor be otherwise circulated in any form or binding or cover other than in which it is published and without a similar condition including this condition being imposed on the subsequent publisher.

Cover design by Bob Budd.

The book is dedicated to the memory of the late Mick Cunningham,
a life-long supporter of AFC Bournemouth and former programme editor,
who took many of the photographs in this book

Printed and bound by 4Edge, Hockley, Essex
www.4edge.co.uk

ISBN: 978-1-905891-97-9

FOREWORD BY THE AUTHOR

Past achievements count for absolutely nothing as AFC Bournemouth strives to consolidate Premier League status. But Cherries' promotion to the top-flight for the first time presents the ideal opportunity to look back and recall all the players who have appeared for the club in the Football League since 1923.

Every player has an equal length profile in this Who's Who book. Football is a team game and no player ever won a match by himself. Club legends such as Ted MacDougall, Harry Redknapp, Sean O'Driscoll and Steve Fletcher have been well documented in the past but it is often the lesser known players who have more interesting life stories.

Football has always meant much more to me than just the 90 minute match. It is a microcosm of life itself. For many it is a religion and the magnificent stadia the new cathedrals. Through the course of researching this book I have interviewed several hundred former Cherries players and also spoken to surviving family of those sadly no longer with us.

I have been able to reunite many former team-mates who had lost contact with each other. It is often overlooked that footballers' wives also form friendships with each other. I reunited former Cherries winger John Meredith with his father who he hadn't seen for over 30 years. His son met his grandfather for the first time.

My interest in AFC Bournemouth began in February 1973 when I moved from Bristol to Christchurch with my parents and two brothers. Two fellow Twynham School old boys, Kevin Reeves and Jamie Redknapp, played for AFC Bournemouth and later became England internationals. Together with my brother Mike, a Cherries season ticket holder, I occasionally played football with another future Cherries player Billy Clark and his brother John. I saw all three players make their League debut for AFC Bournemouth. Not many can say that. All three are still involved with football.

Personal highlights of watching Cherries include the epic FA Cup third round win over holders Manchester United in 1984 and the promotion clincher at Fulham in 1987. That Third Division title triumph inspired me to write the official club history. I compiled another club history publication after Cherries' 2003 promotion play-off success and wrote several series in the 'Daily Echo' newspaper.

AFC Bournemouth's promotion to the top-flight in 2015 under Eddie Howe, and Callum Wilson's hat-trick in Cherries' first Premier League victory at West Ham, are recent landmark achievements to savour.

Leigh Edwards
October 2015

ACKNOWLEDGEMENTS

I would like to thank the many former Cherries players who have kindly assisted me with information relating to their football career and life, also the surviving family of those sadly no longer with us. Jim Creasy and Mike Davage helped with pre-war player details, Barry Hugman with post-war League career details and Alan Platt with non-League career details. Neil Fissler helped me to trace surviving family of pre-war players. Photographs were provided by the late Mick Cunningham, Max Fitzgerald and John Treleven. This is the second of my books on AFC Bournemouth published by Tony Brown.

ROD ADAMS

Versatile winger Rod Adams was a young member of Freddie Cox's squad at Dean Court. He impressed with Frome Town prior to joining Bournemouth in June 1966 and made his League debut in the 0-0 draw at home to Grimsby Town on the final day of the 1966-67 season. Scoring four times in 17 Third Division games for Cherries, he moved to Weymouth in February 1969 and was ever-present as they won the Southern League Cup in 1973. He joined Yeovil Town in July 1975 and was a Southern League Cup finalist again in 1976, then played for Chard Town. Now living in Lantzville, British Columbia, Canada.

MILES ADDISON

Former England U-21 defender Miles Addison featured in AFC Bournemouth's 2012-13 promotion campaign. He turned professional with Derby County in July 2007 and was given his Premier League debut in their 3-1 defeat at Blackburn ten months later. Capped by England U-21s against Greece in September 2009, he was sidelined by foot trouble, then had a loan spell with Barnsley prior to joining Cherries initially on loan in February 2012. His only goal in 34 League games clinched the following month's 1-1 draw at home to Carlisle. He was loaned to Rotherham, Scunthorpe and Blackpool before released in May 2015.

PAUL AIMSON

Experienced striker Paul Aimson briefly partnered Phil Boyer in AFC Bournemouth's attack. Initially with Manchester City, he joined York City in July 1964 and was top scorer in their 1964-65 promotion success. He had spells with Bury, Bradford City and Huddersfield prior to rejoining York for £11,000 in August 1969 and starred in their 1970-71 promotion campaign. Reunited with Boyer at Dean Court for £12,000 in March 1973, he scored twice in nine League games for Cherries before being sold to Colchester United for £8,000 in August 1973. He became a physical recreation officer and died in Christchurch in January 2008.

LIONEL AINSWORTH

Ex-England Youth winger Lionel Ainsworth had a loan spell at AFC Bournemouth at the start of the 2006-07 campaign. He turned professional with Derby County in September 2005 and made his League debut in their 1-0 win over Plymouth five months later. Loaned to Cherries in August 2006, he played seven League One games, making two starts, whilst at Dean Court. He then had a loan spell at Wycombe Wanderers as a replacement for Kevin Betsy before joining Hereford United in August 2007, then Watford, Huddersfield Town, Shrewsbury Town and Rotherham United. He joined Motherwell initially on loan in August 2013.

PETER AITKEN

Former Welsh U-23 international Peter Aitken's solitary League appearance for AFC Bournemouth was in the 5-1 defeat at Newport County in November 1982. Signing professional for Bristol Rovers in July 1972, he featured in their 1973-74 promotion campaign and was ever-present in 1974-75. He joined Bristol City in November 1980 but was released after the 'Ashton Gate Eight' crisis and had spells with York City and Hong Kong side Bulova before briefly joining Cherries on trial. Later playing for Trowbridge Town, he was assistant-manager at Bath City and Cheltenham Town and is now Bristol Rovers' community officer.

WALLY AKERS

Teenage winger Wally Akers appeared for Bournemouth during the 1935-36 season. He was an amateur with Preston before turning professional with Wolves in July 1934. Moving to Cherries in May 1935, he netted four goals in 15 League games prior to joining Newport County in August 1936. He then had spells with Chelsea and Mansfield Town, moving to Gillingham in July 1946. Starring as they won the Southern League and Cup 'double' in 1946-47, he joined Corby Town in July 1948 and became player-boss, plotting two United Counties League title triumphs, then managed Kettering Town. He died in Kettering in March 1975.

DENIS ALLEN

Inside-forward Denis Allen was an experienced member of Cherries' 1970-71 promotion squad. From a notable football family with QPR links, he turned professional with Charlton Athletic in August 1956 and scored on his League debut. He moved to Reading in June 1961 and was leading marksman four times before following John Sainty to Dean Court in August 1970. Scoring three goals in 17 Fourth Division games for Cherries, he had a spell in Belgian soccer with Ostend before managing Cheltenham Town, then scouted for several clubs and England until his death in July 1995. His son Martin now manages Barnet.

IAN ALLEN

Scottish winger Ian Allen contested a first-team slot with Peter Harrison and Roy Littlejohn while at Dean Court. He impressed with Beith Juniors prior to joining QPR in September 1952 and made his League debut in their 1-0 victory at Bournemouth in April 1954. Jack Bruton signed him three months later and he scored 11 times in 52 League games for Cherries before moving to Salisbury with Peter Rushworth in July 1957, starring in their 1957-58 Western League title triumph. Later a joiner with GW Chilcott builders, Kandic Design & Construction, the Ambassador Hotel and Prowting Homes, he settled in West Parley.

KENNY ALLEN

Giant goalkeeper Kenny Allen was ever-present for AFC Bournemouth in 1978-79. He had spells with Tow Law, Hartlepool, Hellenic, West Brom and Workington before joining Bath City in September 1973, starring in their 1977-78 Southern League title triumph. Moving to Dean Court for £7,000 in August 1978, he contested a first-team slot with Ian Leigh during Cherries' 1981-82 promotion campaign and made 152 League appearances. He reunited with David Webb at Torquay United in March 1984, then played for Swindon Town, Torquay again, Bath City and Salisbury. Now a driver for a hospital in Newton Abbot.

KEVIN ALLEN

Young left-back Kevin Allen's solitary League appearance for AFC Bournemouth was in the 2-0 defeat at Huddersfield Town in March 1980. A former Cherries apprentice, he turned professional in August 1979 and understudied Phil Ferns while at Dean Court. He moved with Brian Benjafield to Oxford City in July 1980, where Harry Redknapp was assisting Bobby Moore, before reuniting with several former Cherries, including Brian Chambers and John Evanson, at Poole Town in August 1981. Moving to Newport (IW) in June 1984, he settled back on the Isle of Wight, running Appley Ltd plastic windows in Wootton Bridge.

RYAN ALLSOP

Former England Youth goalkeeper Ryan Allsop helped AFC Bournemouth to clinch promotion in 2012-13, appearing in the final ten matches of that campaign. Initially with West Brom, he joined Millwall in May 2011 and had a spell with Icelandic side Hottur before joining Leyton Orient in July 2012. He was given his League debut in their 1-0 defeat at Crawley Town two months later. Moving to Dean Court in January 2013, he made 22 League appearances before displaced by Lee Camp during a stop-start two years which featured a bout of glandular fever and spending the first half the 2014-15 season on loan to Coventry City.

TOMMY ANDERSON

Fast inside-right Tommy Anderson briefly played for Cherries during the 1958-59 season. A former Scottish Schoolboy international, he had spells with Hearts, Queen of the South and Watford prior to joining Bournemouth in June 1958. His solitary goal in five League games came in the 2-0 win over Norwich City three months later and he joined QPR in November 1958. He played for Torquay United, Stockport County, Doncaster Rovers, Wrexham, Barrow, Watford again, Orient and Limerick before settling in Australia where he became a Sydney soccer reporter and later hosted his own radio programme.

DARREN ANDERTON

Ex-England international winger Darren Anderton had a spell as AFC Bournemouth's captain. Initially with Portsmouth, he was 'Player of the Year' and scored as they took eventual winners Liverpool to an FA Cup semi-final replay in 1991-92. He moved to Spurs for £1,750,000 in June 1992 and overcame a series of injury problems to feature in their 1999 League Cup final triumph. Capped 30 times, 'Sicknote' joined Birmingham in August 2004 and moved via Wolves to Cherries in September 2006. He scored 12 goals in 66 League games, including the late winner on his farewell appearance against Chester in December 2008.

IAN ANDREWS

Ex-England Youth goalkeeper Ian Andrews starred in AFC Bournemouth's 1994-95 relegation escape. Signing professional for Leicester City in December 1982, he was ever-present in the top-flight in 1986-87 and joined Celtic for £300,000 in July 1988. He moved to Southampton for £200,000 in December 1989 and was Mel Machin's first signing for Cherries at £15,000 in September 1994. Playing 64 League games before leaving to care for his dying wife, he rejoined Leicester in March 1997 and became physio at their Academy. He has since been physio at Team Bath and Exeter City, also with a practice in Nottingham.

STEV ANGUS

Young central defender Stev Angus had a loan spell at AFC Bournemouth during the 2000-01 campaign. A former West Ham trainee, he helped them win the FA Youth Cup shortly before turning professional in July 1999. He was loaned to Cherries in August 2000 and made his League debut in that month's 1-1 draw at Bristol Rovers, playing nine Second Division games overall whilst at Dean Court. Moving to Cambridge United in July 2001, he had loan spells at Hull City and Scunthorpe United, then played for Grays Athletic, Torquay United, Barnet, Fisher Athletic and Bishop's Stortford. Now a coach at Brooke House College.

JOHN ARCHER

Inside-left John Archer featured prominently in Cherries' 1961-62 promotion near-miss. Initially with Port Vale, 'Dan' moved to Bournemouth in July 1961 and helped beat Newcastle United in the 1963-64 League Cup third round, scoring 37 goals in 139 League games before being sold to Crewe Alexandra for £3,000 in September 1966. He was exchanged for Huddersfield Town's Kevin McHale in January 1968 and moved to Chesterfield for £1,000 in May 1969, skippering their 1969-70 Fourth Division title triumph. Later Sandbach Ramblers' player-manager, he was greenkeeper of a golf course near Sandbach until retirement.

DAVID ARMSTRONG

Ex-England international midfielder David Armstrong played for AFC Bournemouth during the 1987-88 season. Starting with Middlesbrough, he was a key figure in their 1973-74 Second Division title triumph and joined Southampton for £600,000 in August 1981. He was ever-present 'Player of the Year' as Saints were League Championship runners-up in 1983-84 and joined newly promoted Cherries in July 1987. Scoring twice in nine League games until an ankle injury ended his career, he became the club's community officer and later worked in various other commercial and community departments before office supplies.

JIMMY ARMSTRONG

Right-back Jimmy Armstrong understudied Jack Hayward while at Bournemouth. Initially with hometown Chester-le-Street, he joined Barnsley in April 1921 and featured as they missed promotion to the top-flight on goal average in 1921-22. He moved to Dean Court in June 1925, making 17 League appearances for Cherries prior to joining Accrington Stanley in July 1927. Twice ever-present, making 150 consecutive appearances, he was their player-coach before moving to Stalybridge Celtic in August 1934. He settled in Barnsley, working as a commissionaire at a large works, also scouting for the Tykes until his death.

JOE ARMSTRONG

Inside-left Joe Armstrong featured in Bournemouth's 1923-24 Football League debut campaign. He played for Scotswood before joining Portsmouth in December 1913, helping to win the Southern League title in 1919-20. Following Bob Brown to Sheffield Wednesday with Ernie Thompson in May 1921, he joined Norwich City in exchange for George Gray six months later. He moved to Dean Court in June 1923 and made his debut in Cherries' first home League match against Swindon. Scoring twice in 29 Third Division (South) games, he left in May 1924 and worked for Portsmouth Trams. He died in Cosham in May 1966.

JOHN ARNOTT

Versatile right-half John Arnott was an early Freddie Cox signing for Bournemouth. Turning professional with West Ham in July 1954, he moved to Shrewsbury Town in August 1955. He joined Cherries in July 1956 and helped to qualify for the newly-formed Third Division in 1958, scoring 21 times in 173 League outings prior to reuniting with Cox at Gillingham in August 1962. Starring in their 1963-64 Fourth Division title triumph, he moved to Dover in June 1969, then coached Maidstone United. He still lives in Gillingham and spent 23 years as a PE teacher at Kingsdale Secondary School in Dulwich until retiring in July 1998.

HARRY ARTER

Republic of Ireland international midfielder Harry Arter was an important figure in AFC Bournemouth's 2014-15 Championship title triumph. The brother-in-law of England international Scott Parker, he began with Charlton Athletic and was loaned to Staines Town and Welling United before joining Woking in June 2009. He moved to Cherries in June 2010 and made his League debut in the 1-0 defeat at Charlton two months later. Returning from a loan spell at Carlisle United, he helped Cherries to win promotion in 2012-13 and made his full international debut in Republic of Ireland's 0-0 draw against England in June 2015.

JAMIE ASHDOWN

Big goalkeeper Jamie Ashdown had a loan spell at AFC Bournemouth at the start of the 2002-03 promotion campaign. He turned professional with Reading in November 1999 and made his League debut in their 5-0 win over Oldham ten months later. He was loaned to Cherries in August 2002, playing in the 1-1 draw with Oxford United and 1-0 win at Macclesfield. Also loaned to Rushden & Diamonds, he joined Portsmouth in July 2004 and was a non-playing substitute in the 2008 and 2010 FA Cup finals. He moved to Leeds United in July 2012, then Crawley Town and Oxford United. Now runs online business Trusted Pro Supplements.

JOE ASHWORTH

Tall, versatile left-half Joe Ashworth played alongside Roy Gater and Jimmy White whilst at Dean Court. Initially with Bradford PA, he joined York City in May 1962 and helped win promotion in 1964-65. He moved to Bournemouth in June 1965 and scored twice in 60 Third Division games before joining Southend United in July 1967. Moving to Rochdale in July 1968, he starred in their 1968-69 promotion success and 1970-71 FA Cup run. He later played for Chester and Stockport County, then spent 23 years as a prison officer at Hull, Strangeways and New Hall until retirement. Settling in Rochdale, he died in May 2002.

PHIL ASHWORTH

Much-travelled striker Phil Ashworth was a member of John Benson's squad at Dean Court. Starting with Nelson, he moved via Blackburn Rovers to AFC Bournemouth for £2,000 in September 1975 and scored twice in 31 Fourth Division games prior to joining Workington in July 1976. He later played for Southport and Rochdale, then featured in Portsmouth's 1979-80 promotion campaign. Later with Scunthorpe United, Cambridge City, Rossendale, Clitheroe, Bottesford and Brigg, he was Burnley's commercial manager. Now living in Brigg, he is a driver for a stationery business. His daughter married Hull City star Andy Dawson.

WARREN ASPINALL

Ex-England Youth midfielder Warren Aspinall had two spells with AFC Bournemouth. Initially with Wigan Athletic, he joined Everton for £150,000 in May 1986, then Aston Villa for £300,000 in February 1987. He was top scorer in their 1987-88 promotion success and moved to Portsmouth for £315,000 in August 1988. Loaned to Cherries in August 1993, he returned for £20,000 four months later and scored nine goals in 33 League games before joining Carlisle United in March 1995. He later played for Brentford, Colchester United and Brighton until an ankle injury ended his career, since becoming a warehouseman.

TREVOR AYLOTT

Striker Trevor Aylott was an important figure in Cherries' 1986-87 Third Division title triumph. Starting with Chelsea, he joined Barnsley for £50,000 in November 1979 and starred in their 1980-81 promotion success. He played for Millwall and Luton Town, then joined Crystal Palace in July 1984 and was leading scorer in 1984-85. Moving to Dean Court for £15,000 in August 1986, he also featured in Cherries' 1988-89 FA Cup run and scored 27 times in 147 League games prior to joining Birmingham City for £40,000 in October 1990. Later with Oxford United, Gillingham and Bromley, he is now a London black cab driver.

DANNY BAILEY

Midfielder Danny Bailey was a Cherries apprentice who made his League debut as a 16 year-old in the 1-0 defeat at Hereford in November 1980. Also featuring in the 2-0 reverse at Lincoln the following month, he had spells with Dagenham and Walthamstow before reuniting with David Webb at Torquay in March 1984. He played for Grays and Wealdstone, then featured in Exeter's 1989-90 Fourth Division title campaign and later appeared for Reading, Exeter again, Slough, Telford, Forest Green Rovers, Welling United, Grays again, Aylesbury and Waltham Forest. He runs Bailey Elite Football Academy with his brother Trevor.

JOHN BAILEY

Tigerish midfielder John Bailey scored AFC Bournemouth's goal in the 1998 Auto Windscreens Shield final at Wembley. He appeared for Croydon and Dagenham, then joined Enfield in July 1992 and was 'Player of the Tear' in 1992-93, helping win the Isthmian League title and reach the FA Cup third round in 1994-95. Mel Machin paid £40,000 for him in July 1995 and he netted six goals in 148 Second Division games for Cherries until a back injury ended his League career in October 2000. He then had spells with Brockenhurst, Lymington & New Milton and Lymington Town while working as a painter and decorator.

ALEX BAIN

Scottish centre-forward Alex Bain featured in Cherries' 1961-62 promotion near-miss. He impressed with Cockenzie Star prior to joining Motherwell in August 1954 and scored in the 1955 Scottish League Cup final. Moving to Huddersfield Town in August 1957, he joined Chesterfield in February 1960 and had a spell with Falkirk before reuniting with Bill McGarry at Bournemouth in August 1961. He netted four goals in eight Third Division outings while at Dean Court prior to joining Poole Town in July 1962. Later rejoining Falkirk, he was a parks maintenance man for Grangemouth Council and died in November 2014.

KIERON BAKER

Popular goalkeeper Kieron Baker gave AFC Bournemouth loyal service over 11 years. A former Fulham amateur, he turned professional with Cherries in July 1967 and made his League debut in place of Roger Jones in the 3-0 defeat at Orient in November 1969. He was loaned to Brentford before becoming first-choice keeper in 1973-74, making 217 League appearances while at Dean Court prior to joining Ipswich Town for £20,000 in August 1978. Later playing for Phoenix Fire, Oxford City, Weymouth and Yeovil Town, he has settled near Ringwood and installs fibre optic cabling for communication systems.

STEVE BAKER

Versatile right-back Steve Baker briefly played for Cherries at the start of the 1991-92 season. Signing professional for Southampton in December 1979, he helped them finish League Championship runners-up in 1983-84 and reach two Cup semi-finals before being sold to Leyton Orient for £50,000 in March 1988. He joined AFC Bournemouth in August 1991 and made six League appearances prior to joining Aldershot in December 1991, later playing for Farnborough Town and Basingstoke Town. He has since coached at Saints' Academy and worked as an analyst for the PA, working as a stevedore at Southampton Docks.

JOHN BARCLAY

Scottish centre-forward John Barclay understudied Johnny Mackenzie in Cherries' 1947-48 promotion near-miss. 'Mitch' was a prolific goalscorer for Haddington Athletic either side of the Second World War and joined Bournemouth in December 1947, scoring on his League debut in the 2-0 Boxing Day win at Southend United. He also featured in the return fixture the following day and netted twice in five Third Division (South) games overall for Cherries prior to joining Trowbridge Town in August 1949. Later playing for their Western League rivals Chippenham United, he died in Surrey in September 1996.

STUART BARFOOT

Young full-back Stuart Barfoot briefly played for AFC Bournemouth during the 1994-95 campaign. A former trainee at Dean Court, he turned professional in July 1994 and made his first-team debut two months later in Cherries' 1-0 defeat at Chelsea in the League Cup second round first-leg. He appeared as a substitute in consecutive Second Division matches at Hull City and Shrewsbury Town, both lost in early October, then was loaned to Dorchester Town before joining Trowbridge Town in April 1995. Later playing for Bashley and Andover, he settled in Southampton and became a fabricator for Mitsui Badcock.

LEE BARNARD

Ex-England Youth striker Lee Barnard appeared on loan during AFC Bournemouth's 2012-13 promotion campaign. Starting with Spurs, he had limited top-flight opportunities and was loaned to several clubs before joining Southend United in January 2008. He was top scorer in three successive seasons, moving to Southampton in January 2010 and partnering Rickie Lambert as they won promotion in two consecutive years. Loaned to Cherries in August 2012, he scored on his debut to clinch a 1-1 draw at Portsmouth, netting four goals in 15 League games overall. He returned to Southend initially on loan in January 2014.

BOBBY BARNES

Ex-England Youth winger Bobby Barnes was once AFC Bournemouth's most expensive signing. Initially with West Ham, he gained top-flight experience and joined Aldershot in March 1986. He starred in their 1986-87 promotion success and moved to Swindon Town in October 1987. Joining Cherries for a then record £110,000 in March 1989, he made 14 League appearances before being sold to Northampton Town for £70,000 in October 1989, then played for Peterborough United, Partick Thistle, Kettering Town and in Hong Kong. He was a consultant with Friends Provident and is now assistant chief executive of the PFA.

ADAM BARRETT

Experienced central defender Adam Barrett played for AFC Bournemouth during the 2011-12 season. A former Leyton Orient trainee, he joined Plymouth Argyle in January 1999, then had spells with Mansfield and Bristol Rovers before joining Southend United in July 2004. He helped win promotion in 2004-05 and the League One title in 2005-06. Moving via Crystal Palace to Cherries in July 2011, he scored once in 21 League outings, joining Gillingham in August 2012, He skippered their 2012-13 League Two title triumph and was loaned to AFC Wimbledon before rejoining Southend in January 2015, helping clinch promotion.

BILLY BARROW

Former Welsh Schoolboy winger Billy Barrow scored as Bournemouth hammered Walthamstow Avenue 8-1 in the 1935-36 FA Cup first round replay. Starting with Clapton Orient, he had a spell with Margate before moving to Southend United in February 1934, making his League debut in that month's 4-1 win at Bournemouth. He became one of Bob Crompton's earliest signings for Cherries in June 1935, scoring four goals in 26 League games prior to joining Wrexham in May 1936. Later with Barry Town, he served in the RAF, then ran a ship stores with his brother in his native Cardiff until 1981. He died in September 2000.

PAT BARRY

Experienced left-back Pat Barry contested a first-team slot with Ian Drummond. He began with hometown Southampton and served in the RAF during the Second World War. After a spell with Hyde United, he joined Blackburn Rovers in May 1948 and followed Jack Bruton to Bournemouth in May 1950. He was given his League debut in the 5-0 win over Leyton Orient four months later and played four Third Division (South) games, joining Harry Lowe's Yeovil Town in July 1952. The son-in-law of former Manchester United star Teddy Partridge, he worked for Ford Motors in Southampton and died in November 1994.

MARVIN BARTLEY

Hard-tackling midfielder Marvin Bartley also played in central defence during AFC Bournemouth's 2009-10 promotion campaign. Previously with Burnham, Hayes, Didcot Town and Hampton & Richmond Borough, he moved to Dean Court in July 2007 and was given his League debut in Cherries' 3-1 defeat at Tranmere Rovers five months later. He helped to qualify for the League One play-offs in 2010-11, scoring three goals in 113 League outings before sold to Burnley for £310,000 in January 2011. Moving to Leyton Orient initially on loan in August 2013, he helped them qualify for the League One play-offs in 2013-14.

FRANK BARTON

Ex-England Youth midfielder Frank Barton had two spells at AFC Bournemouth. Starting with Scunthorpe United, he joined Carlisle United in January 1968 and scored in both legs of the 1969-70 League Cup semi-final. He played for Blackpool and Grimsby Town before moving to Dean Court for £6,000 in June 1976. Leading marksman in 1976-77, he joined Hereford United in January 1978 but returned to Cherries for £8,000 just eight months later and netted 15 goals in 88 League games overall before joining Seattle Sounders in March 1979. He has settled in the United States, working for a car company near Seattle.

VINCE BARTRAM

Goalkeeper Vince Bartram was ever-present for AFC Bournemouth in 1991-92. Signing professional for Wolves in August 1985, he was loaned to several clubs prior to joining Cherries for £65,000 in July 1991. He made 132 League appearances while at Dean Court before sold to Arsenal for £400,000 in August 1994, gaining top-flight experience as David Seaman's understudy. Reuniting with Tony Pulis at Gillingham in March 1998, he helped win promotion in 1999-2000 but his career was ended by a wrist injury in February 2004. Later a summariser for BBC Radio Kent, he is now goalkeeping coach at Southampton's Academy.

MATHIEU BAUDRY

French defender Mathieu Baudry briefly featured as AFC Bournemouth qualified for the League One play-offs in 2010-11. Starting with the Le Havre Academy, where his father was a coach, he played for Troyes before moving to Dean Court in July 2010. He was given his League debut in Cherries' 2-0 defeat at Exeter City in March 2011 and his solitary goal in ten League games came in the following month's 2-1 victory at home to Bristol Rovers. He was loaned to Dagenham & Redbridge prior to joining Leyton Orient in July 2012 and appeared in the 2014 League One play-off final when they lost on penalties to Rotherham United.

DAVID BAYNHAM

Welsh full-back David Baynham provided cover for Jack Hayward and Jimmy Blair whilst at Dean Court. Previously playing in the Football League with hometown Aberdare, he joined Bournemouth in July 1927 and was given his debut in the 2-2 draw at home to Luton two months later. He made seven Third Division (South) appearances for Cherries, including a 4-3 win over Bristol Rovers, before moving to Yeovil & Petters in July 1928. He joined Scunthorpe United in July 1929 and starred in their 1929-30 FA Cup run. Settling in Scunthorpe, he was employed at the steelworks and died in nearby Crowle in September 1974.

PETER BEADLE

Much-travelled striker Peter Beadle had a loan spell at AFC Bournemouth during the 1992-93 campaign. Initially with Gillingham, he was sold to Spurs for £300,000 in June 1992 and moved to Dean Court on loan in March 1993, netting twice in nine League outings for Cherries. He joined Watford in September 1994, moving to Bristol Rovers in November 1995 where he was top scorer in 1996-97. Later playing for Port Vale, Notts County, Bristol City, Brentford, Barnet and Team Bath, he managed Taunton, Newport County and Clevedon, then was Hereford United's director of youth and manager of the new Hereford FC.

RUSSELL BEARDSMORE

Versatile former England U-21 midfielder Russell Beardsmore captained AFC Bournemouth in the 1998 Auto Windscreens Shield final. Signing professional for Manchester United in September 1986, he featured in their triumphant 1990-91 ECWC campaign and was loaned to Blackburn Rovers before joining Cherries in June 1993. He scored four times in 178 Second Division games until a back injury curtailed his career in December 1999 and had a testimonial match against Southampton in 2000. Later assistant community officer at Bolton Wanderers, he has since been a coach in AFC Bournemouth's Community Sports Trust.

JOHN BECK

Midfielder John Beck was an experienced figure in AFC Bournemouth's 1984 Associate Members Cup final triumph. Initially with QPR, he moved via Coventry City to Fulham for £80,000 in October 1978 and joined Cherries in February 1983 after a loan spell. He became captain and netted 13 goals in 137 League games before moving to Cambridge United in July 1986. Appointed manager in January 1990, he plotted their meteoric rise, then managed Preston, Lincoln, Barrow and Cambridge again. He assisted Steve Fallon at Histon, then managed Kettering and has since worked for the Football Association in coach education.

BRIAN BEDFORD

Centre-forward Brian Bedford scored Cherries' goal against Manchester United in the 1956-57 FA Cup sixth round. Signing professional for Reading in April 1954, he moved via Southampton to Bournemouth in August 1956 and scored 32 times in 75 League outings prior to joining QPR in July 1959. He was leading marksman in each of his six seasons at Loftus Road. Moving to Scunthorpe United in September 1965, he was top scorer in 1965-66, then played for Brentford, Atlanta Chiefs and Bexley United. Later coaching tennis for the ILEA in Barnes, he became QPR's clerk of works and now lives in Cardiff in retirement.

ASMIR BEGOVIC

Giant goalkeeper Asmir Begovic had a loan spell at AFC Bournemouth during the 2007-08 campaign. He began with Portsmouth but was third choice behind David James and Jamie Ashdown. He made his League debut on loan to Macclesfield Town and was loaned to Cherries in August 2007. Playing in the opening eight League games, he lost his place after a series of errors and rejoined Harry Redknapp's Pompey. He appeared in the top-flight and was loaned to Yeovil Town and Ipswich Town before joining Stoke City for £3,250,000 in February 2010. The Bosnia & Herzogovina international was ever-present in 2012-13.

GEORGE BELLIS

Strong-tackling left-back George Bellis was ever-present for Cherries in 1935-36. Born in India, where his father served in the Royal Engineers, he grew up on Merseyside and played for Southport and Wrexham before joining Wolves in June 1929. He helped clinch the Second Division title in 1931-32 and moved to Burnley in December 1932. Starring as they reached the FA Cup sixth round in 1932-33, he joined Bournemouth in July 1935 and made 56 League appearances, moving to Wellington Town in July 1937. Settling in Liverpool, he spent 27 years with Napiers (English Electric) until his death in January 1969.

BRIAN BENJAFIELD

Teenage midfielder Brian Benjafield briefly played for AFC Bournemouth during the 1978-79 campaign. Signing professional for Cherries in January 1979, he featured in the 2-1 defeat at Rochdale three months later as well as the 2-0 defeat by Barnsley. He joined Oxford City with Kevin Allen in July 1980, where Harry Redknapp was assisting Bobby Moore, then moved via Poole Town to Weymouth in July 1982 and starred in their 1982-83 FA Cup run. Reunited with Geoff Butler at Salisbury, he played for Poole again and Swanage T&H, working for Legal & General, becoming Dorchester Town's commercial manager.

DAVE BENNETT

Ex-England Schoolboy winger Dave Bennett featured in Cherries' 1961-62 promotion near-miss. Starting with Arsenal, helping to win the SE Counties League title in 1955-56, he moved via Portsmouth to Dean Court in December 1960 and made his League debut in Bournemouth's 3-1 defeat at Bradford City two months later. He scored twice in 12 Third Division games as Billy Coxon's understudy prior to joining Guildford City in July 1962, helping to win the Southern League Cup in 1963. Later at Cambridge United, Weymouth and Salisbury, he was a probation officer at Portland and died in Weymouth in December 2009.

KEN BENNETT

Inside-forward Ken Bennett helped Cherries finish third in the Third Division (South) in 1948-49. Initially a junior at Spurs with his elder brother Les, he moved to Southend United in June 1946 and scored on his League debut in their 5-1 victory at Norwich City five months later. He joined Bournemouth in June 1948 and netted once in 19 League games before moving to Guildford City in June 1949, then had spells with Brighton, Crystal Palace, Tonbridge, Headington United (now Oxford United), Plessey and Clacton Town. Later a storeman for Gestetner and a grocer in Walthamstow, he died in Rochford in December 1994.

JOHN BENSON

Versatile defender John Benson had two spells with AFC Bournemouth. Previously with Manchester City and Torquay United, skippering promotion in 1965-66, he reunited with John Bond at Dean Court for £12,000 in October 1970 and helped clinch promotion. Following Bond to Norwich City in December 1973, he rejoined Cherries as player-boss in January 1975, making 150 League appearances overall before resigning in January 1979. He was coach/manager at Manchester City, Burnley, Norwich, Al-Nasr and Wigan Athletic. Assisting Steve Bruce at Birmingham, Wigan and Sunderland, he died in October 2010.

NARADA BERNARD

Versatile full-back Narada Bernard featured in AFC Bournemouth's 2002-03 promotion campaign. The son of a former Bristol rugby union player, he was named after singer Narada Michael Walden. Initially a Spurs trainee, he joined Arsenal in July 1999 and moved to Cherries in July 2000. He played 29 League games before joining Woking in August 2003, then had a spell with Torquay United. Capped by Jamaica against Republic of Ireland in June 2004, he later appeared for Welling, Farnborough, Dover, Yeading, Fisher, Rushden & Diamonds, Weymouth, Maidenhead United, Bishop's Stortford, Margate and St Albans City.

BILL BERRY

Experienced winger Bill Berry contested a first-team slot with Jack Russell as struggling Cherries were forced to seek re-election in 1933-34. Initially with Royal Naval Depot (Chatham), he joined Charlton Athletic in August 1923, moving via Gillingham to Brentford in May 1926. He featured in their 1926-27 FA Cup run and 1932-33 Third Division (South) title campaign before joining Crystal Palace in November 1932. Moving to Cherries in June 1933, he scored twice in 12 League games. Later trainer with French sides Lille and Nice, then Tunisia's Hamman Lif, he settled in Manor Park and died in September 1972.

MOHAMED BERTHE

Central defender Mohamed Berthe played for AFC Bournemouth during the 1998-99 season. A former Paris St Germain junior, he had spells with fellow French clubs Noisy-le-Sec, Chateauroux and Gazelac Ajaccio before moving to West Ham in March 1998 but failed to make an impact. He joined Cherries four months later and scored twice in 18 Second Division games while at Dean Court prior to briefly joining Hearts in March 1999, then moved to Swiss side Bellinzona. Later playing in Belgium with Strombeek, Zulte-Waregem, Cercle Brugge, Tirlemont, KVK Tienen and Dilbeek, he also holds Guinean citizenship.

RYAN BERTRAND

England Youth left-back Ryan Bertrand had a loan spell with AFC Bournemouth during the 2006-07 campaign. A former Chelsea trainee, he turned professional in August 2006 and was loaned to Cherries three months later. He made his League debut in the 4-2 defeat at Swansea and played five consecutive League One games while at Dean Court. Unable to secure a regular first-team slot at Stamford Bridge despite representing Team GB in the 2012 Olympic Games and gaining full England honours, he has since had loan spells with Oldham Athletic, Norwich City, Reading, Nottingham Forest and Aston Villa.

DAVID BEST

Goalkeeper David Best was ever-present for Cherries in three successive seasons. Signing professional in October 1960, he starred in Cherries' 1961-62 promotion near-miss and made 230 League appearances before sold to Oldham Athletic for £15,000 in September 1966. He reunited with Bill McGarry at Ipswich Town for £25,000 in October 1968 and helped them qualify for the UEFA Cup. Moving to Portsmouth in February 1974, he rejoined Cherries in July 1975 and became Dorchester Town's player-boss in February 1976. He later managed various local clubs and worked as a driver for Air Bearings in Holton Heath.

GEORGE BEST

Former Northern Ireland international George Best is arguably the most famous player ever to appear for AFC Bournemouth. He starred as Manchester United were League Champions in 1963-64 and 1966-67, then won the European Cup in 1968, when 'Footballer of the Year' and European 'Player of the Year', but a rift developed between club and player after Matt Busby retired. Later with Fulham, Hibernian and clubs in the United States, he joined Cherries in March 1983 and made five League appearances. He had a spell with Brisbane Lions, then worked in the media and corporate hospitality until his death in November 2005.

LEON BEST

Republic of Ireland Youth striker Leon Best had a loan spell at AFC Bournemouth in 2006-07. Initially with Southampton, he was an FA Youth Cup finalist in 2005 and loaned to QPR and Sheffield Wednesday before Cherries in August 2006, scoring three times in 15 League One games while at Dean Court. Loaned to Yeovil before helping Saints reach the Championship play-offs in 2006-07, he moved via Coventry City to Newcastle United in January 2010 and helped clinch the Championship title. The Republic of Ireland international joined Blackburn Rovers in July 2012, since loaned to Wednesday again, Derby and Brighton.

SAMMY BESWICK

England Amateur inside-forward Sammy Beswick was the first Cherries player to gain international recognition, against Wales in 1929-30. He had a spell with Stockport County before joining Tranmere Rovers in November 1922, then grabbed a hat-trick in Northern Nomads' 1926 Amateur Cup final triumph. Tranmere's top scorer in 1928-29, he also appeared for Rhyl before moving to Cherries in August 1929. Helping to reach the FA Cup fourth round in 1931-32, he netted 11 goals in 54 League games prior to joining Poole in July 1933. He worked for Bluebird Caravans and died in Bournemouth in December 1966.

KEVIN BETSY

Former England Semi-Pro winger Kevin Betsy had a loan spell at AFC Bournemouth in 1999-2000. Initially with Farnborough Town, he moved via Woking to Fulham for £100,000 in September 1998. He was loaned to Cherries in September 1999 and made five League appearances. Sold to Barnsley for £200,000 in February 2002, he was top scorer in 2003-04, moving via Oldham Athletic and Wycombe Wanderers to Bristol City for £200,000 in January 2007. Helping them to clinch promotion, he joined Southend United in August 2008, then returned to Woking. He is now an Academy coach at Fulham.

NICK BIGNALL

Striker Nick Bignall had a loan spell at AFC Bournemouth during the 2010-11 campaign. A former Reading scholar, he was a prolific scorer for their Academy side and turned professional in July 2008. He failed to secure a regular first-team slot with his hometown club and was loaned to Northampton Town, Cheltenham Town, Stockport County and Southampton before joining Cherries on loan in November 2010. Making five successive League appearances while at Dean Court, he then had loan spells at Brentford, Exeter City and Wycombe Wanderers. He moved from Reading to Basingstoke Town in March 2014.

LOUIS BIMPSON

Experienced centre-forward Louis Bimpson played for Cherries during the 1960-61 campaign. Initially with Burscough, he joined Liverpool in January 1953 and understudied Scotland international Billy Liddell. Moving to Blackburn Rovers in November 1959, he was an FA Cup finalist in 1960 and reunited with Don Welsh at Bournemouth in February 1961. His only goal in 11 League games came in that month's 4-4 draw at home to Colchester United. He joined Rochdale in August 1961 and was a League Cup finalist in 1962, then had spells with Wigan Athletic and Burscough. Settling in Burscough, he became a fork-lift driver.

JOE BIRCH

Speedy full-back Joe Birch understudied Jack Hayward whilst at Dean Court. A former miner, he played for Cannock and Hednesford before joining Birmingham in March 1928. He failed to secure a regular slot in the top-flight and moved to Bournemouth in May 1929. Making 26 League appearances, he joined Fulham in October 1931 and helped them clinch the Third Division (South) title. He moved to Colchester United in July 1938 and starred as they won the Southern League title in 1938-39. Later landlord of the Stockwell Arms in Colchester, then the Crown Inn in Lexden, he died in Colchester in December 1980.

KEN BIRD

Ex-England Schoolboy goalkeeper Ken Bird was a key figure in Cherries' 1947-48 promotion near-miss. Starting with Willenhall Rovers, he joined Wolves in May 1937 and moved to Dean Court in October 1938. He formed a memorable defensive quartet with Fred Marsden, Joe Sanaghan and Fred Wilson, starring as Bournemouth won the Third Division (South) Cup in 1946. Twice ever-present, he made 249 League appearances before becoming Dorchester's player-boss in August 1954. A publican in Dorchester, he was then a sales rep for Southern Tiling and later Swanage piermaster. He died in Swanage in October 1987.

DAVID BIRMINGHAM

Young defender David Birmingham had two spells with AFC Bournemouth. Initially a trainee at Dean Court, he overcame a broken leg to join Portsmouth in August 1999 and made his League debut in their 3-0 defeat at Bolton six months later. He was released by player-boss Steve Claridge and moved to Bognor Regis in December 2000 and rejoined Cherries on a non-contract basis in March 2001. Playing four Second Division games during 2001-02, he also appeared regularly for Bognor that season. He played alongside his older brother Mike at Bognor until moving to Gosport Borough in July 2006, settling in Portsmouth.

IAN BISHOP

Skilful midfielder Ian Bishop starred as AFC Bournemouth took Manchester United to an FA Cup fifth round replay in 1988-89. Initially with Everton, he moved via Carlisle United to Cherries for £35,000 in July 1988 and scored twice in 44 League games, joining Manchester City in a £465,000 deal involving Paul Moulden in August 1989. Moving to West Ham four months later, the England B international twice helped them win promotion and rejoined Manchester City in March 1998, then Miami Fusion, Rochdale, Burscough, Radcliffe Borough and New Orleans Shell Shockers. He is now a youth coach in Florida.

JIMMY BLAIR (Snr)

Former Scotland international left-back Jimmy Blair was an experienced figure as Cherries took Liverpool to an FA Cup third round replay in 1926-27. He played for Bonnyrigg Thistle and Glasgow Ashfield before representing the Scottish League with Clyde. Moving to Sheffield Wednesday in July 1914, he followed Jimmy Gill to Cardiff City in November 1920 and starred in their 1920-21 promotion success. He joined Bournemouth in December 1926, making 61 League appearances before hanging up his boots. Returning to Cardiff as trainer, he settled in Sheffield after his wife's death in October 1948 and died in February 1964.

JIMMY BLAIR (Jnr)

Ex-Scotland international inside-forward Jimmy Blair featured prominently in Cherries' 1947-48 promotion near-miss. A former amateur with Cardiff City, where his father was trainer-coach, he turned professional with Blackpool in June 1935 and was capped against Wales in October 1946. Harry Lowe paid £5,000 for him in October 1947 and he scored eight goals in 80 League games for Cherries before joining Leyton Orient in December 1949. He became Ramsgate's player-boss, then had a spell with Canterbury City and was landlord of the 'Cherry Tree' pub in Faversham. Later a prison officer, he died in Llanelli in July 1983.

ALEC BLAKEMAN

Experienced inside-forward Alec Blakeman helped Cherries finish third in the Third Division (South) in 1948-49. He played for Oxford City prior to joining Brentford in May 1946 and netted four goals in his first two First Division games, also playing in the top-flight after moving to Sheffield United in November 1948. Joining Bournemouth in February 1949, he scored eight times in 25 League outings while at Dean Court before moving to March Town in July 1950. Settling in Kidlington, he worked for Morris Motors, then was a foreman for Knowles & Sons builders in Oxford. He died in Deddington in November 1994.

ALAN BLAYNEY

Northern Ireland U-21 goalkeeper Alan Blayney had a loan spell at AFC Bournemouth during the 2002-03 promotion campaign. Signing professional for Southampton in July 2001, he was loaned to Cherries in December 2002 and made two Third Division appearances. He was given his Premier League debut in May 2004 and moved to Doncaster Rovers for £50,000 in January 2006, making his full international debut four months later. He has since played for Oldham Athletic, Bohemians, Ballymena United, Linfield (helping win the Irish League and Cup 'double' in three successive years), Ards, Glenavon and Ballymena again.

BERT BLISS

Former England international Bert Bliss briefly appeared for Cherries during the 1925-26 campaign. He played for Willenhall Pickwick and Willenhall Swifts before joining Tottenham Hotspur in April 1912. Noted for his blistering shot, he was top scorer three times including Spurs' 1919-20 Second Division title triumph when ever-present and played in their 1921 FA Cup final success. He gained his only England cap against Scotland in April 1921 and joined Clapton Orient in December 1922. Moving to Bournemouth in July 1925, he played six League games before hanging up his boots. He died in Wood Green in June 1968.

LUTHER BLISSETT

Ex-England international striker Luther Blissett was AFC Bournemouth's leading marksman three times. Signing professional for Watford in July 1975, he starred in their meteoric rise under Graham Taylor and joined AC Milan for £1,000,000 in June 1983. He returned to Watford in August 1984 and Harry Redknapp paid £60,000 for him in November 1988. Scoring four goals on his home debut against Hull City, he was a key figure in that season's FA Cup run and netted 56 goals in 121 League games for Cherries, rejoining Watford in August 1991. He has held coaching posts including back at Watford and managed Chesham.

LES BLIZZARD

Tall right-half Les Blizzard briefly appeared as Cherries finished Third Division (South) runners-up in 1947-48. Initially with QPR, he moved to Bournemouth in May 1947 and deputised for Ernie Tagg in the 2-0 victory at home to Northampton in April 1948. He joined Yeovil Town three months later and featured in their epic 1948-49 FA Cup fourth round win over Sunderland, following Alec Stock to Leyton Orient in July 1950. Starring in their 1955-56 Third Division (South) title triumph, he later played for Headington United (now known as Oxford United) and Whitstable Town. He died in Northampton in December 1996.

ROGER BOLI

Former French U-21 striker Roger Boli was plagued by injuries whilst at AFC Bournemouth. Born in Adjame, Ivory Coast, he played for French side Lens before joining Walsall in August 1997. Top scorer in 1997-98, selected for the PFA Second Division team, he netted against Cherries in the Auto Windscreens Shield southern final second-leg.

He moved to Dundee United for £150,000 in July 1998 and joined Cherries for a cut-price £50,000 three months later. Although a lot was expected from him, injuries restricted him to six League appearances and he retired in July 1999. He is now a football agent in France.

RONNIE BOLTON

Versatile left-half Ronnie Bolton had two spells with Cherries. Initially with Crompton Recs, he turned professional at Dean Court in April 1958 and was Bournemouth's top scorer in 1960-61, also featuring in the 1961-62 promotion near-miss. He reunited with Bill McGarry at Ipswich Town for £10,000 in October 1965. Rejoining Cherries for £5,000 in September 1967, he scored 48 times in 264 League games overall before moving to Durban City in May 1969, achieving South African League and Cup success. Later with Poole Town, Andover, Dorchester Town and Ringwood Town, he is a retired carpenter in Bournemouth.

KEVIN BOND

Former England B defender Kevin Bond was AFC Bournemouth's 'Player of the Year' in 1991-92. Initially an apprentice at Dean Court, he followed his father John to Norwich City in June 1974 and had a spell with Seattle Sounders before rejoining his father at Manchester City in September 1981. He joined Southampton in September 1984 and returned to Cherries in August 1988, starring in the 1988-89 FA Cup run. Scoring four goals in 126 League games, he joined Exeter City in August 1992. He has assisted Harry Redknapp at Portsmouth, Southampton, Spurs and QPR, also managing Cherries from October 2006 until August 2008.

KIM BOOK

Young goalkeeper Kim Book understudied England U-23 international Roger Jones while at Dean Court. The younger brother of Tony Book, he impressed with Frome Town before moving to Bournemouth in July 1967. He made two Third Division appearances prior to joining Northampton Town in October 1969 and starred in their 1969-70 FA Cup run. Later playing for Doncaster Rovers, Trowbridge, Weston-Super-Mare, Bath City, Gloucester City, Forest Green Rovers, Yeovil Town and Paulton Rovers, he became a bricklayer in his native Bath. His son Steve was an England Semi-Pro keeper with Cheltenham Town.

GARY BORTHWICK

Midfielder Gary Borthwick was a member of John Benson's squad at AFC Bournemouth. He had spells with Windsor & Eton, Aylesbury United and Barnet prior to joining Cherries in March 1978, scoring four times in 74 League outings before moving to Yeovil Town in July 1980. Joining Weymouth in April 1981, he starred in their 1982-83 FA Cup run, then played for Yeovil and Weymouth again before reuniting with Keith Miller at Dorchester in June 1986. He helped win promotion in 1986-87, then was Havant's player-coach and Weymouth's player-boss before Bridport and Dorchester again. He works in the building trade.

ARTUR BORUC

Polish international goalkeeper Artur Boruc starred on loan in AFC Bournemouth's 2014-15 Championship title campaign. He played for Pogon Siedice and Legia Warsaw in his native country before joining Celtic in July 2005. Helping them to win the Scottish League title three times, Scottish Cup in 2007 and Scottish League Cup in 2006 and 2009, 'The Holy Goalie' moved to Italian side Fiorentina in July 2010. He joined Southampton in September 2012 but was displaced by the arrival of Fraser Forster and loaned to Cherries in September 2014. Making 37 Championship appearances, he joined on a permanent basis in May 2015.

WILLIAM BOW

Welsh goalkeeper William Bow made his only Third Division (South) appearance for Cherries in the 8-2 defeat at Swindon Town in January 1926, the club's then-record League defeat. Previously with hometown Merthyr, gaining Third Division (South) experience as Albert Lindon's understudy, he moved to Dean Court in July 1925 and provided cover for George Wilson, gaining his first-team chance after Bournemouth lost 7-2 at Bristol Rovers on Boxing Day. He moved to Coventry City in July 1926 but failed to make an impact and later returned to Merthyr, then in the Welsh League. Settling in Merthyr, he died in May 1985.

DANNY BOXSHALL

Versatile winger Danny Boxshall created numerous chances for Doug McGibbon while at Dean Court. He played for Alston Works, Wilsden and Salem Athletic in the Bradford Amateur League before joining QPR in January 1946. Helping them to pip Bournemouth to the Third Division (South) title in 1947-48, he moved to Bristol City in May 1948. He joined Cherries in July 1950 and netted eight goals in 51 League outings prior to joining Rochdale in July 1952, then played for Chelmsford City. Employed as an insurance agent for Prudential in Chelmsford for 25 years until April 1981, he died in Shipley in November 2009.

PHIL BOYER

Phil Boyer formed a lethal striking partnership with Ted MacDougall whilst at AFC Bournemouth. Initially with Derby County, he followed MacDougall from York City to Cherries for £20,000 in December 1970 and helped clinch promotion. He scored 46 goals in 141 League games before reuniting with MacDougall at Norwich City for £140,000 in February 1974 and was their first England international. Following Mac to Southampton, he was leading scorer in their 1977-78 promotion success, then played for Manchester City, Bulova, Grantham and Stamford. He scouted for Graham Carr and worked for Securicor in Nottingham.

LEE BRADBURY

Ex-England U-21 international Lee Bradbury was an experienced figure in AFC Bournemouth's 2009-10 promotion success. A former soldier, the striker moved from Cowes to Portsmouth in August 1995 and was 'Player of the Season' in 1996-97.

Sold to Manchester City for £3,000,000 in August 1997, he moved via Crystal Palace back to Pompey in October 1999, then had spells with Sheffield Wednesday, Derby County, Walsall, Oxford United and Southend United before joining Cherries in August 2007. Successfully switched to right-back, he netted ten goals in 127 League games and had a brief spell as player-manager.

JACK BRADFORD

Experienced left-half Jack Bradford was an influential figure as Cherries took West Ham to an FA Cup fifth round replay in 1928-29. Initially with Hucknall Byron, he moved via Grimsby Town to Wolves in March 1924 and helped clinch the Third Division (North) title. He joined Bournemouth in October 1927 and was ever-present in 1929-30. His solitary goal in 113 Third Division (South) games came in that season's 4-2 victory at home to Merthyr Town and he became Letchworth Town's player-coach in May 1931. A cousin of Walsall stalwart Bill Bradford, he resided in Hitchin until his death in August 1969.

PHIL BRIGNULL

Ex-England Schoolboy central defender Phil Brignull starred in AFC Bournemouth's 1981-82 promotion success. Turning professional with West Ham in September 1978, he made his League debut eight months later. His second cousin David Webb signed him in August 1981 and he was ever-present in 1982-83, then 'Player of the Year' in 1983-84 as Cherries beat holders Manchester United in the FA Cup third round and won the Associate Members Cup. He netted 11 goals in 129 League games before joining Cardiff City in February 1986, then Newport County and Weymouth, becoming a financial adviser in Cheltenham.

JASON BRISSETT

Enigmatic winger Jason Brissett played for AFC Bournemouth in the 1998 Auto Windscreens Shield final. A former Arsenal trainee, he joined Peterborough United in June 1993 and featured in their 1993-94 League Cup run. Mel Machin signed him in December 1994 and he helped Cherries avoid relegation that season. Regularly featuring as a substitute, he netted eight goals in 124 League games prior to joining Walsall in August 1998. He was an influential figure in their 1998-99 promotion success, then played for Cheltenham Town, Leyton Orient and Stevenage Borough until an ankle injury curtailed his career.

KARL BROADHURST

Versatile defender Karl Broadhurst featured in AFC Bournemouth's 2002-03 promotion campaign but missed the play-off final triumph through injury. A former trainee, he turned professional with Cherries in July 1998 and helped beat top-flight Charlton Athletic in the 1999-2000 League Cup second round. He starred as Cherries narrowly failed to reach the Second Division play-offs in 2000-01 and became captain. Plagued by a nagging back problem, he netted three goals in 192 League games before joining Hereford United in July 2007, then Crawley Town, AFC Telford United and Solihull Moors, where assistant-boss.

LEN BROOKS

Len Brooks displaced long-serving Dick Mellors as Cherries' goalkeeper early in the 1937-38 season. He turned professional with Fulham in June 1934 and made his League debut in place of Alf Tootill in their 1-0 defeat at home to Swansea in April 1936. Unable to secure a regular first-team slot at Craven Cottage, he joined Bournemouth in June 1937 and played 39 League games before quitting football shortly after the 4-0 defeat at home to Southend in September 1938. He received a 28 day FA suspension after reviving his career with Colchester United the following season. He died in Binstead, Isle of Wight, in October 1994.

SHAUN BROOKS

Ex-England Youth midfielder Shaun Brooks helped AFC Bournemouth finish in their then highest-ever position in 1988-89. The son of former England international Johnny Brooks, he turned professional with Crystal Palace in October 1979 and moved via Orient to Dean Court for £20,000 in June 1987. He scored 13 goals in 128 League games for Cherries until leaving in May 1993. Later with Wimborne, Salisbury, Dorchester, Cherries again, Orient, Poole and Ringwood, he managed Poppies and Poole Borough. He was Portsmouth's youth coach, then coached Cherries, managed Winchester and coached Poole Town.

AARON BROWN

Tall central defender Aaron Brown had a loan spell at AFC Bournemouth during the 2005-06 season. He played for Studley before joining Tamworth in July 2004, helping them win at Dean Court in the 2005-06 FA Cup first round. Moving to Reading in November 2005, he was loaned to Cherries in February 2006 and played as a striker, making four League One appearances while at Dean Court. He joined Yeovil Town in August 2008 and has since had spells with Redditch United, Burton Albion, AFC Telford United, Truro City, Leyton Orient, Stockport County, Aldershot Town, Preston, Floriana, Limerick and Worcester City.

BERTIE BROWN

Outside-right Bertie Brown briefly appeared for Cherries during the 1937-38 campaign. He played for Boots Athletic and Ilkeston Town, then was an amateur with Arsenal prior joining Cherries in March 1937. Given his League debut in place of the injured Bob Redfern in the 1-0 defeat at Southend five months later, he made two further Third Division (South) appearances before his career was curtailed by a shoulder injury. Later with Nottinghamshire Police, he represented England Police and was a constable stationed at Sutton-in-Ashfield, Mansfield and Clipstone, then a sergeant at Retford until his sudden death in July 1963.

IRVIN BROWN

Versatile defender Irvin Brown was a member of Don Welsh's squad at Dean Court, The eldest of three footballing brothers, he turned professional with Brighton in October 1952 and reunited with Welsh at Bournemouth for £2,000 in September 1958. He scored twice in 65 League games for Cherries prior to joining Poole Town in June 1963 and was ever-present in their 1964-65 promotion success, then managed Hamworthy United for 14 years. Employed as a joiner by Rawlings Builders and Lytchett Minster Joinery, he was physio at Poppies, Wimborne, Lymington and Hamworthy. He died in Poole in December 2005.

JOE BROWN

Influential left-half Joe Brown starred as Cherries reached the FA Cup sixth round in 1956-57. Initially with Middlesbrough, he also played in the top-flight for Burnley before moving to Bournemouth in June 1954. He was twice ever-present, scoring five times in 215 League games prior to joining Aldershot in July 1960. Returning to Burnley as a coach, he was later their chief scout and manager, then became Manchester United's youth team coach in September 1977. He was United's youth development officer, recruiting Ryan Giggs, David Beckham, Paul Scholes and the Neville brothers, until May 1996 and died in October 2014.

KEITH BROWN

Young right-back Keith Brown understudied Brian Farmer while at Dean Court. Born locally, he played for Pokesdown Old Boys prior to joining Bournemouth in September 1960 and was given his first-team debut in the 2-1 League Cup fourth round defeat at top-flight Stoke City in November 1963. 'Bootsie' made 15 Third Division appearances for Cherries including nine consecutive games during the closing weeks of the 1964-65 campaign. Moving to Poole Town in June 1965, he then played for Christchurch, Pokesdown Old Boys again and Ringwood Town, working in the family fruit and veg wholesale business at Pokesdown.

KEN BROWN

Winger Ken Brown played for Cherries during the 1957-58 campaign. Signing professional for Coventry City in January 1956, he had spells with Corby and Nottingham Forest prior to joining Bournemouth in July 1957. His solitary goal in six Third Division (South) games came on his League debut in Cherries' 4-0 win at Shrewsbury Town two months later and he moved to Torquay United in July 1958, then had spells playing for Hinckley Athletic, Lockheed Leamington, Burton Albion, Atherstone Town, Bedworth United and Redditch United. He settled in his native Coventry and was a finisher for Triumph, then a postman.

KENNY BROWN

Experienced midfielder Kenny Brown was a John Benson signing for AFC Bournemouth. A former Barnsley apprentice, he made his League debut in their 2-0 victory at Halifax two months before turning professional in April 1970 and was ever-present as the Tykes finished sixth in the Fourth Division in 1976-77. He reunited with Mick Butler at Dean Court in June 1978 and netted four goals in 32 Fourth Division games, including two in Cherries' 3-1 win over Stockport in April 1979, prior to joining Frickley Athletic in July 1980. Settling in his native Barnsley, he became a building services officer at Barnsley College.

ROGER BROWN

Central defender Roger Brown skippered AFC Bournemouth's 1984 Associate Members Cup final triumph. A former Walsall apprentice, he starred in AP Leamington's 1975-76 promotion success, joining Cherries in February 1978. He moved to Norwich City for £85,000 in July 1979, then Fulham for £100,000 in March 1980, helping win promotion in 1981-82. Rejoining Cherries in December 1983, he featured in the 1983-84 FA Cup win over Manchester United, scoring eight times in 147 League games. Later managing Poole Town, Colchester United and Bolehall Swifts, he was a probation officer and died in August 2011.

SAM BROWN

Scottish left-back Sam Brown partnered long-serving Jack Hayward in Cherries' defence. He impressed with Rutherglen Glencairn prior to joining Third Lanark in July 1922 and had loan spells with King's Park (later known as Stirling Albion) and East Stirlingshire. Moving to Dean Court in May 1929, he was given his League debut in Bournemouth's 2-0 victory at Coventry City four months later and made 59 Third Division (South) appearances before joining Brighton in May 1931. He later played for Chester and Swindon Town. Returning to Scotland with Stranraer, he settled back in Glasgow and died in June 1961.

MARCUS BROWNING

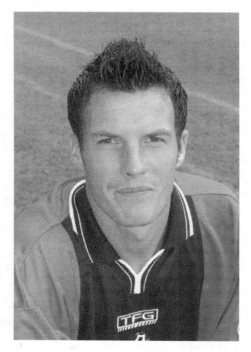

Welsh international midfielder Marcus Browning starred in AFC Bournemouth's 2002-03 Third Division play-off final success. Initially with Bristol Rovers, he was a key figure as they reached the Second Division play-off final in 1994-95 and gained the first of five caps against Italy in November 1995. He joined Huddersfield Town for £500,000 in February 1997, then Gillingham for £150,000 in March 1999. Moving to Cherries in August 2002, he netted three goals in 188 League games before joining Weymouth in July 2007, then Bath City and Poole. He has since been a window cleaner and Cherries' youth coach.

JEFF BRYANT

Ex-England Youth defender Jeff Bryant was a member of Alec Stock's squad at AFC Bournemouth. He starred as Wimbledon won the Southern League in three successive seasons and scored their first-ever Football League goal against Halifax Town in August 1977. Helping them win promotion in 1978-79, he joined Cherries in June 1979 and netted twice in 16 Fourth Division games before moving to Gravesend & Northfleet in February 1980. He later had spells with Dagenham, Crawley Town, Tooting & Mitcham, Worthing, Three Bridges and Billingshurst, becoming a self-employed electrical contractor in Southwater.

BOB BRYCE

Scottish winger Bob Bryce starred as Cherries took West Ham to an FA Cup fifth round replay in 1928-29. Initially with Grange Rovers in his native Grangemouth, he had spells with Falkirk, East Stirlingshire and Stenhousemuir before moving to Bournemouth in July 1928. He made his League debut in the 6-2 victory at home to Bristol Rovers three months later, netting 24 goals in 63 Third Division (South) games prior to joining Luton Town in July 1930. Later playing for King's Park (later known as Stirling Albion) and Raith Rovers, he was a foreman at Grangemouth Docks. He died while on holiday in Bridlington in July 1970.

CAMERON BUCHANAN

Scottish inside-right Cameron Buchanan played alongside Jack Cross in Cherries' attack. Initially with Wolves, he was the youngest-ever debutant in English senior soccer at 14 years 57 days in September 1942 and moved to Bournemouth in August 1949. He scored 19 goals in 83 Third Division (South) games for Cherries before joining Canadian side Montreal Ukraina in April 1955, then had a spell with Norwich City and was

Barnstaple's player-boss. Later linen service manager at hospitals in Newcastle and Dundee until July 1993, he moved back to Barnstaple for a period, then settled in Tayport and died in September 2008.

JIM BUCHANAN

Scottish winger Jim Buchanan was an influential figure as Bournemouth took eventual winners Bolton Wanderers to an FA Cup fourth round replay in 1925-26. Previously with Hibernian, he joined Cherries in July 1924 and also helped take Liverpool to an FA Cup third round replay in 1926-27, He scored ten goals in 65 Third Division (South) games and was loaned to Raith Rovers, moving via East Stirling to Nelson in August 1928. Playing in the Third Division (North), he then had spells with Ashton National, Clitheroe, Accrington Stanley, Bray Unknowns, Shamrock Rovers, Leith Athletic and Bangor. He died in June 1955.

WILF BUCKNALL

Robust full-back Wilf Bucknall provided cover for Tom King and George Bellis during the 1935-36 season. Starting with Lichfield Amateurs, he had spells with Wolves and Linfield before moving to Wellington Town (later known as Telford United) in July 1934, starring in their 1934-35 Birmingham League title triumph. Bob Crompton signed him in May 1935 and he played for Cherries in the first two League matches of the season, against Southend United and Luton Town, but made just three further Third Division (South) appearances while at Dean Court. He settled in Wolverhampton and died in May 1991.

WILF BUDDEN

Forward Wilf Budden featured in Cherries' 1923-24 Football League debut campaign. Previously with Bournemouth Poppies, he joined Boscombe (as the club was then known) in March 1923 and scored on his debut in that month's 3-1 victory at Swindon Town Reserves. He helped to finish Southern League runners-up in 1922-23 and made his Football League debut in Cherries' 1-0 defeat at Swansea in January 1924. His only goal in ten Third Division (South) games came in the 3-3 draw at home to Merthyr in April 1924 but he was unable to prevent Cherries having to seek re-election. He died in Southampton in December 1971.

ALEC BUGG

Young goalkeeper Alec Bugg briefly played for Cherries on loan during the 1969-70 campaign. Signing professional for Ipswich Town in June 1967, he was given his First Division debut in their 3-0 defeat at Sunderland in August 1968 but had few top-flight opportunities and was loaned to struggling Bournemouth in February 1970. He made four League appearances in place of Kieron Baker. Moving to King's Lynn in June 1970, he then spent 30 years as a policeman, serving in the Sussex and Suffolk Constabularies. He became head of equine security for Darley Stud Management at the Godolphin stables in Newmarket.

RAY BUMSTEAD

Long-serving winger Ray Bumstead starred in Cherries' 1961-62 promotion near-miss. Initially with Ringwood Town, he moved to Dean Court in May 1958 and made his League debut in the 5-1 defeat at Doncaster Rovers nine months later. He was twice ever-present and featured in Bournemouth's League Cup wins over Newcastle in 1963-64 and Sheffield Wednesday in 1969-70. Scoring 55 goals in a then record 415 League games prior to joining Weymouth in June 1970, he was a Southern League Cup finalist in 1971. Settling in his native Ringwood, he later became a property developer and died in March 2013.

MIKE BURGESS

Versatile centre-forward Mike Burgess was Cherries' leading marksman in 1958-59. Born in Montreal, he grew up in Bradford and played for Frickley Colliery prior to joining Bradford Park Avenue in August 1952. He had spells with Leyton Orient and Newport County before moving to Dean Court in June 1957. Scoring 34 times in 109 League outings for Cherries, he joined Halifax Town in July 1961 and reunited with Freddie Cox at Gillingham in March 1963. He was ever-present in their 1963-64 Fourth Division title triumph, then played for Aldershot. He is now a retired electronics technician, living in Broadstone.

MEYNELL BURGIN

Centre-forward Meynell Burgin scored as Cherries trounced Walthamstow Avenue 8-1 in the 1935-36 FA Cup first round replay. Initially with Rossington Main Colliery, he joined Wolves in May 1933 and had a loan spell at Tranmere Rovers, helping to win the Welsh Cup shortly before joining Bournemouth in May 1935. He understudied Joe Riley and his only goal in five League outings came in the 2-0 win at Torquay in November 1935. Moving to Nottingham Forest in July 1936, he joined West Brom in May 1938 and guested for Chesterfield and Sheffield Wednesday during the war. He died in Sheffield in August 1994.

CHARLIE BURKE

Scottish right-half Charlie Burke featured in Cherries' first post-war League match at Notts County in August 1946. Initially with Ardeer Recreation, he moved to Bournemouth in June 1939 and netted seven goals in 25 Third Division (South) games prior to joining Clyde in July 1947. He reunited with Paddy Gallacher at Weymouth in August 1949 and helped them reach the FA Cup third round in 1949-50 before rejoining Clyde. Later a PGA professional at Dunnikier, then greenkeeper at Lee-on-the-Solent, Huyton, Royal Winchester and Queen's Park Golf Clubs, he lived in Bournemouth until his death in October 1995.

CHRIS BURNS

Versatile midfielder Chris Burns had a loan spell at AFC Bournemouth during the 1993-94 campaign. He impressed with Cheltenham Town prior to joining Portsmouth in March 1991 and was ever-present as they were FA Cup semi-finalists in 1991-92. Loaned to Cherries in March 1994, he scored once in 14 League games. He joined Swansea City in November 1994, then had spells with Northampton Town, Gloucester City and Forest Green Rovers. Later player-manager of Gloucester City and Cinderford Town, he assisted Cirencester, becoming Cheltenham's youth coach, also managing Bishop's Cleeve and Brockworth Albion.

DEREK BURNS

Young defender Derek Burns briefly featured as Cherries finished fourth in the Third Division in 1968-69. Born locally, he turned professional at Dean Court in January 1968 and was given his League debut in Bournemouth's 1-0 defeat at home to Plymouth Argyle seven months later. He made three further League appearances before joining Salisbury in August 1970, then played for Christchurch, Poole Town and Ringwood Town. Reuniting with Tony Nelson back at Poole in July 1975, he later had spells with Wimborne Town and Swanage T&H. He settled in Bournemouth, becoming a self-employed gardener.

ROY BURNS

Winger Roy Burns was one of many former Wolves players signed by Charlie Bell during his reign at Dean Court. Initially with Walsall Wood, he joined Birmingham League champions Wellington Town (later known as Telford United) in August 1935. He then had spells with Wolves and Port Vale prior to joining Bournemouth in July 1936, making his League debut in the 3-1 win at Aldershot on the opening day of the season. Scoring three times in 18 Third Division (South) games for Cherries, he left in May 1937 and worked for Bournemouth Trams, playing for their works team. He died in Petersfield in December 1983.

DENNIS BUSHBY

Right-half Dennis Bushby played for Cherries during the 1957-58 campaign. Initially with Poppies, then Bournemouth Gasworks, he moved to Dean Court initially as an amateur in August 1956. He was given his League debut in Bournemouth's 1-1 draw at Watford in December 1957 and made six Third Division (South) appearances in place of Alan Rule. Moving to Peterborough United in July 1959, he later played for Poole Town, Cowes, Parley Sports, Christchurch and Ringwood. Settling in Bournemouth, he was a self-employed electrician and then worked in the building trade, running Peach Developments Ltd.

GEOFF BUTLER

Experienced right-back Geoff Butler was a member of John Benson's squad at Dean Court. He began with Middlesbrough and starred in their 1966-67 promotion success, joining Chelsea in September 1967. Moving via Sunderland to Norwich City in October 1968, he featured in two promotion campaigns and the 1973 League Cup final. He joined Cherries in March 1976 and scored once in 119 League games prior to joining Peterborough United in August 1981. Later Salisbury's player-boss, he twice plotted promotion during an 18 year reign, then managed Weymouth and Bashley. He ran a building company in Shrewton.

MICK BUTLER

Striker Mick Butler was AFC Bournemouth's leading marksman in two consecutive seasons. Initially with Worsbrough Bridge MW, while an electrician at Dodworth Colliery, he joined Barnsley in February 1973 and twice topped their goalscoring charts. He moved to Huddersfield Town for £30,000 in March 1976 and was top scorer in 1977-78. Joining Cherries for £15,000 in July 1978, he netted 19 goals in 69 League outings before being sold to Bury for £8,000 in August 1980. He has settled in Royston and was an electrician at Woolley Colliery, then a chargehand at Riccall Mine until its closure in January 2005.

STEVE BUTLER

Loan striker Steve Butler played in Cherries' 0-0 draw at home to Hull City in December 1992. A former soldier, he represented the Combined Services and played for Windsor & Eton and Wokingham prior to joining Brentford in December 1984. He moved to Maidstone United in June 1986 and gained England Semi-Pro honours, setting their League goalscoring record before joining Watford in March 1991. Later with Cambridge United, Gillingham and Peterborough United, he then assisted Peter Taylor at Gillingham, Leicester City, Brighton and Hull City and is now head coach at Soccer Showcase Elite Training Academy.

LEN BUTT

Small right-half Len Butt was ever-present in Cherries' 1923-24 Football League debut campaign. He turned professional with hometown Southampton in April 1912, then worked and played for Thorneycrofts before rejoining Saints in August 1920. Helping win the Third Division (South) title in 1921-22, he joined Boscombe in June 1922. He starred as Cherries took eventual winners Bolton to an

FA Cup fifth round replay in 1925-26 and scored twice in 139 League outings prior to joining Cowes in June 1928. Later a publican at The Sailors Home and Edinburgh Hotel in Southampton, he died in Sholing in December 1993.

STEVE BUTTLE

Winger Steve Buttle starred as AFC Bournemouth went close to regaining Third Division status at the first attempt in 1975-76. Signing professional for Ipswich Town in January 1971, he failed to make an impact and moved to Dean Court for £8,000 in August 1973. He scored 12 goals in 139 League games for Cherries before reuniting with Jimmy Gabriel at Seattle Sounders in February 1977. Playing alongside several former Cherries, he later coached Pittsburgh Spirit and Tacoma Stars, then worked for a medical delivery company in Washington State. He became a trade unionist in his native Norwich and died in June 2012.

DAVID BUTTON

Ex-England Youth goalkeeper David Button had a loan spell at AFC Bournemouth in 2008-09. He turned professional with Tottenham Hotspur in March 2006 and was loaned to Cherries in January 2009. Given his League debut in that month's 1-0 defeat at Rotherham, he also played in the next three League matches. He was loaned to Luton Town, an unused substitute in their 2009 Johnstone's Paint Trophy final triumph, then Dagenham & Redbridge, Crewe, Shrewsbury, Plymouth, Leyton Orient, Doncaster and Barnsley. Briefly with Charlton Athletic, he joined Brentford in July 2013 and starred in their 2013-14 promotion success.

LEWIS BUXTON

Versatile defender Lewis Buxton featured in AFC Bournemouth's 2002-03 promotion campaign. A former Portsmouth trainee, he turned professional in April 2001 and made his League debut in their 1-0 victory at Stockport four months later. He had few first-team chances and Harry Redknapp loaned him to Cherries in January 2003. Returning for a second loan spell in October 2003, he made 43 League appearances overall for Cherries. He reunited with Tony Pulis at Stoke City in December 2004, moving to Sheffield Wednesday in January 2009. Helping them to win promotion in 2011-12, he joined Rotherham United in June 2015.

NATHAN BYRNE

Teenage defender Nathan Byrne had a loan spell at AFC Bournemouth at the start of the 2011-12 season. Starting with Harry Redknapp's Tottenham Hotspur, he failed to secure a first-team slot and made his League debut while on loan to Brentford in February 2011. He was loaned to Cherries in August 2011 and appeared in the opening nine League One games of the campaign which produced three wins and six defeats. Following a loan spell at Crawley Town, he joined Swindon Town initially on loan in March 2013 and helped them to qualify for the League One play-offs that season, then repeated the feat in 2014-15.

RICHARD CADETTE

Diminutive striker Richard Cadette had a loan spell at AFC Bournemouth during the 1989-90 campaign. Initially with Wembley, he moved via Orient to Southend United in August 1985 and was leading marksman in their 1986-87 promotion success. He joined Sheffield United in July 1987, then Brentford in July 1988. Loaned to Cherries in March 1990, his solitary goal in eight Second Division games came in the following month's 4-2 defeat at home to Sheffield United. Later playing for Falkirk, Millwall, Shelbourne, Clydebank and Gloucester City, he coached at Millwall's Academy and managed Tooting & Mitcham.

BILL CAMERON

Scottish inside-right Bill Cameron briefly appeared for Bournemouth early in the 1934-35 campaign. Previously with Middlesbrough, where his older brother Kenny also played, he failed to secure a top-flight slot behind Bobby Bruce and former Boro' captain Billy Birrell brought him to Dean Court in July 1934. He impressed in the reserves before making his solitary Third Division (South) appearance in place of Alfie White in Cherries' 2-0 defeat at Millwall two months later. Moving to Stenhousemuir in July 1935, he had various jobs back in his native Glasgow including working in the docks and died in September 1995.

LEE CAMP

Northern Ireland international goalkeeper Lee Camp played nine times in Cherries' 2014-15 Championship title campaign. He turned professional with Derby County in July 2002 and was loaned to Burton Albion, QPR (promotion in 2003-04) and Leicester City before rejoining QPR for £300,000 in August 2007. Ever-present in 2007-08, he reunited with Billy Davies at Nottingham Forest in July 2009 and was twice ever-present. He played for England U-21s five times before making his Northern Ireland debut against Serbia in March 2011. Moving via Norwich and West Brom, he joined Cherries initially on loan in November 2013.

JOSH CARMICHAEL

Scotland Youth midfielder Josh Carmichael briefly played in AFC Bournemouth's 2012-13 promotion campaign. He progressed through the ranks at Dean Court and made his League debut as a substitute in Cherries' 2-0 win over Exeter City in September 2011. Starting a League match for the first time in the 3-1 defeat at Crawley Town in October 2012, he had a loan spell with Gosport Borough the following season and played for them in the 2014 FA Trophy final at Wembley Stadium. He was loaned to Welling United during 2014-15 and had made four League appearances overall for Cherries by the end of that season. He went on loan to Torquay United in August 2015.

STEVE CARTER

Winger Steve Carter helped AFC Bournemouth clinch promotion in 1981-82. Initially with Manchester City, he gained top-flight experience prior to joining Notts County in February 1972. He featured in their 1972-73 promotion campaign and was swapped for Derby County's Don Masson in August 1978. Briefly rejoining Notts County, he joined Cherries in March 1982 and played against Manchester United in the 1982-83 League Cup second round, scoring once in 46 League outings before reuniting with David Webb at Torquay United in July 1984. He has since run a confectionery business, settling in Wilmslow.

JIMMY CASE

Former England U-23 midfielder Jimmy Case starred as Cherries won at Newcastle United in the 1991-92 FA Cup third round replay. He amassed a vast collection of honours during eight years at Liverpool and moved to Brighton as part of the Mark Lawrenson deal in August 1981, featuring in the 1983 FA Cup final. Joining Southampton in March 1985, he was their 'Player of the Year' in 1989-90 and moved to AFC Bournemouth in June 1991. He scored once in 40 Third Division outings before joining Halifax Town in May 1992. Later managing Brighton and Bashley, he has since been a summariser for Saints and Liverpool.

TOM CASEY

Tough-tackling left-half Tom Casey was capped 12 times by Northern Ireland after leaving Dean Court. He moved to Leeds United from Bangor in May 1949 and joined Cherries in August 1950, scoring once in 66 League outings before being sold to Newcastle United for £7,000 in August 1952. Featuring in their 1955 FA Cup final triumph, he appeared in the World Cup shortly before joining Portsmouth in June 1958, then played for Bristol City and was Gloucester City's player-boss. He was coach/manager at clubs including Grimsby Town, then a mobile fishmonger in Portbury for 17 years and died in Nailsea in January 2009.

CHRIS CASPER

England U-21 central defender Chris Casper had a loan spell at AFC Bournemouth in 1995-96. The son of former Burnley striker Frank Casper, he helped Manchester United win the FA Youth Cup in 1992 and turned professional at Old Trafford in February 1993. He was loaned to Cherries in January 1996 and scored once in 16 League outings while at Dean Court. Sold to Reading for £300,000 in September 1998, his career was ended by a broken leg 15 months later. He became Bury's youth coach, then manager, before coaching at Bradford City and Grimsby Town, then joined the Premier League as a club support manager.

MICKEY CAVE

Popular midfielder Mickey Cave had two spells at AFC Bournemouth. Initially with hometown Weymouth, he followed Frank O'Farrell to Torquay United in July 1968 and reunited with John Bond at Dean Court for £15,000 in July 1971. He featured in Cherries' 1971-72 promotion near-miss and was sold to York City for £18,000 in August 1974. Top scorer in 1975-76, he returned to Cherries in February 1977, netting 20 goals in 141 League games overall. Joining Seattle Sounders in February 1978, he coached Pittsburgh Spirit and died in November 1985. AFC Bournemouth's 'Player of the Season' award is named in his memory.

DAVE CHADWICK

Winger Dave Chadwick featured in Cherries' 1971-72 promotion near-miss. Born in India, he grew up in Lymington and turned professional with Southampton in October 1960. He understudied Terry Paine and John Sydenham, moving to Middlesbrough in July 1966. Helping win promotion in 1966-67, he played for Halifax Town prior to joining Cherries in February 1972. He scored four times in 36 League games before moving to Gillingham in September 1974, then Dallas Tornado and Fort Lauderdale. Achieving success as a coach in the United States, he became involved with youth soccer, notably AFC Lightning in Atlanta.

STEVE CHALK

Young goalkeeper Steve Chalk understudied Kieron Baker while at AFC Bournemouth. A former apprentice at Dean Court, he turned professional in October 1975 and was given his League debut in Cherries' 1-1 draw at Doncaster six months later. He played 11 Fourth Division games prior to joining Charlton Athletic in June 1978. Reunited with Stuart Morgan at Weymouth in February 1979, he later played for Oxford City and Eastleigh.

Now living in Hedge End, he spent 17 years as a dog handler with the British Transport Police before becoming an instructor at the police dog training centre in Tadworth.

WILLIE CHALMERS

Scottish inside-left Willie Chalmers was ever-present as Cherries finished sixth in the Third Division (South) in 1936-37. Starting with hometown Kirkcaldy Waverley, he worked as a joiner and had a brief spell with Raith Rovers before joining Bournemouth in July 1932. He made his League debut in the 4-0 defeat at Gillingham five months later and grabbed a hat-trick in Cherries' 8-1 win over Walthamstow Avenue in the 1935-36 FA Cup first round replay. Scoring 17 goals in 153 League outings, he moved to Barrow in June 1938 but was killed whilst serving in the Royal Artillery in Grimsby in October 1943.

BRIAN CHAMBERS

Ex-England Schoolboy midfielder Brian Chambers was an experienced member of Alec Stock's squad at Dean Court. Initially with Sunderland, he was sold to Arsenal for £30,000 in May 1973 and also appeared in the top-flight for Luton Town prior to joining Millwall in July 1977. He featured in their 1977-78 FA Cup run and joined Cherries for £12,000 in July 1979, netting seven goals in 42 League outings prior to joining Halifax Town in March 1981. Later with Poole Town, Salisbury, Dorchester Town and Swanage T&H, he rejoined Poole as player-boss and became a financial planning consultant with Allied Dunbar.

TOM CHARLESTON

Right-back Tom Charleston contested a first-team slot with Edgar Saxton during the 1924-25 season. Previously with Wrexham, where understudy to stalwart Alf Jones, who held their appearance record for many years, he moved to Dean Court in July 1924 and was given his League debut in Cherries' 2-1 victory at home to Luton Town two months later. He played seven Third Division (South) games, appearing alongside James Lamb in defence, before losing his place and joining Poole in July 1925. Helping them to win the Western League Second Division title in 1925-26, he resided in Poole until his death in May 1965.

KEVIN CHARLTON

Goalkeeper Kevin Charlton contested a first-team slot with Kieron Baker while at Dean Court. He turned professional with Wolves in September 1972 and joined AFC Bournemouth in December 1973, making 21 Third Division appearances before moving to Hereford United in June 1975. Starring in their 1975-76 Third Division title triumph, he had a spell with Bangor City, then spent 13 seasons with Telford United. He gained England Semi-Pro recognition and was twice an FA Trophy winner, also helping them to reach the FA Cup fifth round in 1984-85. Briefly with Scarborough, he is now a book salesman in Menai Bridge.

DENIS CHENEY

Versatile forward Denis Cheney partnered Doug McGibbon and Jack Cross in Cherries' attack. Signing professional for Leicester City in November 1941, he starred as they won the Football League (South) title in 1941-42 and was loaned to Watford before Harry Lowe paid £2,500 for him in October 1948. He scored 47 goals in 157 League games for Bournemouth prior to joining Aldershot in June 1954. Reuniting with Ken Bird at Dorchester Town in July 1956, he was top scorer three times, then played for Portland United. He worked for Vigar & Co, Max Factor, then Poole Pottery and died in Christchurch in October 2008.

PERCY CHERRETT

Inside-right Percy Cherrett featured as Cherries took West Ham to an FA Cup fifth round replay in 1928-29. Born locally, he appeared for Bournemouth Poppies and Boscombe prior to joining Portsmouth in February 1921. He was top scorer in 1921-22 and repeated the feat with Plymouth Argyle in 1923-24, then Crystal Palace in two consecutive seasons. Moving to Bristol City with Cecil Blakemore in May 1927, he rejoined Cherries in July 1928 and netted 19 goals in 36 League games before joining Cowes in May 1929. Later landlord of the 'Brunswick Hotel' in Malmesbury Park, he died in Bournemouth in February 1984.

BILL CHIVERS

Inside-left Bill Chivers briefly appeared for Bournemouth during the 1927-28 campaign. Initially with Lowton St Mary's, he joined Stockport County in September 1912 and was given his League debut in the following month's 2-1 defeat at Leeds City. He moved to Eccles Borough in March 1914, then had spells at Merthyr Town, Newport County and Swindon Victoria before joining Swindon Town in July 1927. Leslie Knighton brought him to Dean Court and his solitary League appearance for Cherries was in the 4-3 victory at home to Bristol Rovers in December 1927. He settled back in Stockport and died in September 1971.

GARY CHIVERS

Versatile full-back Gary Chivers was a Tony Pulis signing for AFC Bournemouth. He turned professional with Chelsea in July 1978 and featured in their 1981-82 FA Cup run. Moving via Swansea City to QPR in February 1984, he then had a spell with Watford before joining Brighton in March 1988. Helping clinch promotion straight back to the Second Division, he was granted a testimonial in August 1992 and briefly played for Lyn Oslo prior to joining Cherries in November 1993. He scored twice in 31 League games before moving to Stamco in January 1995, then was Worthing's player-boss. Now a London taxi driver.

IYSEDEN CHRISTIE

Young striker Iyseden Christie had a loan spell at AFC Bournemouth during the 1996-97 campaign. Signing professional for Coventry City in May 1995, he was loaned to Cherries in November 1996 and made four League appearances. He joined Mansfield Town in June 1997, then spent three seasons with Leyton Orient before rejoining Mansfield in August 2002. Top scorer in 2002-03, he helped qualify for the Third Division play-offs in 2003-04, then played for Kidderminster Harriers, Rochdale, Kidderminster again, Stevenage, Torquay United, Tamworth, Kettering, Nuneaton, Tamworth again and Halesowen.

JEAN-FRANCOIS CHRISTOPHE

French midfielder Jean-Francois Christophe had a six-month loan spell at AFC Bournemouth in 2007-08. Initially with RC Lens in his native country, he joined Portsmouth in August 2007 and was loaned to Cherries a week later. He made his League debut in the 0-0 draw at Nottingham Forest on the opening day and returned from a broken hand to score his only goal in ten League One outings as Cherries lost 3-2 at Brighton on New Year's Day 2008. Following a loan spell at Yeovil Town, he has since appeared for Southend United, Oldham Athletic, Compiegne, Lincoln City, Tienen, Avion and Boussu Dour Borinage.

STEVE CLARIDGE

Striker Steve Claridge played League football for 15 different clubs, an all-time record for an outfield player. A former Portsmouth apprentice, he moved via Fareham to AFC Bournemouth in November 1984 and scored once in seven League outings before being sold to Weymouth for £10,000 in October 1985. He then had spells at Crystal Palace, Aldershot, Cambridge United, Luton, Birmingham, Leicester, Wolves, Portsmouth, Millwall, Weymouth again, Brighton, Brentford, Wycombe, Gillingham, Bradford City and Walsall before playing in Cherries' 4-0 defeat by Port Vale in December 2006. Now working in the media.

BILLY CLARK

Young central defender Billy Clark was a fringe member of AFC Bournemouth's 1986-87 Third Division title squad. Locally born, he signed professional for Cherries in September 1984 and made four League appearances before joining Bristol Rovers initially on loan in October 1987. He helped them reach the Third Division play-off final in 1988-89 and moved to Exeter City in October 1997. Joining Forest Green Rovers in July 1999, he featured in the 2001 FA Trophy final, then played for Newport County, Weston-Super-Mare and Clevedon Town. He has since been youth coach at Bristol Rovers and Bath City.

BRIAN CLARK

Striker Brian Clark was AFC Bournemouth's leading marksman in 1972-73. The son of former Bristol City favourite Don Clark, he starred in Bristol City's 1964-65 promotion triumph and moved via Huddersfield to Cardiff City in February 1968. Top scorer three times, he joined Cherries in a £100,000 deal with Ian Gibson in October 1972 and netted 12 goals in 30 League games before being sold to Millwall for £30,000 in September 1973. He rejoined Cardiff and helped them to win promotion in 1975-76, then played for Newport County. Settling in Cardiff, he became a sales rep for safety equipment and died in August 2010.

COLIN CLARKE

Northern Ireland international striker Colin Clarke was Cherries' leading goalscorer in 1985-86. A former Ipswich Town apprentice, he played for Peterborough United and Tranmere Rovers before moving to Dean Court for £22,500 in June 1985. He netted 26 goals in 46 League games for Cherries and starred for his country in the World Cup shortly before sold to Southampton for £400,000 in July 1986. Twice top scorer, he rejoined Cherries on loan in December 1988, then played for QPR and Portsmouth. He has coached United States sides including Richmond Kickers, San Diego Flash, FC Dallas and Carolina Rail Hawks.

LEW CLAYTON

Right-half Lew Clayton featured as Cherries reached the FA Cup sixth round in 1956-57. Initially with Monkton Athletic, he joined Barnsley in March 1942, then played for Carlisle United, Barnsley again and QPR before Jack Bruton signed him in May 1955. His only goal in 40 League games came in Cherries' 3-2 defeat at Southampton nine months later. He joined Swindon Town in June 1957, then played for Wisbech, Poole Town and Gainsborough Trinity. Later trainer/physio at Cambridge City, Doncaster Rovers, Cardiff City, Middlesbrough, Swansea City and Darlington until May 1989, he died in Redcar in January 2010.

PAT CLIFFORD

Winger Pat Clifford starred as Cherries took West Ham to an FA Cup fifth round replay in 1928-29. Initially with Merthyr Town, he moved to Dean Court with Les Roberts in December 1924 after they impressed against Cherries and their arrival contributed to a significant improvement in results. He also helped take eventual winners Bolton to an FA Cup fourth round replay in 1925-26, netting 17 goals in 188 League games before joining Chester in May 1930. Later with Stalybridge Celtic, Prescot Cables and Bacup Borough, he was a porter at Stalybridge railway station until a fatal heart-attack in March 1948.

SHAUN CLOSE

Striker Shaun Close was once AFC Bournemouth's most expensive signing. A former Tottenham Hotspur apprentice, he turned professional in August 1984 and gained top-flight experience before Harry Redknapp paid £90,000 for him in January 1988. He helped Cherries achieve their then highest final placing in 1988-89 and netted eight goals in 39 Second Division games prior to joining Swindon Town in September 1989. Featuring in their 1992-93 promotion campaign, he joined Barnet in August 1993, then Bishop's Stortford and St Albans City. He was a publican in Hoddesdon, becoming a sports coach for Epping Forest Council.

JOE COEN

Young Scottish goalkeeper Joe Coen contested a first-team slot with Billy Gold. He represented Glasgow Schools against London in 1928-29 and played for Clydebank before joining Celtic in March 1931. After loan spells at Clydebank, Nithsdale and Stenhousemuir, he moved to Guildford City in August 1932. He joined Bournemouth in January 1933, after Gold broke a finger, making his debut in that month's 6-1 win over Bristol City. Playing 36 League games, he moved to Luton Town in July 1934 and helped to clinch the Third Division (South) title in 1936-37. He was killed whilst training to be an RAF pilot in October 1941.

DAVID COLEMAN

Young left-back David Coleman was a member of Harry Redknapp's squad at AFC Bournemouth. Signing professional at Dean Court in September 1984, he made his League debut in the 2-0 defeat at Blackpool in April 1986 and provided reliable defensive cover for Paul Morrell. He scored twice in 50 League outings for Cherries prior to joining Farnborough Town in August 1992. Moving to Dorchester Town in August 1993, he later appeared for Salisbury, Wimborne Town, Amesbury Town and Warminster Town while managing the sports shop at Southampton University until his tragic death from meningitis in May 1997.

BILL COLEY

Hard-tackling wing-half Bill Coley appeared for Bournemouth during the 1937-38 campaign. He turned professional with hometown Wolves in September 1933 and made his First Division debut in their 1-0 win at Chelsea in March 1937. Charlie Bell signed him in September 1937 and he played 13 League games for Cherries prior to joining Torquay United in July 1938. He guested for Northampton, Bristol City, Chester and Tranmere during the war, returning to Northampton in August 1947. Later with Exeter and St Austell, he was Northampton's reserve coach, then ran a guest house in Torquay until his death in August 1974.

OWEN COLL

Republic of Ireland U-21 international Owen Coll briefly succeeded Mark Morris in the heart of AFC Bournemouth's defence. Initially with Enfield, he moved to Tottenham Hotspur in July 1994 but failed to secure a first-team slot and joined Cherries in March 1996. He made his League debut in that month's 2-1 victory at home to Bristol Rovers and played 24 Second Division games until sidelined by a knee injury. After a spell with Stevenage, he joined Aldershot Town in December 1998 and later played for Grays Athletic, Hitchin Town and Cheshunt, working for a company involved in the underpinning of buildings.

GEORGE COLLIN

Left-back George Collin starred as Cherries took eventual winners Bolton Wanderers to an FA Cup fourth round replay in 1925-26. Initially with West Stanley, he joined Arsenal in February 1924 and followed Leslie Knighton to Bournemouth with Arthur Roe in August 1925. He made 48 League appearances before breaking a leg in December 1926, then revived his career back at West Stanley. Moving to Derby County in November 1927, he helped finish League Championship runners-up in 1929-30 and 1935-36, then had spells with Sunderland, Port Vale and was Burton Town's player-boss. He died in Derby in February 1989.

DES COLLINS

Winger Des Collins played for Cherries during the 1950-51 campaign. Initially with Chesterfield, starring in wartime football, he joined Halifax Town in November 1946, then had spells with Carlisle United and Barrow before moving to Bournemouth in August 1950. His only goal in five League games clinched that month's 2-2 draw at Gillingham and he joined Shrewsbury in August 1951, then played for Accrington Stanley, Boston United and Spalding United. He settled back in his native Chesterfield and was a precision engineer for Sheepbridge Stokes, then Rhodes Engineering and ran his own company until retirement.

JACK COLLISON

Welsh international midfielder Jack Collison had a loan spell at AFC Bournemouth during the 2013-14 campaign. A former West Ham scholar, he turned professional in August 2007 and made his Premier League debut in their 2-0 defeat at Arsenal on New Year's Day 2008. He was Young Hammer of the Year in 2008-09 and returned from a serious knee injury to feature in their 2011-12 Championship play-off final triumph. Loaned to Cherries in October 2013, he made four League appearances, then joined Wigan on loan and was an FA Cup semi-finalist in 2014. He moved via Ipswich to Peterborough United in May 2015.

JOHN COMPTON

Experienced left-back John Compton was a member of Reg Flewin's squad at Dean Court. Signing professional for Chelsea in February 1955, he had limited top-flight opportunities and moved to Ipswich Town in July 1960. He helped Alf Ramsey's side win the Second Division title in 1960-61 and League Championship in 1961-62, joining Bournemouth in July 1964. His solitary goal in 27 Third Division games came on his debut in the following month's 3-2 victory at home to Reading. A knee injury curtailed his career in May 1965 and he then spent over 30 years as a petrol tanker driver for Texaco, settling in Poole.

PAUL COMPTON

Central defender Paul Compton featured in AFC Bournemouth's 1981-82 promotion campaign. A former Cardiff City apprentice, he moved via Trowbridge to Cherries for £10,000 in October 1980 and made 64 League appearances before joining Aldershot in December 1983. He reunited with David Webb at Torquay United in February 1984, then played for Newport County, Weymouth, Bashley and became Torquay's manager from May 1992 until March 1993. Since then he has been youth team coach/YDO at Preston, Torquay, Swansea City, Cirencester, West Brom, Cardiff City, Dorchester Town and Torquay again.

ALAN CONNELL

Young striker Alan Connell was sidelined by a knee injury for much of AFC Bournemouth's 2002-03 promotion campaign. Initially with Ipswich Town, he moved to Dean Court in July 2002 and regularly featured as a substitute for Cherries. He joined Torquay United in July 2005, then had spells with Hereford United and Brentford prior to rejoining Cherries in August 2008. Helping to clinch promotion in 2009-10, he scored 13 goals in 104 League games overall, moving to Grimsby Town in July 2010. He has since been at Swindon Town, Bradford City, Northampton, Grimsby again, Havant & Waterlooville and Poole Town.

MATTHEW CONNOLLY

Ex-England Youth defender Matthew Connolly was loaned to AFC Bournemouth in 2006-07. He turned professional with Arsenal in July 2005 and played in Dennis Bergkamp's testimonial in July 2006. Loaned to Cherries in November 2006, he was given his League debut in that month's 0-0 draw at Bradford City and his only goal in five League One games came in the 2-0 win at home to Nottingham Forest. Following a loan spell at Colchester United, he joined QPR for £1,000,000 in January 2008 and starred in their 2010-11 Championship title triumph. He repeated the feat with Cardiff City in 2012-13, then loaned to Watford.

STEVE COOK

Versatile central defender Steve Cook was ever-present in AFC Bournemouth's 2014-15 Championship title triumph. A former Brighton trainee, he made his first-team debut in their 2008-09 League Cup second round win over Manchester City and was loaned to Havant & Waterlooville before turning professional in April 2009. He joined Cherries initially on loan in October 2011 and starred in the 2012-13 promotion success, helping take eventual winners Wigan Athletic to an FA Cup third round replay. Forming a fine partnership with skipper Tommy Elphick, he netted nine goals in 143 League games by the end of 2014-15.

RICHARD COOKE

England U-21 winger Richard Cooke helped AFC Bournemouth clinch the Third Division title in 1986-87. Signing professional for Spurs in May 1983, he scored on his First Division debut at Luton six months later and Harry Redknapp paid £27,500 for him in January 1987. He helped Cherries take Manchester United to an FA Cup fifth round replay in 1988-89 and joined Luton Town for £75,000 in March 1989. Rejoining Cherries in March 1991, he netted 17 times in 125 League games overall until a knee injury ended his career in March 1993. He had a testimonial against Spurs in July 1994 and became a London taxi driver.

STEPHEN COOKE

Ex-England Youth midfielder Stephen Cooke had three spells at AFC Bournemouth. Signing professional for Aston Villa in February 2000, he was loaned to Cherries in March 2002 and made his League debut in that month's 5-1 victory at home to Northampton. He returned to Dean Court on loan in January 2004. Following a loan spell at Wycombe Wanderers, he rejoined AFC Bournemouth on a permanent basis in July 2005 but had injury problems, netting three goals in 51 League games overall. He joined Halesowen Town in August 2007, then played for Weymouth, Halesowen again, Bloxwich United and Pelsall Villa.

TOM COOKE

Versatile left-back Tom Cooke helped Bournemouth to finish sixth in the Third Division (South) in 1936-37, the club's then-highest placing. A former miner, he began with Sheepbridge and had a spell at New Brighton before joining Mansfield Town in May 1934, making his League debut in their 2-1 defeat at York City in April 1935. Moving to Dean Court in July 1936, he played 19 Third Division (South) games prior to joining Luton Town in July 1938. He guested for Bradford City during the Second World War and later appeared for Sutton Town. Returning to the mining industry, he died in Chesterfield in August 1974.

SHAUN COOPER

Versatile central defender Shaun Cooper featured prominently as AFC Bournemouth qualified for the League One play-offs in 2010-11. He turned professional with Portsmouth in April 2001 and made his League debut in their 0-0 draw at Crystal Palace in March 2002. Unable to secure a regular first-team slot at Fratton Park, he had loan spells at Leyton Orient and Kidderminster Harriers before joining Cherries in August 2005. He returned from a hip injury to help clinch promotion in 2008-09 and scored once in 211 League outings, moving to Crawley Town in July 2012, then Portsmouth again and Torquay United.

JACK CORK

Ex-England Youth midfielder Jack Cork had two loan spells at AFC Bournemouth during the 2006-07 campaign. The son of Wimbledon legend Alan Cork, he turned professional with Chelsea in July 2006 and was loaned to Cherries in November 2006, playing seven League One games. Also loaned to Scunthorpe United ('Player of the Year' in 2007-08), Southampton, Watford, Coventry City and Burnley, he rejoined Saints in July 2011 and was ever-present in their 2011-12 promotion success. He gained England U-21 honours and played for Team GB in the 2012 Olympic Games, moving to Swansea City in January 2015.

LEO COTTERELL

Ex-England Youth midfielder Leo Cotterell played for AFC Bournemouth during the 1996-97 campaign. Signing professional for Ipswich Town in July 1993, he made his Premier League debut as a substitute in their 3-1 defeat at Southampton in October 1994 but failed to start a match and Mel Machin signed him in June 1996. He made his Cherries debut as a substitute in the 3-2 defeat at Bristol Rovers three months later but injury problems restricted his progress and he made nine League appearances, moving to Rushden & Diamonds in September 1997. Later playing for King's Lynn, he settled back in his native Cambridge.

STEVE COTTERILL

Striker Steve Cotterill was AFC Bournemouth's leading marksman and 'Player of the Year' in 1993-94. Initially with hometown Cheltenham, he had spells with Alvechurch and Burton Albion prior to joining Wimbledon in February 1989. Tony Pulis paid £80,000 for him in August 1993 and he netted 15 goals in 45 Second Division outings for Cherries before a knee injury ended his League career. He has since managed Sligo Rovers, Cheltenham's meteoric rise, Stoke City, Burnley, Notts County's 2009-10 League Two title success, Portsmouth, Nottingham Forest and Bristol City's 2014-15 League One title triumph.

DENIS COUGHLIN

Centre-forward Denis Coughlin twice topped Cherries' goalscoring charts. He represented England Boys Clubs and turned professional with Barnsley in October 1957, playing for Yeovil Town during National Service in the Army before Bill McGarry paid £1,500 for him in March 1963. He netted 41 goals in 88 Third Division games for Bournemouth prior to being swapped for Swansea's Ken Pound in August 1966, then played for Chelmsford City, King's Lynn, Bedford Town and South Shields. Now living in Hetton-le-Hole, he worked at Billingham ICI, then was a pipe-fitter with Amec Oil Rigs until retiring in June 1994.

MOHAMED COULIBALY

Senegalese winger Mohamed Coulibaly was a fringe member of Cherries' 2014-15 Championship title squad. He began his career in France with Gueugnon and Saint-Louis Neuweg, then joined Swiss side Dornach in June 2011 and helped Grasshoppers to finish Swiss League runners-up in 2012-13 before moving to AFC Bournemouth in July 2013. Given his debut in the 2-1 win over Charlton Athletic on the opening day, he had injury problems while at Dean Court, making seven Championship appearances. He was loaned to Coventry City and Port Vale prior to joining Spanish side Racing Santander in July 2015.

JAMES COUTTS

Young midfielder James Coutts made his first start for AFC Bournemouth in the 2005-06 League Cup second round match at eventual finalists Wigan Athletic. A former Southampton junior, he joined Cherries in July 2004 and was given his League debut in the 2-1 defeat at Brentford two months later. He regularly featured as a substitute, playing 11 League games. Following a loan spell at Grays Athletic, he joined hometown Weymouth in July 2007, then Newport County, Dorchester Town, AFC Totton, Weymouth on loan, Gosport Borough and Totton again before Australian sides Twin City Wanderers and Murray United.

IAN COX

Stylish central defender Ian Cox skippered AFC Bournemouth in the 1998 Auto Windscreens Shield final. He impressed with Whyteleafe and Carshalton prior to joining Crystal Palace in March 1994, moving to Dean Court in March 1996. Top scorer and 'Player of the Season' in 1996-97, he was twice ever-present for Cherries and netted 16 goals in 172 League games before sold to Burnley for £500,000 in February 2000. Joining Gillingham in June 2003, the Trinidad & Tobago international joined Maidstone United in March 2008, then reunited with Nicky Southall at Whitstable. He is a prison officer and Ramsgate's head coach.

JACK COXFORD

Commanding centre-half Jack Coxford made a significant contribution as Cherries progressed to the FA Cup fourth round in 1931-32. Starting with North Seaton Colliery, he moved via Stakeford United to Sunderland in May 1924. He also had limited top-flight opportunities after joining Birmingham in April 1927, following Frank Richards to Bournemouth in May 1930. A distinctive figure with his high forehead, he netted three goals in 134 Third Division (South) games for Cherries prior to briefly joining Poole Town in May 1934, then finished his career with Northfleet United. He died in Bury St Edmunds in May 1978.

BILLY COXON

Outside-left Billy Coxon featured prominently in Cherries' 1961-62 promotion near-miss. Initially with Derby County, he moved via Ilkeston to Norwich City in May 1952 and scored on his League debut at Aldershot seven months later. He had a spell with Lincoln City prior to joining Bournemouth in November 1958. Featuring in the League Cup wins over Cardiff City in 1961-62 and Newcastle United in 1963-64, he netted 37 goals in 200 Third Division games for Cherries before moving to Poole Town in June 1966. Later Parley Sports player-coach, he was a local hotelier and taxi driver, then settled in Spondon, near Derby.

FRANK CRAIG

Welsh inside-forward Frank Craig played for Cherries during the 1926-27 season. Initially with Llanelly, he impressed in the Southern League prior to joining Fulham in November 1924 but failed to secure a first-team slot at Craven Cottage and moved to Bournemouth in August 1926. He scored on his League debut in the following month's 6-2 defeat at Coventry City and briefly played alongside record goalscorer Ron Eyre in Cherries' attack, making six further Third Division (South) appearances while at Dean Court. Later playing football back in Wales, he had various jobs back in his native Swansea and died in May 1967.

MARTIN CRANIE

England Youth defender Martin Cranie had a loan spell at AFC Bournemouth in 2004-05. A former Southampton trainee with Gareth Bale and Theo Walcott, he made his Premier League debut in their 4-0 defeat at Chelsea four months before turning professional in September 2004. He was loaned to Cherries in October 2004 and made three League appearances. Captaining Saints to the 2005 FA Youth Cup final, he followed Harry Redknapp to Portsmouth for £150,000 in July 2007. The England U-21 international was loaned to QPR and Charlton prior to joining Coventry City in August 2009, then played for Barnsley.

ANDY CRAWFORD

Striker Andy Crawford was an influential figure in AFC Bournemouth's 1981-82 promotion success. He turned professional with Derby County in January 1977 and scored on his First Division debut. Sold to Blackburn Rovers for £50,000 in October 1979, he was top scorer in their 1979-80 promotion triumph. He reunited with David Webb at Dean Court for £40,000 in November 1981, netting ten goals in 33 League outings for Cherries prior to joining Cardiff City in August 1983. Later with Middlesbrough, Scarborough, Stockport, Torquay United, Poole Town and Bournemouth Sports, he is now a builder in his native Filey.

GEORGE CRAWFORD

Centre-half George Crawford contested a first-team slot with Alex Forbes during the 1929-30 season. Starting with hometown Sunderland, he failed to make an impact at Roker Park and joined Gillingham in May 1927. He was given his League debut in their 2-1 win at Southend United six months later. Moving to Bournemouth in May 1929, he played in the opening three matches of the 1929-30 campaign but then lost his place and made just one further League appearance, at QPR in February 1930. He joined Northampton Town in May 1930 where injury ended his career. Settling back in Sunderland, he died in February 1975.

CHARLIE CRICKMORE

Outside-left Charlie Crickmore starred in consecutive promotion challenges while at Dean Court. Initially with hometown Hull City, he moved to Bournemouth for £3,000 in July 1962 and helped beat Newcastle in the 1963-64 League Cup third round. He scored 17 times in 128 League games prior to joining Gillingham in June 1966 as Jimmy White, David Stocks and Rodney Taylor moved in the opposite direction. Playing for Rotherham United and Norwich City before moving to Notts County in

March 1970, he was ever-present in their 1970-71 Fourth Division title triumph. Now a retired fireman in Thorngumbald, near Hull.

JOHNNY CROSLAND

Former England B international centre-half Johnny Crosland was ever-present for Cherries in two consecutive seasons. Starting with St Annes United, he was awarded the DSC during wartime service in the Fleet Air Arm and joined Blackpool in May 1946. He featured in the 1948 FA Cup final and moved to Bournemouth in June 1954. Appointed captain, he made 106 League appearances prior to joining Wisbech Town in July 1957, starring in their 1957-58 FA Cup run. Reunited with Stan Mortensen at Lancaster City, he was a publican and hotelier back in Blackpool, then ran a taxi business and died in Ely in May 2006.

JACK CROSS

Centre-forward Jack Cross was Cherries' leading marksman in two consecutive seasons. A former Blackpool amateur, he played for Hendon and Guildford City before following Harry Lowe to Dean Court in June 1947. He scored 64 goals in 137 League games for Bournemouth prior to joining Northampton Town for £4,000 in October 1953, then played for Sheffield United, Reading, Headington United (now known as Oxford United), Weymouth and Poole Town. Spending 31 years with the UK Atomic Energy Authority, based at Harwell, Winfrith, Risley and Winfrith again, he died in Broadstone in February 2006.

JAMIE CRUMLEY

Scottish goalkeeper Jamie Crumley helped Bournemouth to reach the FA Cup fifth round in 1928-29. Initially with Dundee Hibernian, he joined Swansea in December 1919 and featured in their first-ever Football League match at Portsmouth in August 1920. He moved via Bristol City to Darlington in June 1924 and was ever-present in their 1924-25 Third Division (North) title triumph. Leslie Knighton signed him in August 1926 and he played 51 League games. Married to a Londoner, he later had three fish and chip shops in London and died in Raynes Park in April 1981. His brother Bob was a keeper with Arbroath.

LES CRUMP

Winger Les Crump briefly appeared for Cherries at the start of the 1927-28 campaign. A great nephew of long-serving FA official Charles Crump, he had represented Birmingham Schools against Scotland and impressed with his works team Sunbeam Motors prior to joining Kilmarnock in May 1925. He played in the Scottish First Division before moving to Bournemouth in July 1927 but made only four League appearances while at Dean Court before losing his place to Tot Pike. Later manager of the Heaton & Benton laundry company in Newcastle-upon-Tyne, he settled in Newcastle and died in December 1983.

WARREN CUMMINGS

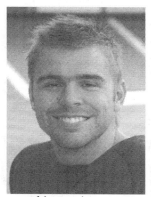

Scotland U-21 left-back Warren Cummings featured in AFC Bournemouth's 2002-03 Third Division play-off final triumph. Initially with Chelsea, he was loaned to Cherries in October 2000, making his League debut in that month's 5-2 victory at Bury. He also had loan spells at West Brom and Dundee United before returning to Dean Court in February 2003. Overcoming a broken leg, he helped Cherries win promotion in 2009-10 and netted seven goals in 259 League games overall. He was loaned to Crawley Town in 2011-12, helping clinch promotion, then joined AFC Wimbledon in June 2012, Poole and Havant & Waterlooville.

IAN CUNNINGHAM

Ex-Scotland Youth right-back Ian Cunningham was a popular member of John Benson's squad at Dean Court. He captained AFC Bournemouth's youth team and helped the reserves win the Football Combination title in 1973-74. Signing professional in August 1974, 'Jock' made his League debut in Cherries' 3-2 defeat at Halifax Town four months later. He scored four goals in 188 League games until leaving in May 1981, then appeared for Swanage T&H, Poole Town, Poppies and was Sturminster Marshall's player-boss. He managed the 'Dorset Soldier' pub for ten years before running his own taxi business in Corfe Mullen.

LAURIE CUNNINGHAM

Long-serving right-back Laurie Cunningham was ever-present four times while at Dean Court. Initially with Consett, he flew Mosquitos as an RAF pilot in 151 Squadron during the war and joined Barnsley in November 1945. He moved to Bournemouth in June 1948 and formed a notable partnership with Ian Drummond, making 273 Third Division (South) appearances before reuniting with Ken Bird at Dorchester Town in July 1957. Later Wareham Rangers' player-boss, he was briefly Cherries' A team coach and ran a newsagent in Bennett Road until retiring in April 1987. He remained local until his death in October 2013.

JAMIE CURETON

England Youth striker Jamie Cureton had a loan spell at AFC Bournemouth during the 1995-96 campaign. Signing professional for Norwich City in February 1993, he was loaned to Cherries in September 1995 and made five substitute appearances while at Dean Court. He moved to Bristol Rovers for £250,000 in September 1996 and was leading marksman in 1998-99, joining Reading for £250,000 in August 2000. A promotion winner in 2001-02, he has since played for Busan Icons, QPR, Swindon Town, Colchester United, Norwich City, Exeter City, Leyton Orient, Exeter again, Cheltenham and Dagenham & Redbridge.

JOHN CURRIE

John Currie was one of nine different players who featured at outside-right for Cherries during the 1946-47 season as the Football League returned to normal after the Second World War. Previously with Stafford Rangers, he moved to Bournemouth as an amateur in October 1946 and made his League debut in that month's 3-0 victory over Port Vale. He played on the opposite flank to Jack McDonald and his solitary goal in seven Third Division (South) games came in Cherries' 3-1 win at home to Southend United. Joining Port Vale in June 1947, he was unable to secure a regular first-team slot. He died in Bromley in April 1984.

ALBERT CURWOOD

Centre-forward Albert Curwood briefly led Bournemouth's attack midway through the 1934-35 campaign. Initially with Llanelly, he moved via Blackpool to Dean Court and made his League debut in Cherries' 2-1 defeat at QPR in December 1934. He played seven Third Division (South) games and joined Swansea in June 1935, then Fleetwood until a knee injury ended his career. Settling back in Blackpool, he was a tram driver, then worked for Hawker aircraft, at Solwick nuclear power station and the Premium Bonds in St Anne's. He died in November 1971. His grandson Steve Curwood is now Fleetwood's chief executive.

REG CUTLER

Outside-left Reg Cutler brought a goal crashing down and scored in Cherries' 1956-57 FA Cup fourth round win at Wolves. Initially with West Brom, he appeared in the top-flight and followed Freddie Cox to Dean Court in June 1956. He netted 21 goals in 96 League games for Bournemouth before reuniting with Cox again at Portsmouth in September 1958, featuring in their 1961-62 Third Division title triumph. Later with Stockport County, Worcester City, Dudley Town and Bromsgrove Rovers, he was a supervisor for Seamless Tubes in Wednesfield, then ran Oakvale Nurseries near Wolverley and died in April 2012.

LAURI DALLA VALLE

Finland U-21 striker Lauri Dalla Valle had a loan spell at AFC Bournemouth in 2010-11. He played youth football for JIPPO and Inter Milan before moving to Liverpool in January 2008. Gaining Europa League experience, he joined Fulham as part of the Paul Konchesky deal in August 2010 and was loaned to Cherries in March 2011. He scored on his League debut in that month's 3-0 victory at home to Oldham and 3-1 defeat at home to Southampton, making eight League appearances. Also loaned to Dundee United, Exeter City and Crewe Alexandra, he has since played for Molde, Sint-Truiden and now Crewe again.

CHARLIE DANIELS

Defender Charlie Daniels missed just four matches in AFC Bournemouth's 2014-15 Championship title campaign. He turned professional with Tottenham Hotspur in July 2005 but failed to make an impact and was loaned to Chesterfield, Leyton Orient and Gillingham before rejoining Orient in January 2009. Moving to Dean Court initially on loan in November 2011, the deal was made permanent two months later and he helped Cherries to win promotion in 2012-13 when selected for the PFA League One 'Team of the Year'. He had netted seven goals in 120 League games for AFC Bournemouth by the end of the 2014-15 season.

HUGH DAVEY

Irish centre-forward Hugh Davey was leading marksman in Bournemouth's 1923-24 Football League debut campaign. He began with Belfast United, then helped Glentoran win the FAI Cup in 1921 and moved to Dean Court in June 1923, featuring in Cherries' first-ever League match at Swindon. Scoring 22 goals in 43 Third Division (South) games, he joined Reading in January 1925. He was top scorer in the 1925-26 Third Division (South) title triumph, moving to Portsmouth in November 1927, then Belfast Celtic. Capped five times by Northern Ireland before a knee injury, he was a publican and grocer in Omeath. He died in 1982.

LORENZO DAVIDS

Dutch U-21 international Lorenzo Davids briefly appeared in AFC Bournemouth's 2012-13 promotion campaign. A cousin of Edgar Davids, the midfielder of Surinamese descent played youth football for SC Voorland, FC Omniworld and FC Utrecht before joining Feyenoord in July 2006. He moved to NEC in February 2007 and was ever-present in 2008-09, then 'Player of the Year' in 2009-10. Following two years with German side FC Augsburg, he joined Cherries in August 2012. Making three League appearances, he was released after Eddie Howe returned as manager and joined Danish side Randers in February 2013.

IAN DAVIDSON

Midfielder Ian Davidson featured in AFC Bournemouth's 1971-72 promotion near-miss. Signing professional for Hull City in February 1965, he had a lengthy loan spell at Scunthorpe before moving to York City in June 1969. He helped them win promotion in 1970-71 and joined Cherries in exchange for Eddie Rowles in July 1971. Making nine League appearances, he moved to Stockport County in May 1972, then Worcester City and Scarborough, featuring in the 1975 FA Trophy final. He has settled in his native Goole, working on the Humber Bridge construction, then spent 25 years with Hygena Kitchens distribution.

FRED DAVIES

Experienced goalkeeper Fred Davies was a key figure in Cherries' 1970-71 promotion success. Initially with Llandudno, he joined Wolves in April 1957 and helped them to regain top-flight status in 1966-67, moving to Cardiff City for £10,000 in January 1968. He joined Bournemouth for £6,000 in July 1970 and was ever-present in 1971-72, making 134 League appearances before following John Bond to Norwich City in December 1973. Returning to Dean Court as John Benson's assistant, he later assisted Bond at Swansea, Birmingham and Shrewsbury where he became manager, then had two spells in charge of Weymouth.

TOM DAVIES

Welsh left-half Tom Davies briefly deputised for Charlie Smith during the 1925-26 campaign. Starting with his local club Troedyrhiw Carlton, he turned professional with Luton Town in September 1924 and joined Bournemouth in August 1925. Given his League debut in that month's 1-1 draw at Northampton, following a 7-2 hammering at Plymouth, he made five consecutive Third Division (South) appearances, then spent two seasons in the reserves. He joined Chelsea in August 1929 but failed to make an impact before moving to Watford in July 1933. Later playing for Exeter City and Walsall, he died in Surbiton in March 1971.

ERIC DAVIS

Centre-forward Eric Davis was top scorer for Bournemouth Reserves in 1936-37. Initially with Frickley Colliery, he moved via Bangor City to Dean Court in July 1936 and was handed his League debut in Cherries' 5-2 win at home to Swindon Town two months later. He also deputised for Joe Riley in the next match, a 1-0 defeat at Gillingham, but did not get another first-team chance and joined Bath City in August 1937. Joint top scorer in 1937-38, he moved to Folkestone in August 1938, then New Brighton in May 1939 before the Second World War ended his career. Settling in Sheffield, he died in September 1995.

DEREK DAWKINS

Versatile right-back Derek Dawkins featured in AFC Bournemouth's 1981-82 promotion campaign. Signing professional for Leicester City in November 1977, he joined Mansfield Town in December 1978 and reunited with David Webb at Dean Court in August 1981. He made eight League appearances for Cherries, then had a spell with Weymouth before linking up with Webb again at Torquay United in February 1984. Helping to reach the Fourth Division play-off final in 1987-88, he later played for Newport County, Yeovil Town and Gloucester City. He has since run a mobile accessories business in Torquay.

KEVIN DAWTRY

Midfielder Kevin Dawtry featured in AFC Bournemouth's 1981-82 promotion campaign. Signing professional for Southampton in June 1976, he gained top-flight experience before joining Crystal Palace in May 1980 and moved to Dean Court in March 1981. He netted 11 goals in 65 League outings for Cherries prior to joining Road Sea Southampton in August 1983, then played for Salisbury, Fareham Town, Gosport Borough, Salisbury again and was Blackfield & Langley's player-coach. He became a production planner for Exxon Chemical at Fawley Oil Refinery, managing Totton & Eling for five years until February 2013.

JAMIE DAY

Ex-England Schoolboy midfielder Jamie Day helped Cherries to beat Charlton Athletic in the 1999-2000 League Cup second round. He turned professional for Arsenal in July 1997, moving to AFC Bournemouth for £20,000 in March 1999. Also featuring in a defensive role, his only goal in 20 Second Division games came in the 2-0 victory at Cambridge United in December 1999. He joined Dover Athletic in July 2001 and moved to Welling United in May 2004, becoming their player-boss in November 2009. Later managing Ebbsfleet United, he reunited with Adrian Pennock as Forest Green Rovers' assistant-boss in May 2015.

MIKE DEAN

Midfielder Mike Dean was a young member of Mel Machin's squad at AFC Bournemouth. A former trainee at Dean Court, he made his League debut in Cherries' 1-0 victory at home to Blackpool five months before turning professional in July 1996. He was regularly a substitute as Cherries narrowly failed to reach the Second Division play-offs in 1998-99 and played 34 League games prior to joining Weymouth in July 2000. Moving to Wessex League newcomers Winchester City in June 2003, he featured in their triumphant 2004 FA Vase run but missed the final, then played for Wimborne Town, settling in his native Weymouth.

JERMAIN DEFOE

England Youth striker Jermain Defoe scored in ten consecutive matches for AFC Bournemouth during the 2000-01 season. A former Charlton Athletic trainee, he joined West Ham for £400,000 in October 1999 and moved to Dean Court on loan in October 2000. He scored 18 goals in 29 League games, including a brilliant solo goal at Oxford United, as Cherries narrowly failed to reach the Second Division play-offs. Twice West Ham's leading marksman, the England international joined Tottenham Hotspur for £7,000,000 in February 2004. He has since played for Portsmouth, Spurs again, Canadian side Toronto and Sunderland.

JIM DE GARIS

Young midfielder Jim De Garis featured in AFC Bournemouth's 1971-72 promotion near-miss. A former Arsenal apprentice, he turned professional in June 1970 and helped win the FA Youth Cup, SE Counties League Cup and Combination Cup in 1970-71. Unable to secure a first-team slot, John Bond signed him in September 1971 and he made his League debut in Cherries' 2-2 draw at Bradford City two months later. He played 12 Third Division games prior to joining Torquay United in March 1974, then had a spell at Ilford. Later rejoining Arsenal as a youth team coach under Don Howe, he has held various other coaching posts.

JOHN DELANEY

Ex-England Amateur international central defender John Delaney had a spell as AFC Bournemouth's captain. A former QPR junior, he spent six seasons with Slough Town, helping to win promotion in 1963-64, before joining

Wycombe Wanderers in July 1969. He skippered them to two Isthmian League titles and moved to Dean Court in August 1973, making 25 League appearances for Cherries before returning to Wycombe in July 1975. Later playing for Hayes, Sutton United and Oxford City, he then managed Tring and Chesham while a cargo agent for Plane Handling at Heathrow Airport. He lives in Holmer Green.

FRANK DEMOUGE

Dutch U-21 striker Frank Demouge briefly featured in AFC Bournemouth's 2012-13 promotion campaign. Starting with NEC, gaining UEFA Cup experience, he joined FC Eindhoven in July 2005, then spent three seasons with Willem II before moving to FC Utrecht in August 2010. He joined Cherries in June 2012 and made his League debut in the 2-1 defeat at home to Walsall three months later. Unlucky to suffer a broken nose and concussion in the following week's 3-1 defeat at Crawley Town, he never played in the first-team again and joined Roda JC Kerkrade on loan in January 2013, with the deal made permanent that summer.

MURDOCH DICKIE

Scottish outside-right Murdoch Dickie understudied Johnny McKenzie as Cherries were Third Division (South) runners-up in 1947-48. Initially with Crewe Alexandra, he joined Port Vale in May 1939 and had a spell with Guildford City before moving to Chelsea in April 1945. He briefly appeared in the top-flight and joined Bournemouth in February 1947, scoring once in 17 Third Division (South) games prior to joining newly-formed Tonbridge in July 1948. Later a security guard in Great Yarmouth and Nuneaton, he ran Meadow View Caravan Park in Huttoft, Lincs, with his wife Margaret until his death in February 2004.

CHARLIE DIXON

Centre-half Charlie Dixon starred as Cherries took West Ham to an FA Cup fifth round replay in 1928-29. He played for Rugeley Villa and Cannock Town before joining Sunderland in March 1927 but failed to make an impact and moved to Dean Court in July 1928. Given his League debut in Bournemouth's 1-0 win at home to Fulham two months later, he made 25 League appearances prior to joining Connah's Quay & Shotton in July 1929. Later with Southport, Nelson (in their final League season) and Hednesford Town, he was an insurance agent and died in Stafford in March 1983. His son Graham played for Stafford Rangers.

RYAN DOBLE

Welsh U-21 midfielder Ryan Doble had a loan spell at AFC Bournemouth during the 2011-12 campaign. He turned professional with Southampton in February 2007 but failed to make an impact and made his League debut while on loan to Stockport County in February 2011. Also loaned to Oxford United that season, he joined Cherries on loan in August 2011 and made his debut in the 2-0 win over Sheffield Wednesday, playing seven League One games while at Dean Court. He then had a similar loan spell at Bury before joining Shrewsbury Town in July 2012 and has since appeared for AFC Telford United.

GEORGE DONOWA

Outside-left George Donowa briefly appeared in Cherries' 1923-24 Football League debut campaign. Born in Southampton, he played for Harland & Wolff before moving to Dean Court and made his solitary Third Division (South) appearance in Bournemouth's 3-1 victory at home to QPR in March 1924. He joined Salisbury in May 1924 but quit football soon after and worked as a lorry driver's mate for Southampton Council until his retirement in December 1965, residing in Southampton until his death in December 1973. His son Roy, who still lives in Southampton, spells his surname Donana after it was changed by his mother.

DICKIE DOWSETT

Centre-forward Dickie Dowsett was Cherries' leading marksman three times. Christened Gilbert, he impressed with Sudbury Town prior to joining Tottenham Hotspur in May 1952. He played for Southend United and Southampton, moving to Bournemouth in June 1957 and scoring 79 goals in 169 League games prior to joining Crystal Palace in November 1962. Later with Weymouth, helping to retain the Southern League title in 1965-66, he was Cherries' commercial manager between June 1968 and January 1984, then production manager of Icarus (Toys) in West Howe. His wife Cynthia had a spell as Cherries' secretary.

BOB DRUMMOND

Scottish forward Bob Drummond played for Bournemouth during the 1927-28 campaign. He impressed with Bathgate before joining Burnley in May 1924 and made his First Division debut in their 0-0 draw at home to Cardiff City three months later. Unable to maintain a regular slot in the top-flight, he moved to Pembroke Dock in July 1925, then had a spell with Bristol City prior to joining Cherries in July 1927. His solitary goal in seven Third Division (South) games clinched the 1-1 draw at Charlton Athletic eight months later and he rejoined Bathgate in July 1928. Settling in Bathgate, he died in December 1966.

IAN DRUMMOND

Long-serving Scottish left-back Ian Drummond was ever-present for Cherries in 1954-55. Starting with Jeanfield Swifts, he joined Portsmouth in May 1945 and moved to Bournemouth in June 1949. He formed a notable defensive pairing with Laurie Cunningham, scoring twice in 265 League games prior to joining Poole Town in July 1956. Featuring in their 1956-57 Western League title triumph, he was later Bluebird Sports player-boss. He settled in Oakdale and spent nearly 20 years as a supervisor during two spells with Bluebird Caravans, then was a storeman for a local engineering firm until retiring in August 1988.

MICHAEL DUBERRY

Young central defender Michael Duberry had a loan spell at AFC Bournemouth during the 1995-96 season. Signing professional for Chelsea in June 1993, he made his Premier League debut in their 2-1 defeat at home to Coventry in May 1994. He was loaned to Cherries in September 1995 and played seven League games. Helping Chelsea win the League Cup and ECWC in 1997-98, the England U-21 international joined Leeds United for £4,000,000 in July 1999. He moved to Stoke City in October 2004, then Reading, Wycombe, St Johnstone and Oxford United. Now a motivational speaker, journalist and sports pundit.

SAM DUDLEY

Outside-left Sam Dudley briefly appeared for Cherries midway through the 1928-29 campaign. Starting with Tipton Excelsior, he turned professional with Preston in April 1927 but failed to secure a first-team slot and joined Bournemouth in June 1928, making his League debut in the 6-3 defeat at Exeter City on Boxing Day. He also featured in Cherries' 4-4 draw at Southend three days later. Moving to Coleraine in May 1929, he joined Clapton Orient in July 1930 and scored on his debut, then briefly played in the top-flight for Chelsea before joining Exeter City in July 1934. He died in his native Dudley in January 1985.

TOMMY DUFF

Tommy Duff was one of six different players who appeared on the left wing for Cherries during the 1928-29 season. Initially with Bishop Auckland, he had a spell with Huddersfield Town but failed to make an impact in the top-flight before moving to Dean Court in June 1928. He was given his League debut in Bournemouth's 2-1 defeat at Luton Town three months later and also featured in the next two matches against Coventry City and Northampton Town. Following a trial spell at Darlington, he joined Crook Town in September 1930. He later worked in the mining industry and died in Canterbury in September 1951.

MARTIN DUFFIELD

Ex-England Youth midfielder Martin Duffield played for AFC Bournemouth on loan during the 1983-84 campaign. A former QPR apprentice, he turned professional in January 1982 and made his League debut in their 1-1 draw at Grimsby Town in May 1983. He was loaned to Cherries in September 1983 and his only goal in six League games came on his debut in that month's 5-1 defeat at John Bond's Burnley. Joining Enfield in July 1985, he helped them win the Conference title in 1985-86 and moved to Hendon in June 1988. He later played for Sutton United, St Albans City and Hendon again, settling in Leighton Buzzard.

GEORGE DUKE

Goalkeeper George Duke understudied Ken Bird while at Dean Court. Initially with Southwick, he moved to Luton Town in January 1939 and made his debut in their first post-war League match against Sheffield Wednesday in August 1946. He was displaced by future England international Bernard Streten and joined Bournemouth in May 1949. Making ten Third Division (South) appearances for Cherries, culminating in a 5-0 defeat at Newport County, he moved to Guildford City in July 1950. Ever-present in 1950-51, he later played for Snowdown CW and Ramsgate in the Kent League. He died in Worthing in March 1988.

GEORGE DUMBRELL

Centre-forward George Dumbrell was unable to prevent Cherries from having to seek re-election for only the second time in 1933-34. He had spells with Botwell Mission, Nunhead, Catford South End, Cray Wanderers and Dartford before joining Brentford as a full-back in May 1928. Moving to Leicester City in May 1930, he partnered record appearance holder Adam Black in the top-flight. He joined Bournemouth in November 1933 and scored twice in 13 Third Division (South) games. Rejoining Brentford in August 1934, he helped them finish a best-ever fifth in the top-flight in 1935-36. He died in Gravesend in March 1990.

KEITH EAST

Striker Keith East was Cherries' leading marksman in 1968-69. Initially with Portsmouth, he moved via Swindon Town to Stockport County in December 1966 and helped clinch the Fourth Division title that season. He joined Bournemouth in November 1967, starring as Cherries took Liverpool to an FA Cup third round replay two months later and netting 34 goals in 94 League games prior to joining Northampton Town in July 1970. Later playing for Crewe Alexandra, Folkestone Town, Johannesburg Rangers, Berea Park, Poole Town and Corinthian Casuals, he has since worked as a car salesman and now lives in Epsom.

ANTHONY EDGAR

Teenage winger Anthony Edgar briefly appeared for AFC Bournemouth on loan during the 2009-10 season. A cousin of Jermain Defoe, he turned professional with West Ham in July 2009 and was a regular member of their reserve team before joining Cherries on loan in October 2009. He made his League debut in a 0-0 draw at Port Vale but played just two further League games while at Dean Court. A late substitute in West Ham's FA Cup third round defeat by Arsenal in January 2010, he joined Yeovil Town in July 2011 and has since played for Barnet, Dagenham & Redbridge, Italian side Triestina and Bishop's Stortford.

PAUL EDMUNDS

Ginger-haired winger Paul Edmunds featured in AFC Bournemouth's 1981-82 promotion success. He gave up his place in the British squad for the World Student Games in Mexico to join Leicester City in April 1979. Helping them win the Second Division title in 1979-80, he moved to Cherries in May 1981 and scored twice in 14 League games prior to joining Bentley Victoria in July 1982. He later played for Grantham, Burton Albion and Armthorpe Welfare while a schoolteacher, then managed Doncaster Belles women's team between 1987 and 1995 where his wife Sheila was the founder/captain and later physio.

EFAN EKOKU

Striker Efan Ekoku starred in Cherries' 1991-92 FA Cup third round replay win at Newcastle United. The 'Chief' impressed with Sutton United before joining Cherries for £100,000 in May 1990, netting 21 goals in 62 League games. Sold to Norwich City for £765,000 in March 1993, he joined Wimbledon for £920,000 in October 1994 and was twice top scorer, including when FA Cup and League Cup semi-finalists in 1996-97. The Nigerian international then played for Grasshoppers Zurich, Sheffield Wednesday, Brentford and Dublin City. Later an insurance salesman, he now works for Premier League Productions and ESPN.

BILL ELLAWAY

Inside-forward Bill Ellaway was an early Freddie Cox signing for Cherries and a fringe member of the 1956-57 FA Cup run squad. He played for Barnstaple prior to joining Exeter City in November 1953 and scored on his League debut in their 2-1 defeat at Brighton three months later. Moving to Cherries in June 1956, he understudied Ollie Norris and made four League appearances while at Dean Court before joining Poole Town in June 1958, then played for Barnstaple and Crediton. Settling in his native Crediton, he was a machinist for Hardinge Machine Tools, then a porter at Exeter University until retiring in October 1997.

BILLY ELLIOTT (1)

Outside-right Billy Elliott gained England wartime international honours after leaving Bournemouth. Starting with Carlisle United, he joined Wolves in July 1937 and followed the well-worn trail to Dean Court in May 1938. His solitary goal in ten League games came in Cherries' 4-0 win over Bristol City five months later and he moved to West Brom in December 1938. He gained two wartime caps and was a key figure as the Baggies regained top-flight status in 1948-49, becoming Bilston's player-manager in July 1951. Later a publican in Handsworth, he died while on holiday in the Canary Islands in November 1966.

BILLY ELLIOTT (2)

Young midfielder Billy Elliott played for AFC Bournemouth during the 1980-81 campaign. Initially with hometown Poole, where his father of the same name was manager, he turned professional with Plymouth Argyle in March 1979 and joined Cherries in May 1980. His solitary goal in 11 League games clinched the 1-0 win at home to Hereford United three months later and he joined Weymouth in June 1981. Featuring in their 1982-83 FA Cup run, he later played for Yeovil Town, Poole again, Swanage T&H and Wimborne Town. He went into partnership with his wife Annette in the Rags to Stitches curtain shop in Wimborne.

MARK ELLIOTT

Welsh winger Mark Elliott had a loan spell at AFC Bournemouth during the 1979-80 season. Starting with Ton Pentre, he joined Brighton in February 1977 and made his League debut in the following month's 4-0 win over Shrewsbury, helping clinch promotion. He moved to Cardiff City in September 1979 and was loaned to Cherries in January 1980, making four League appearances. Returning to Ton Pentre, he joined Wimbledon in February 1982 and scored in the League Group Cup final. He later played for Walton & Hersham, then spent ten seasons with Tonyrefail where he runs a catering business with his wife Sandra.

STUART ELLIOTT

Central defender Stuart Elliott played on loan for AFC Bournemouth during the 1999-2000 campaign. He began with Newcastle United and was loaned to Hull City, Swindon Town, Gillingham, Hartlepool and Wrexham before joining Cherries on loan in December 1999, making eight League appearances while at Dean Court. Moving to Darlington in July 2000, he has since played for Plymouth Argyle, Carlisle United, Exeter City, Halifax Town, Harrogate, Harrow Borough, Waltham Forest, Gateshead, Northwich Victoria, York City, Grays Athletic, Durham City, Bedlington Terriers, Newcastle Benfield and Ashington.

WADE ELLIOTT

Ex-England Schoolboy winger Wade Elliott starred in AFC Bournemouth's 2002-03 Third Division play-off final triumph. He impressed with Bashley prior to joining Cherries for £5,000 in February 2000 and scored on his full League debut in the following month's 2-0 win over Wycombe. Voted 'Player of the Year' in 2000-01, he netted 31 goals in 220 League games, joining Burnley with Garreth O'Connor in July 2005. He was ever-present in 2007-08 and scored their 2008-09 Championship play-off final winner. Moving via Birmingham to Steve Cotterill's Bristol City in January 2014, he became their U-21 coach in June 2015.

TOMMY ELPHICK

Central defender Tommy Elphick was ever-present captain in AFC Bournemouth's 2014-15 Championship title triumph. A former Brighton trainee, following his older brother Gary, he was loaned to Bognor Regis and made his League debut in Brighton's 5-1 defeat at Reading six months before turning professional for his hometown club in June 2006. He was 'Player of the Year' in 2007-08 and starred in the Seagulls' 2010-11 promotion success. Moving to Dean Court in August 2012, he was captain and 'Player of the Year' in Cherries' 2012-13 promotion triumph, netting four goals in 118 League games by the end of 2014-15.

CHUKKI ERIBENNE

Striker Chukki Eribenne was a member of AFC Bournemouth's 2002-03 promotion squad. Starting with Coventry City, he moved to Dean Court in July 2000 and scored on his Second Division debut to clinch Cherries' 1-1 draw at Bristol Rovers the following month, his solitary goal in 47 League outings. Loaned to Hereford United, he joined Havant & Waterlooville in July 2003, then helped Weymouth to win the Conference South title in 2005-06. He played for Grays Athletic and was an unused substitute in Ebbsfleet United's 2008 FA Trophy final success before spells with Sutton United, Hinckley United and Ilkeston.

HUGH EVANS

Welsh inside-left Hugh Evans contested a first-team slot with Cliff Marsh during the 1950-51 season. He grew up in Luton and played representative football for the Army before moving from Redditch United to Birmingham City in December 1947. Given his First Division debut in their 0-0 draw at Preston in January 1949, he was unable to prevent relegation from the top-flight in 1949-50 and joined Bournemouth in June 1950. He netted eight goals in 22 Third Division (South) games while at Dean Court prior to joining Walsall in August 1951, then had a spell with Watford and later ran the family grocery shop in Luton.

RAY EVANS

Inside-forward Ray Evans helped Cherries reach the FA Cup fourth round in 1959-60. Signing professional for Preston North End in May 1951, he was given his First Division debut in their 3-2 defeat at Arsenal in October 1953 and featured as his hometown club finished third in the top-flight in 1956-57. He moved to Bournemouth in August 1959 and scored nine times in 36 League games before reuniting with Joe Dunn at Morecambe in July 1961. Helping them win the Lancashire Combination title in two consecutive seasons, he later played for Chorley and ran his own roof-slating firm in Preston. He died in Chorley in June 2009.

JOHN EVANSON

Midfielder John Evanson was an experienced member of Alec Stock's squad at AFC Bournemouth. Starting with Towcester, he turned professional with Oxford United in February 1965 and was a member of their 1967-68 Third Division title squad. He moved to Blackpool for £40,000 in February 1974, then Fulham for £50,000 in August 1976, playing alongside George Best. Following Stock to Cherries for £20,000 in July 1979, he scored twice in 53 League games prior to joining Poole Town in March 1981. He then worked in the licensed trade and became head of catering at a private health and fitness club in High Wycombe.

LES EYRE

Versatile inside-left Les Eyre partnered Jack Cross in Cherries' early post-war attack. Initially with Bilsthorpe Colliery, he represented the RAF and was an amateur with Cardiff City before following Cyril Spiers to Norwich City in July 1946. Twice leading marksman, he moved to Dean Court for £5,500 in November 1951 and netted ten goals in 38 Third Division (South) games for Bournemouth prior to joining Chelmsford City in July 1953. He returned to mining at Bilsthorpe Colliery, then ran the 'Horse Barracks' pub in Norwich. Later working for Colmans, he resided in Norwich until his death in November 1991.

RON EYRE

Centre-forward Ron Eyre holds Cherries' all-time goalscoring record. Real name Roland, he impressed with Hucknall Colliery before joining Sheffield Wednesday in August 1923. He moved to Bournemouth in January 1925 and his arrival sparked a significant upturn in results. Starring as Cherries took eventual winners Bolton Wanderers to an FA Cup fourth round replay in 1925-26, he was leading marksman in eight successive seasons and netted 202 goals in 302 League games before joining Christchurch in May 1933. He spent 30 years as a foreman ganger for the Southern Electricity Board and died locally in August 1969.

HARRY FALCONER

Young full-back Harry Falconer featured in AFC Bournemouth's 1974-75 relegation battle. A former Burnley apprentice, he turned professional at Dean Court in July 1972 and helped the reserves to win the Football Combination title in 1973-74. He made his League debut in the 1-0 defeat at Blackburn in October 1974 and played seven Third Division games prior to joining Wimbledon in July 1975, featuring in their 1975-76 Southern League title campaign. Also playing semi-professional football for Dulwich Hamlet, Staines Town, Kingstonian and Walton & Hersham, he has since worked in the printing trade in London.

BRIAN FARMER

Right-back Brian Farmer was an experienced figure in Cherries' 1961-62 promotion near-miss. Initially with Stourbridge, he joined Birmingham City in July 1954 and secured a regular slot after the tragic death of Jeff Hall in April 1959. He was a Fairs Cup finalist in two consecutive seasons and moved to Dean Court for £3,800 in January 1962. Helping Bournemouth beat Newcastle United in the 1963-64 League Cup third round, he made 132 League appearances before joining Christchurch in June 1965. He later worked in the finance industry and became chairman of Christchurch, remaining local until his death in June 2014.

GEORGE FARROW

Right-half George Farrow was Cherries' joint leading marksman in 1934-35. He turned professional with Stockport County in October 1930 and joined Wolves in January 1932, gaining top-flight experience as Dickie Rhodes' understudy. Moving to Bournemouth in July 1933, the penalty expert netted 12 goals in 106 League games before joining Blackpool in June 1936. He featured in their 1936-37 promotion success and was swapped for Sheffield United's Walter Rickett in January 1948. Later Bacup Borough's player-manager, he became a progress chaser at Whitburn Area Workshops and died in December 1980.

PETER FEELY

Ex-England Youth striker Peter Feely was a John Bond signing for AFC Bournemouth. He failed to make the grade at Ipswich Town but helped Enfield win the Amateur Cup in 1970 and gained England Amateur honours before moving to Chelsea in May 1970. Joining Cherries for £1,000 in February 1973, he scored twice in nine League games prior to briefly joining Fulham in July 1974. He later played under Len Ashurst at Gillingham and Sheffield Wednesday, then became a chartered surveyor and had an international real estate consultancy in Hong Kong. Now living in Perth, Western Australia, he is president of Subiaco City.

LIAM FEENEY

Fast winger Liam Feeney missed just two matches in AFC Bournemouth's 2009-10 promotion campaign. Initially with Hayes, he impressed alongside Matt Tubbs at Salisbury City in the Conference and had a loan spell at Southend United before moving to Dean Court in February 2009. He was ever-present as Cherries qualified for the League One play-offs in 2010-11 and netted 12 goals in 109 League games prior to joining Millwall in May 2011. Featuring in their run to the FA Cup semi-finals in 2012-13, he was loaned to Bolton Wanderers and Blackburn Rovers before returning to Bolton on a permanent basis in May 2014.

WARREN FEENEY

Northern Ireland international striker Warren Feeney was AFC Bournemouth's leading marksman and 'Player of the Year' in 2001-02. Previously with Leeds United, he joined Cherries initially on loan in March 2001 and made his Northern Ireland debut in

March 2002, joining his grandfather Jim and father Warren as a full international. Featuring in Cherries' 2002-03 promotion campaign, he netted 36 goals in 107 League games before moving to Stockport County in July 2004. The brother-in-law of Stephen Purches, he joined Luton in March 2005, then Cardiff, Oldham, Plymouth and Salisbury, becoming Linfield's player-boss.

NICKY FENTON

Ex-England Youth central defender Nicky Fenton had two loan spells at AFC Bournemouth. Signing professional for Manchester City with his twin brother Tony in November 1996, he featured in two promotion campaigns and was loaned to Cherries in March 2000. He returned on loan in August 2000 and made 13 Second Division appearances overall. Sold to Notts County for £150,000 in September 2000, he moved via Doncaster Rovers to Grimsby Town in August 2006 and was a Johnstone's Paint Trophy finalist in 2008. He then played for Rotherham, Morecambe and Alfreton, becoming Burton Albion's physio.

RIO FERDINAND

Outstanding young central defender Rio Ferdinand had a loan spell at AFC Bournemouth during the 1996-97 campaign. A cousin of Les Ferdinand, he turned professional with West Ham in November 1995 and was loaned to Cherries in November 1996, playing ten consecutive Second Division games while at Dean Court. He gained the first of 81 England caps against Cameroon in November 1997 and was sold to Leeds United for £18,000,000 in November 2000, then Manchester United for a British record £30,000,000 in July 2002. Amassing a vast collection of honours, he reunited with Harry Redknapp at QPR in July 2014.

WAYNE FEREDAY

Former England U-21 winger Wayne Fereday helped AFC Bournemouth reach the FA Cup fourth round in 1990-91. Signing professional for QPR in September 1980, he featured as they won the Second Division title in 1982-83 and reached the League Cup final in 1986, following Jim Smith to Newcastle for £300,000 in July 1989. He joined Cherries as part of the Gavin Peacock deal in November 1990 and played 23 League games before being sold to West Brom for £60,000 in December 1991. Later with Cardiff City, Weymouth, Telford United, Sturminster Marshall and Christchurch, he became a local delivery driver.

PHIL FERNS (Snr)

Versatile right-half Phil Ferns was ever-present for Cherries in 1965-66. Signing professional for Liverpool in September 1957, he featured in their 1963-64 League Championship success and moved to Bournemouth in August 1965. He helped take Burnley to an FA Cup third round replay and made 46 League appearances prior to joining Mansfield Town in August 1966. Appointed Rhyl's player-manager in July 1968, he was later Poole Town's player-coach. Settling in Poole, he spent 24 years as a machine operator at Hamworthy Engineering, then was a security man at the B&Q Supercentre in Fleets Lane and died in August 2007.

PHIL FERNS (Jnr)

Young left-back Phil Ferns played alongside Ian Cunningham in AFC Bournemouth's defence. The son of ex-Cherry Phil Ferns, he impressed with Poole Town before turning professional at Dean Court in

February 1979. He netted six goals in 95 League games for Cherries prior to joining Charlton Athletic for £20,000 in August 1981. Moving to Blackpool in August 1983, he was a promotion winner in 1984-85, then played for Aldershot and skippered Yeovil Town's 1987-88 Isthmian League and Cup 'double' success. Later with Poole, Yeovil again and Trowbridge, he became a constable with Hampshire Police and Dorset Police.

CHRIS FERRETT

Teenage left-back Chris Ferrett briefly appeared for AFC Bournemouth during the 1994-95 season. Born in Poole, he was a trainee at Dean Court and made his only League appearance as a substitute in Cherries' 3-0 defeat at Shrewsbury in October 1994. He was at Portsmouth on a non-contract basis before moving to Fleet Town in October 1995, then Basingstoke, Salisbury, Dorchester, Havant & Waterlooville, Bashley, Salisbury and Bashley again, playing almost 300 games for them overall. Assisting Steve Riley before accompanying him to AFC Totton in July 2012, he is general manager for Fowler Welch in Hilsea.

FRANK FIDLER

Centre-forward Frank Fidler was Cherries' leading marksman in 1953-54. A former Manchester United amateur, he was top scorer as Witton Albion were twice Cheshire League champions and moved via Wrexham to Leeds United in October 1951. Jack Bruton signed him in December 1952 and he netted 32 goals in 61 Third Division (South) games for Bournemouth prior to joining Yeovil Town in July 1955, then played for Hereford United and Bridgwater Town. Employed by Westlands in Yeovil, he later worked for the Post Office until retiring in August 1989. He settled in Farnborough and died in November 2009.

MATT FINLAY

Teenager Matt Finlay briefly appeared for AFC Bournemouth during the 2007-08 season. He was a versatile left-sided player who could occupy a number of positions both in defence and attack. A trainee at Brockenhurst College, he was drafted into the first-team squad during an injury crisis and went on as a substitute in place of fellow debutant Billy Franks for the last 13 minutes of the 2-1 victory at home to Tranmere Rovers in March 2008. It was destined to be the only League appearance either player made for Cherries. He joined Bashley in July 2008, since playing for Basingstoke, Bashley again and Ringwood.

TREVOR FINNIGAN

Striker Trevor Finnigan was a member of John Benson's squad at AFC Bournemouth. A former Port Vale apprentice, he turned professional with Everton in May 1971 and had a spell with Runcorn before moving to Blackpool in March 1977. He joined Cherries for £3,000 in January 1978, scoring five goals in 25 League games before sold to Yeovil Town for £2,000 in January 1979. Featuring in Weymouth's 1982-83 FA Cup run, he rejoined Yeovil as player-manager, then had spells with Bath City, Dorchester, Wimborne, Swanage and Lyme Regis. He installed fibre-optic cabling with Kieron Baker and still lives locally.

JACK FISHER

Hard-tackling left-back Jack Fisher partnered Laurie Cunningham in Cherries' defence. Signing professional for Millwall in May 1946, he played alongside his twin brother George before Harry Lowe paid £1,000 for him in June 1949. He made 52 League appearances for Bournemouth prior to reuniting with Jimmy Blair at Ramsgate in June 1954, helping win the Kent League title in 1954-55. Later with Weymouth and Yeovil Town, he gave Poole Town lengthy service as trainer while a floor layer for Sherry & Haycock. He coached Cherries under son-in-law David Webb, then was a carpenter, settling in Poole.

DARRYL FLAHAVAN

Goalkeeper Darryl Flahavan missed just two matches as AFC Bournemouth reached the League One play-offs in 2010-11. The brother of former Portsmouth keeper Aaron Flahavan, he began with Southampton and moved via Woking to Southend United in October 2000. He played in two LDV Vans Trophy finals and helped win promotion in two consecutive seasons. Joining Crystal Palace in July 2008, he was loaned to Oldham Athletic, then moved via Portsmouth to Dean Court in June 2011. He was sidelined by a shoulder injury in 2011-12 and made 46 League appearances for Cherries before released in May 2015.

JACK FLAHERTY

Inside-forward Jack Flaherty briefly understudied Willie Chalmers during the 1935-36 season. Previously with Wolves, the 'Buckley Babe' failed to secure a first-team slot while at Molineux and was an early Charlie Bell signing for Bournemouth in March 1936. He impressed on his debut for the reserves against Dartford, making his Third Division (South) debut in that month's 4-1 defeat at Watford. The match report states that he faded in the second half after starting well. Destined to be his only League appearance for Cherries, he was released at the end of the season. He later settled in Sheffield and died in February 1980.

ALAN FLETCHER

Inside-left Alan Fletcher scored in Bournemouth's 1938-39 FA Cup third round defeat at Leeds United. He turned professional with Blackpool in January 1937 and had a spell with Port Vale before moving to Dean Court in June 1938. Given his League debut in Cherries' 4-2 defeat at Swindon Town six months later, he made 12 Third Division (South) appearances before joining Bristol Rovers in June 1939, having impressed in Cherries' 3-0 FA Cup second round victory at Eastville Stadium. The Second World War disrupted his career and he moved to Crewe Alexandra in September 1947. He died in Hillingdon in August 1984.

CARL FLETCHER

Welsh international midfielder Carl Fletcher was capped four times while at AFC Bournemouth. Given his League debut in Cherries' 2-1 defeat at Grimsby five months before turning professional at Dean Court in July 1998, he was captain and 'Player of the Year' in the 2002-03 promotion success. He netted 19 goals in 193 League games, then reunited with Peter Grant at West Ham for £250,000 in August 2004 and was an FA Cup finalist shortly before joining Crystal Palace for £400,000 in July 2006. Later at Plymouth Argyle, he became manager, then had a spell with Barnet, rejoining Cherries as youth team boss in January 2014.

JACK FLETCHER

Inside-right Jack Fletcher was unable to prevent Cherries having to seek re-election in 1933-34. He had spells at Boldon Colliery Welfare and Chopwell Institute before joining Aldershot in January 1932, moving via Guildford City to Bournemouth in November 1933. Scoring on his League debut in the next month's 2-1 defeat at home to Charlton, he netted three goals in 26 Third Division (South) games before following Billy Birrell to QPR in June 1935. He later played for Clapton Orient, scoring a hat-trick against Cherries in September 1937, Barrow and Peterborough United. Settling in Peterborough, he died in August 1991.

STEVE FLETCHER

Long-serving striker Steve Fletcher holds AFC Bournemouth's appearance record. The grandson of former England international left-back Jack Howe, he helped hometown Hartlepool win promotion in 1991-92 and was Tony Pulis' first signing at £30,000 in July 1992. He was 'Player of the Year' in 1994-95 and leading scorer as Cherries were Auto Windscreens Shield finalists in 1998. Scoring in the 2002-03 Third Division play-off final triumph, he joined Chesterfield in July 2007, then returned via Crawley in January 2009. He was a promotion winner in 2009-10 and 2012-13, netting 103 goals in a club record 628 League games.

JOHN FLOOD

Former England Schoolboy winger John Flood played for Cherries during the 1958-59 campaign. Initially with Pennington St Marks, he turned professional with Southampton in November 1949 and scored on his League debut in their 6-1 victory at home to Blackburn Rovers in April 1953. Moving to Bournemouth in July 1958, he netted three goals in 17 League games prior to joining Headington United (now known as Oxford United) in July 1959, then reunited with Bill Dodgin at Yiewsley before Cowes. After 18 years as a fitter's mate at Southampton Docks, he worked for the Ordnance Survey until retiring in October 1992.

WES FOGDEN

Versatile midfielder Wes Fogden was a fringe member of AFC Bournemouth's 2012-13 promotion squad. A former Brighton trainee, he turned professional with his hometown club in June 2006 and overcame health problems that threatened his career. He was loaned to Dorchester Town and Bognor Regis before rejoining Dorchester in August 2008. Moving to Havant & Waterlooville in February 2009, he joined Cherries initially on loan in October 2011 and overcame a shoulder injury to score four times in 53 League games while at Dean Court. He joined Portsmouth in January 2014, moving to Yeovil Town in July 2015.

STEVEN FOLEY

Diminutive Republic of Ireland Youth midfielder Steven Foley was a Sean O'Driscoll signing for AFC Bournemouth. Starting with Stella Maris in his native Dublin, he was an Aston Villa trainee, helping win the FA Youth Cup in 2002 and reach the final again in 2004. He turned professional in February 2003 but failed to secure a first-team slot at Villa Park. His full surname is Foley-Sheridan and he joined Cherries for £20,000 in August 2005 after a loan spell. He made his League debut in the following month's 0-0 draw at home to Tranmere Rovers, netting six goals in 53 League games before a back injury curtailed his career.

CHRIS FOOTE

Young midfielder Chris Foote helped Cherries beat top-flight Sheffield Wednesday in the 1969-70 League Cup second round. Born locally, he turned professional at Dean Court in August 1968 and made his League debut in Cherries' 3-0 defeat at Swindon Town eight months later. He starred as Bournemouth were FA Youth Cup semi-finalists in 1968-69 and scored twice in 44 League games prior to joining Cambridge United in March 1971. Featuring prominently in their 1972-73 promotion success, he then played for Weymouth before quitting football in May 1976. He has since been a plumbing and heating engineer.

ALEX FORBES

Scottish centre-half Alex Forbes featured in Bournemouth's 1931-32 FA Cup fourth round defeat at Sheffield Wednesday. Initially with Musselburgh Bruntonians, he joined Luton Town in October 1928 and made his League debut in their 2-1 defeat at home to Torquay six months later. He moved to Dean Court in July 1929 and his solitary goal in 47 Third Division (South) games came in Cherries' 3-1 win over Bristol Rovers in April 1930. Joining Gillingham in July 1932, his career was curtailed by a knee injury in April 1935. Settling back in Bournemouth, he worked for W Hayward & Sons builders and died in January 1979.

TERRELL FORBES

Teenage defender Terrell Forbes had a loan spell at AFC Bournemouth during the 1999-2000 season. A former West Ham trainee, he helped win the FA Youth Cup shortly before turning professional in July 1999. Harry Redknapp loaned him to Cherries in October 1999 and he made three League appearances while at Dean Court. He joined QPR in July 2001 and helped win promotion in 2003-04. Joining Grimsby Town in September 2004, he had a spell with Oldham Athletic, then played under Russell Slade again at Yeovil Town and Leyton Orient before Chesterfield, Aldershot, Dover, Dulwich and Hemel Hempstead.

JAMES FORD

Midfielder James Ford was a young member of Sean O'Driscoll's squad at AFC Bournemouth. He was a trainee at Dean Court and turned professional in April 2000, making his League debut in that month's 1-1 draw at home to Chesterfield. Unable to secure a regular first-team slot, he played 12 League games for Cherries and had a spell with Dorchester Town prior to joining Havant & Waterlooville in July 2002. He helped them qualify for the Conference South in 2003-04 and moved to Fareham Town in January 2005, since appearing for Bognor Regis, Lymington & New Milton, Chichester City and Gosport Borough.

DAVID FORDE

Goalkeeper David Forde featured in AFC Bournemouth's dramatic run in at the end of the 2007-08 season. He had spells with Barry Town, West Ham and Derry City prior to joining Cardiff City in January 2007. Given his League debut in the following month's 4-1 win over Preston, he had a loan spell at Luton Town before loaned to Cherries in March 2008. He made 11 League appearances, including seven wins, as Kevin Bond's side narrowly failed to avoid relegation. Moving to Millwall in July 2008, the Republic of Ireland international has since been ever-present three times including the Lions' 2009-10 promotion success.

DARYL FORDYCE

Northern Ireland Youth midfielder Daryl Fordyce had a loan spell at AFC Bournemouth in 2005-06. He turned professional with Portsmouth in July 2005 and Harry Redknapp loaned him to Cherries in February 2006. Given his League debut in that month's 0-0 draw at home to Oldham Athletic, he also appeared in Cherries' next two matches against Rotherham and Blackpool. He failed to secure a first-team slot with Pompey and moved to Glentoran in July 2007, then joined Linfield in July 2011. Helping them to win the Irish League title in 2011-12, he joined Canadian side FC Edmonton with Albert Watson in February 2013.

CLIFF FOSTER

Outside-left Cliff Foster understudied Harry Maidment during the 1925-26 campaign. Starting with Scunthorpe United, he joined Rotherham County in March 1924 and was given his League debut in their 4-2 defeat at Wigan eight months later. He moved to Bournemouth in May 1925, making four consecutive League appearances prior to joining Shirebrook in March 1926. Moving via Morecambe to Manchester City in April 1927, he featured in their 1927-28 Second Division title campaign, then had spells with Oldham Athletic and Halifax Town. He settled back in his native Rotherham and died in January 1959.

AMOS FOYEWA

Nigerian striker Amos Foyewa was a fringe member of AFC Bournemouth's 2002-03 promotion winning squad. He was a trainee at West Ham but failed to make an impact at Upton Park and joined Cherries in July 2001, making his League debut in the 1-0 defeat at Huddersfield on the opening day of the season. Unlucky to break his leg during Cherries' 2-2 draw at Cardiff City in August 2001, he failed to establish a regular first-team place after returning from injury and made nine League appearances prior to joining Woking in March 2003. He has since played for Lewes, St Albans City, Thurrock and AFC Hornchurch.

SIMON FRANCIS

Ex-England Youth defender Simon Francis missed just four matches in AFC Bournemouth's 2014-15 Championship title campaign. Rejected as a youngster by both Nottingham clubs, he turned professional with Bradford City in May 2003 and joined Sheffield United for £200,000 in March 2004. He was loaned to Grimsby and Tranmere before moving to Southend United for £70,000 in June 2006. Helping reach the League One play-offs in 2007-08, he joined Charlton Athletic in July 2010. He moved to Cherries initially on loan in November 2011 and starred in the 2012-13 promotion success, then ever-present in 2013-14.

BILLY FRANKS

Teenage central defender Billy Franks briefly appeared for AFC Bournemouth during the 2007-08 campaign. Born in Shoreham, he progressed through the youth ranks at Dean Court and had been on the bench a couple of occasions before an injury crisis saw him make his solitary League appearance in Cherries' 2-1 victory at home to Tranmere Rovers in March 2008. Released following injury problems, he failed to make an impact during six months with Exeter City, then played for Eastbourne Borough, Bognor Regis and Worthing, moving to East Preston in October 2012. He returned to Worthing in October 2014.

RYAN FRASER

Scotland U-21 winger Ryan Fraser helped AFC Bournemouth to clinch promotion in 2012-13. Initially with hometown Aberdeen, he turned professional in May 2010 and quickly impressed in the Scottish Premier League before moving to Dean Court for £400,000 in January 2013. He was given his Cherries debut in the following month's 1-0 defeat at home to Sheffield United and regularly featured as a substitute during the 2014-15 Championship title campaign. Scoring four goals in 63 League games, he joined Ipswich Town with Brett Pitman, on a season-long loan, as part of the Tyrone Mings deal in June 2015.

JACK FRIAR

Scottish winger Jack Friar was a promising young member of Billy Birrell's squad at Dean Court. He had spells with Carluke Juniors, Bradford City and Hibernian before joining Portsmouth in April 1932, scoring on his First Division debut at Middlesbrough the following season. Moving to Cherries in July 1933, he netted 11 goals in 34 Third Division (South) games prior to joining Port Vale in July 1934. He returned to the top-flight with Preston four months later, then played for Norwich City and Ipswich Town. Settling back in Scotland, he worked at a pit-head in Lanark until July 1976 and died in Bathgate in May 1979.

TONY FUNNELL

Striker Tony Funnell was leading marksman in AFC Bournemouth's 1981-82 promotion success. Initially with Eastbourne United, he joined Southampton in January 1977 and scored their promotion-clinching goal at Orient in April 1978. He joined Gillingham for £50,000 in March 1979 and moved via Brentford to Dean Court for £5,000 in September 1981. Scoring 22 goals in 64 League outings for Cherries until a back injury, he joined Poole Town in November 1984 and was ever-present in their 1989-90 promotion success, breaking their club goalscoring record. He has since run a community coaching scheme and soccer school.

JIMMY GABRIEL

Former Scotland inter-national Jimmy Gabriel was a key figure in AFC Bournemouth's 1972-73 promotion challenge. Initially with Dundee, he joined Everton in March 1960, starring as they won the League Championship in 1962-63 and FA Cup in 1966. He moved to Southampton for £45,000 in July 1967 and John Bond paid £20,000 for him in July 1972. Scoring four goals in 53 League games for Cherries, he joined Brentford in March 1974, then coached Seattle Sounders and San Jose Earthquakes. He assisted Harry Redknapp at Cherries, then was Everton's assistant-boss before coaching back in the United States.

PADDY GALLACHER

Inside-forward Paddy Gallacher played for Cherries either side of the Second World War. He impressed with Third Lanark prior to joining Blackburn Rovers in October 1936 and moved to Dean Court in June 1938. Helping Bournemouth to win the Third Division (South) Cup in 1946, he featured in the 1947-48 promotion near-miss and scored three times in 35 Third Division (South) games. Appointed Weymouth's player-manager in June 1948, he plotted their 1949-50 FA Cup run and later coached Dundalk. He settled in Bexhill-on-Sea and was employed as an HGV driver, remaining in Sussex until his death in June 1983.

RYAN GARRY

Ex-England Youth central defender Ryan Garry featured prominently in AFC Bournemouth's 2009-10 promotion success. A former Arsenal trainee, he helped them win the FA Youth Cup shortly before turning professional in July 2001 and made his Premier League debut in their 6-1 win over Southampton in May 2003. He joined Cherries in August 2007 and forged a fine partnership with Jason Pearce, netting three goals in 77 League outings before a leg injury curtailed his career in July 2011. Appointed first-team coach and defensive co-ordinator, he left ten months later and rejoined Arsenal as a youth development coach.

ROY GATER

Tough-tackling centre-half Roy Gater was twice ever-present for Cherries. Signing professional for Port Vale in April 1958, he moved to Bournemouth for £5,000 in July 1962 and succeeded Tony Nelson in the heart of defence. He scored three goals in 216 League games while at Dean Court prior to joining Crewe Alexandra in January 1969, then helped Weymouth win the Southern League Cup in 1973 and was ever-present for Dorchester in 1974-75. He had two spells as Christchurch's manager and also coached Poole Town and Poppies. Still living locally, he was a painter and decorator for Furneaux Builders until retiring.

LEN GAYNOR

Inside-forward Len Gaynor partnered the likes of Jack Cross and Frank Fidler in Cherries' attack. He had spells with Ilkeston, Brinsley and Eastwood Colliery prior to joining Hull City in April 1948. Jack Bruton signed him in June 1951 and he scored 12 goals in 51 League games for Bournemouth before moving to Southampton in March 1954. He helped their reserves win the Combination Cup in 1955, then had a spell as Aldershot's captain and played for Oldham Athletic and Yeovil Town until a broken leg ended his career. Settling locally, he was a carpenter, then in partnership with his eldest son Gary as L&G Builders.

CHARLIE GEORGE

Ex-England international striker Charlie George briefly featured in Cherries' 1981-82 promotion campaign. Signing professional for Arsenal in March 1968, he helped them win the Fairs Cup in 1970 and scored the winning goal in the 1971 FA Cup final to clinch the 'double'. He joined Derby County in July 1975 and was top scorer in 1975-76, moving to Southampton for £400,000 in December 1978. After a spell with Bulova, he joined Cherries in March 1982 and played two League games that month before rejoining Derby. He ran a pub near New Milton, then was a partner in a garage business and is now a matchday host at Arsenal.

RICKY GEORGE

Winger Ricky George briefly played for Cherries during the 1965-66 campaign. Initially with Tottenham Hotspur, he joined Watford in August 1964, then Bournemouth in May 1965. He made three League appearances while at Dean Court before joining Oxford United in July 1966, then played for Hastings United, Barnet and Hereford United. Scoring their 1971-72 FA Cup third round replay winner against top-flight Newcastle United, he later had spells playing for Stevenage, Barnet again, Cambridge City, Boreham Wood and Barnet once more. He has since run a sportswear business and become a racehorse owner.

BRIAN GIBBS

Inside-forward Brian Gibbs featured in Cherries' 1961-62 promotion near-miss. A former Portsmouth junior, he moved via Gosport Borough to Bournemouth in October 1957 and netted 15 goals in 58 League games before reuniting with Freddie Cox at Gillingham for £4,000 in October 1962. Top scorer in their 1963-64 Fourth Division title triumph, he joined Colchester United for £6,000 in September 1968 and starred in their 1970-71 FA Cup run. He became Bletchley Town's player-boss and spent 23 years in meat industry management. Later a voluntary ambulance driver, he died in Silverstone in February 2014.

IAN GIBSON

Former Scotland U-23 midfielder Ian Gibson was a John Bond signing for AFC Bournemouth. Initially with Accrington Stanley, he joined Bradford PA in July 1959, then played for Middlesbrough before joining Coventry City for £57,500 in July 1966. He starred in their 1966-67 Second Division title triumph and reunited with Jimmy Scoular at Cardiff City for £35,000 in July 1970. Moving to Cherries in a joint £100,000 deal with Brian Clark in October 1972, he made 20 Third Division appearances. He joined Berrea Park in May 1974, then Gateshead and Whitby. Settling in Redcar, he fitted new seals in gasometers.

SIMON GILLETT

Midfielder Simon Gillett had a loan spell at AFC Bournemouth in 2006-07. He turned professional with Southampton in November 2003 and was loaned to Walsall and Blackpool before joining Cherries on loan in November 2006. His solitary goal in seven League games came in the following month's 3-1 defeat at home to Blackpool. He had another loan spell at Blackpool, featuring in their 2007 League One play-off final triumph, then helped Saints win the 2010 Johnstone's Paint Trophy final. Later playing under Sean O'Driscoll at Doncaster, Nottingham Forest and Bristol City (on loan), he joined Yeovil in August 2014.

MIKE GILMORE

Right-half Mike Gilmore contested a first-team slot with Willie Smith as Cherries finished sixth in the Third Division (South) in 1936-37. Christened Henry Patrick, he began with Shotton CW and joined Hull City in December 1934. He moved to Mansfield Town in July 1935, then Bournemouth in June 1936. Featuring in the 1936-37 FA Cup third round defeat at top-flight Everton, he played 13 consecutive League games for Cherries prior to joining Runcorn in February 1937. Following spells with QPR and Hull City again, he guested for Barnsley during the Second World War. He died in Hartlepool in December 1966.

DICKIE GIRLING

Winger Dickie Girling contested a first-team slot with Tommy Tippett during the 1951-52 campaign. Christened Howard, he turned professional with Crystal Palace in October 1943 and scored their first post-war League goal at Mansfield in August 1946. He joined Brentford in February 1947 but was unable to prevent relegation from the top-flight and moved to Bournemouth in July 1951. Playing four League games, including the 2-2 draw at Torquay on the opening day, he joined Hastings United in July 1952 and starred as they reached the FA Cup third round in consecutive years. He died in Hastings in January 1992.

DON GIVENS

Republic of Ireland international striker Don Givens had a loan spell at AFC Bournemouth during the 1979-80 campaign. Initially with Manchester United, he moved via Luton Town to QPR in July 1972 and starred as they won promotion in 1972-73, then were League Championship runners-up in 1975-76. Joining Birmingham City in August 1978, he reunited with Alec Stock on loan at Dean Court in March 1980 and scored four goals in five League games. Later playing for Sheffield United, he was then player and coach with Neuchatel Xamax, becoming Arsenal's youth coach before managing Republic of Ireland U-21's.

JIMMY GLASS

Goalkeeper Jimmy Glass played for AFC Bournemouth in the 1998 Auto Windscreens Shield final. Signing professional for Crystal Palace in July 1991, he moved to Dean Court in March 1996 and was ever-present in 1997-98. He made 94 League appearances for Cherries prior to joining Swindon Town in June 1998. Loaned to Carlisle United in April 1999, he scored their dramatic late goal against Plymouth Argyle that preserved Football League status that season, then played for Cambridge United, Brentford, Oxford United, Crawley Town, Kingstonian, Salisbury and Brockenhurst, working for a local IT company.

PETER GLEDSTONE

Long-serving left-back Peter Gledstone featured in Cherries' 1961-62 promotion near-miss. Born locally, he helped Bournemouth Gasworks win the Hampshire Senior Cup in 1954 and moved to Dean Court in November 1955. He made his League debut in Bournemouth's 3-1 victory at home to Port Vale in April 1958, scoring twice in 131 League games until a knee injury ended his career in June 1964. After a period with Bournemouth Fire Brigade, he emigrated to New Zealand in March 1967, briefly returning, then was a maintenance engineer in Australia. He settled in Cabarita Beach, NSW and died in December 2014.

HOWARD GODDARD

Striker Howard Goddard had two spells at AFC Bournemouth. He made his debut as a 15 year-old in Cherries' 2-0 defeat at Halifax in April 1973 and turned professional at Dean Court in July 1974. Leading marksman in 1974-75, he joined Swindon Town in June 1976 and moved to Newport County in August 1977. He was twice top scorer and returned to Cherries in December 1981, helping to clinch promotion. Netting 20 goals in 76 League games overall prior to joining Aldershot in August 1982, he later played and coached overseas, working for a computer company. He has managed Andover and Whitchurch United.

TOMMY GODWIN

Republic of Ireland international goalkeeper Tommy Godwin starred as Cherries reached the FA Cup sixth round in 1956-57. Initially with Home Farm, he represented the League of Ireland while at Shamrock Rovers and joined Leicester City in September 1949. Jack Bruton signed him in June 1952 and he was ever-present for Bournemouth on three occasions. The club's first full international against Holland in May 1956, he played 357 League games, moving to Dorchester Town in June 1963. He spent 20 years at British Aerospace (Hurn), then was a parks patrolman for Bournemouth Corporation and died in August 1996.

IVAN GOLAC

Former Yugoslav international right-back Ivan Golac briefly appeared for AFC Bournemouth during the 1982-83 campaign. He starred for Partizan Belgrade before joining Southampton in September 1978 and played in the 1979 League Cup final. Moving to Dean Court in November 1982, he made nine League appearances for Cherries prior to joining Manchester City in March 1983. He later played for Bjelasica, Saints again, Portsmouth and Zumun. Since holding various coaching and managerial posts, he plotted Dundee United's 1994 Scottish Cup final triumph, shuttling between his homes in Vienna and Belgrade.

SCOTT GOLBOURNE

Ex-England Youth full-back Scott Golbourne was one of four Reading players to spend time on loan at AFC Bournemouth during the 2007-08 season. A former Bristol City trainee, he turned professional in March 2005 and was sold to Reading for £150,000 in January 2006. He had limited first-team chances and spent two loan spells with Wycombe before joining Cherries on loan in November 2007, making five League One appearances. Following a loan spell at Oldham Athletic, he joined Exeter City in July 2009. He moved via Barnsley to Wolves in August 2013 and helped them win the League One title in 2013-14.

BILLY GOLD

Former Scotland Junior goalkeeper Billy Gold succeeded Peter McSevich during the 1931-32 campaign. Initially with Bellshill Athletic, he moved via Ballieston Juniors to Dean Court in January 1931 and made his League debut in Cherries' 2-1 defeat at Mansfield a year later. He was unlucky with injuries, suffering a broken arm against Northampton in January 1933, playing 77 Third Division (South) games before joining Wolves in December 1936. Gaining top-flight experience as Alex Scott's understudy, he moved to Chelsea in May 1937, then appeared for Doncaster Rovers. He settled in Doncaster and died in February 1976.

DALE GORDON

Former England U-21 winger Dale Gordon had a spell as AFC Bournemouth's player-coach. Starting with Norwich City, he was ever-present 'Player of the Year' as they were fourth in the top-flight and FA Cup semi-finalists in 1988-89. He joined Glasgow Rangers for £1,200,000 in November 1991 and helped win all three major Scottish honours. Moving to West Ham in July 1993, he reunited with Mel Machin at Dean Court in July 1996 and played 16 League games for Cherries. He later managed Great Yarmouth and Gorleston, then rejoined Great Yarmouth as director of football, since running his own football academy.

DAN GOSLING

Versatile England U-21 defender Dan Gosling regularly featured as a substitute in AFC Bournemouth's 2014-15 Championship title campaign. A former Plymouth Argyle trainee, he made his League debut against Hull City two months before turning professional in February 2007. He joined Everton in January 2008 and scored their 2008-09 FA Cup fourth round replay winner against Liverpool. Appearing in the 2009 FA Cup final, he overcame a serious knee injury and moved to Newcastle United in July 2010. He was loaned to Blackpool before joining Cherries in May 2014, playing three League games in 2014-15.

JEFF GOULDING

England Semi-Pro international striker Jeff Goulding featured in AFC Bournemouth's 2009-10 promotion campaign. He had spells at Molesey, Croydon, Clapton, Egham Town, Hayes, Yeading, Fisher Athletic and Gray Athletic on loan before moving to Dean Court in September 2008. Scoring on his debut in the 3-0 Johnstone's Paint Trophy first round win over Bristol Rovers, he returned from a loan period at Eastbourne Borough to score four goals in 44 League games. He was reunited with Wesley Thomas at Cheltenham Town in June 2010, joining Aldershot Town in February 2013, then Chelmsford City and Dover Athletic.

BRENT GOULET

United States international striker Brent Goulet played for AFC Bournemouth during the 1987-88 season. Previously with Portland, he impressed for Seattle Storm in a friendly against Cherries and moved to Dean Court in November 1987. He made six Second Division appearances and was loaned to Crewe before returning to Seattle Storm. Featuring in the 1988 Olympic Games, he was capped eight times by the United States and also played for Tacoma Stars back in his native country, then for German sides Bonner, Teve Berlin, Bonner again, Rot-Weiss Oberhausen, Wuppertaler and Elversberg where he became coach.

JOSH GOWLING

Central defender Josh Gowling helped AFC Bournemouth to avoid relegation in 2006-07. A former West Brom trainee, he played for Danish side Herfolge before reuniting with Richard O'Kelly at Cherries in August 2005 and made his League debut as a substitute in that month's 2-2 draw at MK Dons. He overcame a serious knee injury in the 2-0 win at Brentford in October 2005 and his solitary goal in 83 League games came in the 3-1 defeat by Rotherham in October 2006. He joined Carlisle United in July 2008, then had a loan spell at Hereford and has since appeared for Gillingham, Lincoln City, Kidderminster and Grimsby.

LEWIS GRABBAN

Striker Lewis Grabban was AFC Bournemouth's leading marksman in 2013-14. He turned professional with Crystal Palace in July 2006 but struggled to make an impact and was loaned to Oldham Athletic and Motherwell before sold to Millwall for £150,000 in January 2008. Featuring in their 2009-10 promotion campaign, he moved via Brentford to Rotherham United in July 2011 and topped their goalscoring charts in 2011-12. He joined Cherries in July 2012 and starred in the 2012-13 promotion success, netting 35 goals in 86 League games. Moving to Norwich City in June 2014, he featured in their 2014-15 promotion triumph.

MAX GRADEL

Exciting winger Max Gradel spent the 2007-08 season on loan at AFC Bournemouth. Born in the Ivory Coast, his full name is Max-Alain. He turned professional with Leicester City in September 2005. He was loaned to Cherries in August 2007 andscored nine goals in 34 League outings while at Dean Court. Featuring in Leicester's 2008-09 League One title triumph, he joined Leeds United in October 2009 and helped to win promotion that season. The Ivory Coast international moved to Saint-Etienne in August 2011 and was top scorer in 2014-15, rejoining Cherries for a reported £7,00,000 in August 2015.

GEORGE GRAHAM

Much-travelled Scottish inside-left George Graham scored as Cherries took West Ham to an FA Cup fifth round replay in 1928-29. Initially with Vale of Clyde, he moved via Shettleston to Morton in July 1925. He joined Cherries in November 1928, scoring on his debut in the following month's 2-2 draw at Gillingham. Playing alongside record goalscorer Ron Eyre, he scored twice in 17 Third Division (South) games before joining Caernarvon Town in June 1929. Following spells with Boston Town and Waterford, he rejoined Morton in July 1931, then appeared for East Stirlingshire, Ards and Jarrow, settling back in Glasgow.

MILTON GRAHAM

Young midfielder Milton Graham scored in AFC Bournemouth's 1983-84 FA Cup third round victory over holders Manchester United. Signing professional for Cherries in May 1981, he netted twice on his League debut five months later and helped clinch promotion in 1981-82. He scored in the 1984 Associate Members Cup final triumph, netting 12 goals in 73 League outings prior to joining Chester in August 1985. Later playing for Peterborough United, Poole Town, Spalding United, Bourne Town, Grantham Town, Holbeach United, Corby Town and Stamford, he has since worked for a boat building company in Oundle.

PETER GRANT

Former Scotland international midfielder Peter Grant had a spell as AFC Bournemouth's player-coach. He turned professional with Celtic in July 1982 and helped twice win the Scottish Premier League title as well as the Scottish Cup in 1989. Sold to Norwich City for £200,000 in August 1997, he moved via Reading to Cherries in August 2000. He played 15 League games before concentrating on coaching, then assisted Alan Pardew at West Ham and returned to Norwich as manager in October 2006. Later assisting Tony Mowbray at West Brom and Celtic, then Alex McLeish at Birmingham, Villa and Forest, he became Fulham's coach.

STEVE GRAPES

Diminutive winger Steve Grapes had a loan spell at AFC Bournemouth during the 1975-76 campaign. Signing professional for hometown Norwich in July 1970, he helped them to regain top-flight status at the first attempt under John Bond in 1974-75. He reunited with John Benson on loan at Cherries in March 1976 and his solitary goal in seven League games came in the following month's 4-2 win at home to Hartlepool. Joining Cardiff City in October 1976, he later played for Torquay United, Bath City, Merthyr Tydfil, Barry Town and Llantwit Major. He has settled in Llantwit Major and since worked for a fitness equipment firm.

HARRY GRAY

Experienced inside-right Harry Gray featured in Cherries' 1947-48 promotion near-miss. Initially with Grimethorpe Rovers, he joined Barnsley in February 1938 and appeared in their first post-war League match at home to Nottingham Forest in August 1946. He moved to Bournemouth in December 1946 and displaced Tommy Paton in attack. Ever-present for the second-half of that season, featuring in five-goal wins over Torquay and

Swindon, he netted seven goals in 30 Third Division (South) games prior to joining Southend United in June 1948, then played for Ashford Town. He died in Sheffield in January 1989.

ADAM GREEN

Young left-back Adam Green had a loan spell at AFC Bournemouth during the 2004-05 season. A former Fulham scholar, he turned professional in July 2003 and made his Premier League debut in their 2-1 defeat at Middlesbrough six months later. He was loaned to Sheffield Wednesday before joining Cherries on loan in March 2005, making three League One appearances while at Dean Court. Following another loan spell at Bristol City, he joined Grays Athletic in July 2006 and has since played for Woking, Hayes & Yeading, Dartford, Basingstoke, Dartford again and Leatherhead, working as a telecommunications engineer.

EDDIE GREEN

Young inside-left Eddie Green provided valuable cover whilst at Dean Court. He turned professional with Bournemouth in March 1929 and was given his League debut in the 1-0 defeat at Norwich in April 1930. Making six League appearances, he joined Derby County in May 1931 and gained top-flight experience, then moved via Manchester United to Stockport County in July 1934. He helped win the Third Division (North) Cup and reach the FA Cup fifth round in 1934-35. Later playing for Cheltenham Town, he worked for S Smith & Sons in Bishop Cleeve and died in Cheltenham after a lengthy illness in November 1949.

BRIAN GREENHALGH

Striker Brian Greenhalgh replaced Phil Boyer in Cherries' attack. Initially with Preston, he joined Aston Villa with Brian Godfrey in September 1967, then played for Leicester City and Huddersfield Town before joining Cambridge United in July 1971. He was top scorer three times including their 1972-73 promotion success and joined Cherries for £35,000 in February 1974. Scoring seven times in 24 League games, he joined Watford in March 1975, then Dartford, Bedford, Hillingdon, Staines, Wealdstone, Cambridge City, Carshalton, Maidenhead and Chesham. He scouted for Everton, Watford, Aston Villa and Newcastle.

JACK GREGORY

Full-back Jack Gregory was a member of Don Welsh's squad at Dean Court. Signing professional for Southampton in December 1944, he appeared in four Combination Cup finals and had a spell as captain before joining Leyton Orient in July 1955. He featured in their 1955-56 Third Division (South) title triumph, moving to Bournemouth in July 1959. Playing 17 League games before reuniting with Ted Ballard at Ashford Town in August 1960, he followed him to Hastings United, then was a boilermaker welder for Vospers ship repairs at Southampton Docks. He resided in Southampton until his death in March 2008.

STEVEN GREGORY

Former England Semi-Pro international midfielder Steven Gregory played for AFC Bournemouth in 2011-12. He progressed through the ranks at Wycombe Wanderers and turned professional in July 2006, featuring in their run to the League Cup semi-finals in 2006-07. Moving to Hayes & Yeading in July 2008, he starred in their 2008-09 promotion success and joined AFC Wimbledon in July 2009. He featured in their 2011 Conference play-off final triumph and moved to Cherries in July 2011. Scoring twice in 28 League One games, he was loaned back to AFC Wimbledon before joining Gillingham in January 2013.

ANTONY GRIFFIN

Versatile defender Antony Griffin briefly featured as AFC Bournemouth narrowly failed to qualify for the Second Division play-offs in 1998-99. Born locally, he turned professional at Dean Court in July 1997 and made his League debut in Cherries' 5-0 win at home to Burnley in November 1998. He played six Second Division games before Steve Cotterill paid £20,000 to sign him for Football League new-boys Cheltenham Town in July 1999. Featuring in their 2001-02 Third Division play-off final triumph, he joined Dorchester Town in June 2004 and was loaned to Lymington & New Milton before injury problems ended his career.

ADAM GRIFFITHS

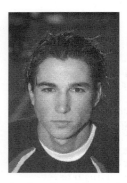

Tall central defender Adam Griffiths briefly appeared for AFC Bournemouth during the 2005-06 campaign. Born in Sydney, the twin brother of Joel Griffiths, he appeared for Sutherland Sharks, Northern Spirit, Eastern Pride and Newcastle KBU in his native country. He then had spells with Belgian side KV Ostende and Watford before joining Cherries in January 2006. Scoring once in seven League games, the Australian international moved to Brentford in July 2006, then played for Newcastle Jets, Gold Coast United, Al-Shabab, Adelaide United, Hangzhou Greentown, Sydney FC, Selangor, Kedah and APIA Leichhardt.

BILL GRIPTON

Centre-half Bill Gripton succeeded Jim Stirling in the heart of Cherries' defence. Initially with Toll End Wesley, he turned professional with West Brom in November 1937 and made most wartime appearances for the Baggies, moving to Luton Town in June 1948. Jack Bruton signed him in July 1950 and he made 79 Third Division (South) appearances for Bournemouth prior to joining Worcester City in June 1952. He became their groundsman, then was groundsman for Vono bedding company in his native Tipton as well as coaching Vono Sports but motor neurone disease forced his early retirement and he died in February 1981.

STEVE GRITT

Midfielder Steve Gritt was a young member of John Benson's squad at Dean Court. Born locally, he turned professional with AFC Bournemouth in July 1976 and scored three goals in six League outings before joining Charlton Athletic in July 1977. He helped them to win promotion in 1980-81 and 1985-86, moving to Walsall in July 1989. Rejoining Charlton in February 1990, he was joint-manager with Alan Curbishley between July 1991 and June 1995, then managed Brighton and was Millwall's assistant-boss. He returned to Charlton as Academy manager before reuniting with Steve Brown as Ebbsfleet United's assistant-boss.

ALAN GROVES

Exciting winger Alan Groves featured in AFC Bournemouth's 1972-73 promotion challenge. Initially with hometown Southport, he moved via Chester to Shrewsbury Town in February 1971 and was ever-present in 1971-72. John Bond paid £44,000 for him in October 1972 and he scored twice on his debut as Cherries triumphed 7-2 at Rotherham United, netting four goals in 36 League outings before being controversially sold to promotion rivals Oldham Athletic for £10,000 in February 1974. He helped them to clinch the Third Division title that season and later played for Blackpool until suffering a fatal heart-attack in June 1978.

JOHN GROVES

Experienced right-half John Groves helped Cherries beat Newcastle United in the 1963-64 League Cup third round. The son of former Derby County star Arthur Groves, he represented Derbyshire Schools with Billy Coxon and turned professional with Luton Town in October 1950. He featured in their 1954-55 promotion success and was an FA Cup finalist in 1959, moving to Dean Court for £2,750 in September 1963. Making 54 League appearances for Bournemouth until a back injury ended his career in June 1965, he settled back in his native Derby and spent 30 years with Courtaulds until retiring in December 1995.

PHIL GULLIVER

Big central defender Phil Gulliver featured in AFC Bournemouth's 2002-03 Third Division play-off final success. A former Middlesbrough trainee, he signed professional in July 2000 but failed to secure a Premiership slot despite captaining their reserve team. He was loaned to Blackpool and Carlisle, then Cherries in March 2003, making six Third Division appearances. After further loan spells at Bury and Scunthorpe, he joined Rushden & Diamonds in August 2004 and was their 'Player of the Year' in 2005-06, moving to Hereford United in July 2006, then Rushden again, Oxford City, Corby Town and King's Lynn.

TERRY GULLIVER

Popular right-back Terry Gulliver featured in Cherries' 1970-71 promotion campaign. Initially with Weymouth, he helped twice win the Southern League title before Freddie Cox signed him in August 1966. He starred as Bournemouth took Liverpool to an FA Cup third round replay in 1967-68 and beat Sheffield Wednesday in the 1969-70 League Cup second round. Scoring twice in 163 League outings, he moved to Cape Town City in June 1972, helping to win the South African title, then played for rivals Hellenic. He returned to the Bournemouth area in March 1986 and became sales manager for a pump manufacturer.

ALISTAIR GUNN

Scottish outside-right Alistair Gunn played for Cherries during the 1954-55 campaign. A former classmate of Ian Drummond at Grove Academy in Broughty Ferry, he started with Dundee Elmwood, then joined Dundee in July 1946 and helped them win the Scottish B Division title in 1946-47. Moving to Huddersfield Town in January 1951, he featured in their 1952-53 promotion campaign and joined Bournemouth in June 1954. He scored twice in 27 League games before leaving in May 1955, then was briefly with Arbroath and spent 23 years as an accountant with NCR in Dundee. Settling in Broughty Ferry, he died in April 2010.

PETER GUTHRIE

Goalkeeper Peter Guthrie deputised for Gerry Peyton while at Dean Court. An FA Vase semi-finalist with Whickham in 1983-84, he moved via Blyth Spartans to Weymouth in July 1987, then Tottenham Hotspur for £100,000 in January 1988. He failed to secure a first-team slot at White Hart Lane and was loaned to Swansea, featuring in their 1987-88 Fourth Division play-off final success. Sold to Barnet for £60,000 in August 1989, he joined Cherries for £15,000 in August 1990 and made ten League appearances. He later played for Sing Tao, Happy Valley and Bedlington Terriers, since becoming a bus driver in Newcastle.

SCOTT GUYETT

Ex-England Semi-Pro central defender Scott Guyett featured in Cherries' 2009-10 promotion campaign. Born in Ascot, he grew up in Australia and played for Brisbane City, then helped Gresley Rovers win the Southern League title in 1996-97. He had spells at

Southport, Oxford United and Chester City, helping win the Conference title in 2003-04, prior to joining Yeovil Town in July 2004. Featuring in their 2004-05 League Two title triumph, he was a League One play-off finalist in 2007 and moved to Cherries in August 2008. Playing 34 League games, he joined Dorchester in July 2010. Now Crystal Palace's fitness coach.

RAY HADDINGTON

Inside-right Ray Haddington briefly played for Cherries at the start of the 1952-53 season. After spells with Bradford PA and Bradford City, he joined Oldham Athletic in August 1947 and was twice top scorer. He joined Manchester City in November 1950, helping them win promotion in 1950-51. Moving to Stockport County in December 1951, he joined Bournemouth in July 1952, appearing in the first two League games of the season, losing 1-0 to both Northampton and Aldershot. Joining Rochdale in October 1952, he later played for Halifax Town and Bedford Town. He emigrated to Australia and died in Adelaide in July 1994.

NEIL HAGUE

Ex-England Youth defender Neil Hague was ever-present for AFC Bournemouth in 1975-76. Initially with Rotherham United, he helped take Leicester City to an FA Cup fifth round replay in 1967-68 and joined Plymouth Argyle in November 1971. He helped reach the League Cup semi-finals in 1973-74 and moved to Dean Court with Derek Rickard in July 1974. Scoring seven times in 89 League games for Cherries, he joined Huddersfield Town in June 1976, then played for Darlington, Phoenix Fire and Columbus Ohio. He became a builder near Barnard Castle and is now a self-employed property developer in Plymouth.

GORDON HAIGH

Hard-working inside-forward Gordon Haigh was an early Jack Bruton signing for Cherries. After a spell with Ransom & Marles, he joined Burnley in November 1945 and helped them win promotion in 1946-47, appearing in the top-flight as Harry Potts' understudy. He moved to Bournemouth in April 1950 and netted three goals in 17 League games prior to joining Watford in August 1951, then played for Rossendale United and Nelson. He ran two fruit and fish shops in Burnley, then spent 20 years as caretaker at Reedley County Primary School until retiring in August 1986. Settling in Brierfield, he died in August 2011.

RICHARD HALL

Young midfielder Richard Hall played for Cherries at Liverpool in the 1967-68 FA Cup third round replay. Starting with hometown Weymouth, he helped them twice win the Southern League title, following Terry Gulliver to Bournemouth in June 1967. He was given his League debut in the 3-1 win over Bristol Rovers on the opening day and made 11 Third Division appearances before rejoining Weymouth in March 1968, featuring in their 1968-69 FA Cup run. Moving to Dallas Tornado in May 1970, he was ever-present five times including their 1971 NASL championship success and since been a college soccer coach in Dallas.

CLIFF HALLIWELL

Popular right-half Cliff Halliwell starred as Cherries took West Ham to an FA Cup fifth round replay in 1928-29. A former Sheffield Wednesday junior, he played for leading Sheffield amateur side Darnall Old Boys before joining Sheffield United in June 1920. He gained top-flight experience as Harold Pantling's understudy, moving to Dean Court in October 1926. Scoring twice in 214 League games before a knee injury ended his career in May 1932, he was briefly landlord of the Old Crown Inn in Sheffield, then spent 38 years at Firth Vickers steelworks. His died in Sheffield in June 1984. Ian Botham is his great nephew.

RAY HAMPSON

Winger Ray Hampson helped Cherries qualify for the newly formed Third Division in 1957-58. A former 'Busby Babe', he turned professional with Manchester United in April 1951 and also spent two seasons as a Reading reserve before joining Aldershot in July 1955. He made his League debut in their 2-2 draw at QPR five months later, moving to Bournemouth in July 1957. Contesting a first-team slot with Brian Loughnane, John Flood and Tommy Southren, he scored twice in 15 League games prior to joining Folkestone in July 1959. He settled in Reading and became a sales development manager during 29 years with Berger Paints.

WALLY HANLON

Outside-left Wally Hanlon created numerous goalscoring chances for Doug McGibbon while at Dean Court. A former Dundee junior, he was captured by the Italians during wartime service in the Army and spent four years as a prisoner of war. He moved via Clyde to Brighton in August 1946 and joined Cherries in May 1948. Contesting a first-team slot with Denis Cheney, he netted three goals in 19 League games before moving to Crystal Palace in July 1949. Later Sudbury Town's player-boss, he settled in Ferndown and spent 20 years as a check weighman for Fatstock Marketing Corporation. He died in April 1999.

BOB HARDY

Centre-half Bob Hardy skippered Cherries' 1953-54 FA Cup first round replay win over Southampton. Christened Gordon, he turned professional with Millwall in August 1945 and moved via Southport to Bournemouth in June 1950. He made 76 Third Division (South) appearances while at Dean Court before moving to Yeovil Town in July 1954. Featuring in their 1954-55 Southern League and Cup 'double' success, he was then player-boss of Street, Frome and Salisbury. He became a sales rep for golf equipment, then ran Premier Sports Agency in Charminster until retiring in May 1988 and died in November 2003.

PETER HARMAN

Young centre-forward Peter Harman made his solitary League appearance for Cherries in the 2-1 defeat at home to Reading in January 1970. A former apprentice at Dean Court, he turned professional in August 1968 and helped Bournemouth to reach the FA Youth Cup semi-finals in 1968-69. He was a fringe member of Cherries' 1970-71 promotion winning squad and joined Reading in August 1971, starring in their 1971-72 FA Cup run. Moving via Bath City to Guildford City in July 1974, he was leading marksman in 1974-75, then played for Molesey. He later emigrated to Australia and is now a retired policeman in Brisbane.

JUSTIN HARRINGTON

Versatile midfielder Justin Harrington played for AFC Bournemouth during the 1997-98 campaign. Born in Truro, he turned professional with Norwich City in July 1994 but failed to make an impact and reunited with Martin O'Neill at Leicester City in August 1996. He moved to Dean Court in July 1997, making his League debut in Cherries' 1-0 win at home to Wigan Athletic the following month. Playing eight Second Division games, he joined Porthleven in August 1998. He moved to rivals St Blazey in July 2000 and starred in successive South-Western League title triumphs, also representing Cornwall against Devon.

FRANK HARRISON

Forward Frank Harrison briefly appeared in the closing weeks of Bournemouth's 1923-24 Football League debut campaign. Born locally, he played for Bournemouth Trams, Bournemouth Gasworks and Lymington, gaining Dorset and Hampshire county honours before joining Boscombe in July 1921. He helped Cherries finish Southern League runners-up in 1922-23 and made four Third Division (South) appearances in place of Jimmy Miller prior to rejoining Bournemouth Trams. Employed by Hants & Dorset Motor Services, he then had a business in Littlehampton before retiring back to Bournemouth. He died locally in May 1975.

PETER HARRISON

Fast outside-left Peter Harrison was ever-present for Cherries in 1952-53. A former Notts County amateur, he reunited with Major Buckley at Leeds United in August 1948 and played alongside his best man John Charles. Moving to Bournemouth for £1,500 in August 1952, he netted 34 goals in 172 League games prior to joining Reading in June 1957. He later played for Southport, Macclesfield Town and Runcorn, then reunited with Lew Clayton as Cardiff City's reserves and youth team trainer. Settling in Cardiff, he was a chargehand at Tremorfa Steelworks until retiring in June 1984 and died in Llandough in July 2006.

CALLUM HART

Rangy full-back Callum Hart was a Sean O'Driscoll signing for AFC Bournemouth. A former Bristol City trainee, he joined Cherries in July 2005 and made his League debut in the following month's 0-0 draw at home to Walsall, quickly becoming a regular in the starting line-up. Called up to the Wales U-21 squad in February 2006, he put club before country to help in Cherries' battle with relegation, making 47 League appearances until released in May 2007. He has since played for Weymouth, Farnborough Town, Bath City, Weston-Super-Mare, Bath again, Salisbury and Sutton United, helping his father in the building trade.

IAN HARTE

Former Republic of Ireland international left-back Ian Harte was an experienced member of Cherries' 2014-15 Championship title squad. He turned professional with Leeds United in December 1995 and helped win the FA Youth Cup in 1997. Playing alongside his uncle, Gary Kelly, he featured as they were European Cup semi-finalists in 2001. He joined Spanish side Levante in July 2004, then had spells with Sunderland, Blackpool and Carlisle United before helping Reading win the Championship title in 2012-13. Moving to Cherries in June 2013, he scored once in 28 Championship games before released in May 2015 and retiring in August 2015.

TREVOR HARTLEY

Versatile winger Trevor Hartley featured in Cherries' 1970-71 promotion campaign. Signing professional for West Ham in July 1964, he appeared in the top-flight before moving to Dean Court for £5,000 in July 1969. He scored twice in 42 League games for Bournemouth prior to joining the coaching staff after injury ended his playing career in June 1972, then was manager between November 1973 and January 1975. Later assisting David Pleat at Luton Town and Tottenham Hotspur, he had a spell as the Malaysian national coach and held various other coaching and scouting posts, then was a supply PE teacher based in Ampthill.

JOE HARVEY

Young wing-half Joe Harvey featured in Cherries' 1-1 draw at home to Newport County in October 1937. Initially with Edlington Rangers, he moved via Bradford PA to Wolves in November 1936 and followed the well-worn trail to Bournemouth in May 1937. He joined Newcastle United for £4,250 in October 1945 and skippered promotion in 1947-48, then FA Cup final glory in 1951 and 1952. Managing Crook, Barrow and Workington, he rejoined Newcastle in June 1962, managing them to promotion in 1964-65, Fairs Cup final success in 1969 and the 1974 FA Cup final. He became their general manager and died in February 1989.

JAMES HAYTER

Versatile striker James Hayter starred in AFC Bournemouth's 2002-03 Third Division play-off final triumph. He turned professional at Dean Court in July 1997 and netted four times in Cherries' 5-2 win at Bury in October 2000, scoring the League's fastest-ever hat-trick in the 6-0 victory at home to Wrexham in February 2004. Leading marksman five times, he netted 94 goals in 358 League games before reuniting with Sean O'Driscoll at Doncaster Rovers for £200,000 in June 2007. He scored their winner in the 2007-08 League One play-off final and moved to Yeovil Town in July 2012, helping win promotion in 2012-13.

DOUG HAYWARD

Outside-left Doug Hayward made his solitary League appearance in Cherries' 1-0 defeat at home to Bristol Rovers in April 1925. Born locally, his long association with the club continued when he joined the board in 1946 and was chairman from 1967 until 1970, thus maintaining the family tradition which had seen his father Wilf and his brother Reg also occupying that position. He left the board in 1974 and was made a life vice-president of the club, with his son Peter later becoming Cherries' chairman. He was chairman of the local building firm W Hayward & Sons and Patron of the Bournemouth FA. He died in November 1978.

JACK HAYWARD

Tough-tackling right-back Jack Hayward starred as Cherries took West Ham to an FA Cup fifth round replay in 1928-29. Born in Mansfield, he developed with Welbeck Colliery and Shirebrook prior to joining Bradford City in March 1924. He moved to Bournemouth in May 1925 and helped take eventual winners Bolton Wanderers to an FA Cup fourth round replay in 1925-26 and Liverpool to a third round replay in 1926-27. Cherries' regular penalty taker, he netted 28 goals in 247 League games before joining Crystal Palace in May 1933. He was a security guard at MEXE in Christchurch and died locally in March 1974.

BILL HEATH

Young goalkeeper Bill Heath understudied Republic of Ireland international Tommy Godwin while at Dean Court. Born locally, he turned professional with Bournemouth in December 1951 and made his League debut in the 2-2 draw with Crystal Palace in December 1956, playing 34 League games prior to joining Lincoln City in exchange for Billy Coxon in November 1958. He moved to Cambridge City in July 1962 and helped win the Southern

League title in 1962-63, then was Newmarket Town's player-manager. A self-employed school and sportswear agent in Cambridge until February 2000, he settled back in Bournemouth.

TOM HEFFERNAN

Irish right-back Tom Heffernan starred in AFC Bournemouth's 1981-82 promotion success. Initially with Dunleary Celtic, he joined Tottenham Hotspur in October 1977 and moved to Cherries in May 1979. He was ever-present in 1980-81 and joined Sheffield United in August 1983, helping win promotion in 1983-84. Rejoining Cherries in June 1985, he featured in the 1986-87 Third Division title campaign and netted 27 goals in 217 League games overall before joining Swanage T&H in July 1988, then Bournemouth Poppies, Sturminster Marshall and Parley Sports. He is now a painter and decorator back in Ireland.

STEPHEN HENDERSON

Republic of Ireland U-21 goalkeeper Stephen Henderson had a loan spell with Cherries in 2013-14 as cover for Ryan Allsop and Darryl Flahavan. From a noted Irish goalkeeper family, he began with Aston Villa and moved to Bristol City in May 2007. He was loaned to York City, Weymouth, Aldershot and Yeovil before joining Portsmouth in July 2011. Moving to West Ham initially on loan in March 2012, he was loaned to Ipswich Town, then Cherries in October 2013. He dislocated his shoulder in only his second match, a 1-1 draw at Nottingham Forest. Rejoining West Ham for treatment, he joined Charlton Athletic in July 2014.

JAMES HENRY

Loan striker James Henry scored both goals on his debut in AFC Bournemouth's 2-0 win at Bristol Rovers in 2007-08. The England Youth international turned professional with Reading in June 2006 but failed to make an impact and was loaned to Nottingham Forest before joining Cherries on loan in November 2007. Scoring four times in 11 League outings while at Dean Court, he then had loan spells at Norwich City and Millwall, joining the Lions on a permanent basis in July 2010. He was an FA Cup semi-finalist in 2013 and followed Kenny Jackett to Wolves in October 2013, helping them to win the League One title in 2013-14.

ALEC HERON

Goalkeeper Alec Heron featured in Bournemouth's first-ever Football League match at Swindon in August 1923. Joining Cherries from Army football shortly after the First World War, he featured in the record 9-0 FA Cup preliminary round victory over Poole St Mary's in 1919-20 and three Southern League campaigns, helping Bournemouth to finish runners-up in 1922-23. He was displaced by the arrival of Bert Lock from Southampton in January 1924, then George Wilson from Clapton Orient in July 1924, making 26 Third Division (South) appearances before leaving in May 1926. Settling in Boscombe, he died in June 1964.

JOHN HILL

Versatile right-back John Hill was a young member of Freddie Cox's squad at Dean Court. A former Cherries apprentice, he turned professional in August 1966 and made his League debut in the 2-1 win at home to Swindon in March 1968. He played four League games before joining Weymouth in March 1971, featuring in that year's Southern League Cup final. Moving to Poole Town in June 1972, he was ever-present three times, then played for Holt United. He has since worked locally in the building trade, notably with A&J Building Services in Highcliffe. His son Richard had a spell as a Cherries youth team player.

ZAVON HINES

Former England U-21 striker Zavon Hines had a loan spell as AFC Bournemouth in 2011-12. Born in Jamaica, he grew up in East London and turned professional with West Ham in July 2007. He was loaned to Coventry City in March 2008 and gained top-flight experience before joining Burnley for £250,000 in August 2011. Loaned to Cherries in March 2012, his only goal in eight League One games came in the following month's 2-1 defeat at Sheffield United. He joined Bradford City in August 2012, helping to win promotion and reach the League Cup final in 2012-13, moving to Dagenham & Redbridge in August 2013.

JACK HOBBS

Centre-forward Jack Hobbs understudied Frank Fidler while at Dean Court. He was a prolific scorer for hometown Swanage prior to joining Bournemouth in October 1952 and made his League debut in the 1-0 defeat at Walsall in November 1953. His only goal in six Third Division (South) games clinched Cherries' 2-2 draw at Bristol City in April 1955 and he moved to Weymouth in July 1955, then helped Poole Town to win the Western League title in 1956-57 before playing for Swanage again. He emigrated to Canada in August 1959 and worked for Michelin, settling in retirement in New Westminster, British Columbia.

KEN HODGSON

Centre-forward Ken Hodgson was Cherries' leading marksman in 1964-65. Initially with Newcastle United, he joined Scunthorpe United for £3,000 in December 1961 and was top scorer in 1963-64. He moved to Bournemouth for £5,000 in June 1964, netting 24 goals in 78 Third Division games before being sold to Colchester United for £4,000 in July 1966. Later with Poole Town, Christchurch, Parley Sports, Eastern Suburbs (NZ) and Ringwood Town, he was a branch manager for Amplivox Ultratone hearing aids in Bournemouth, Leeds and Newcastle until retirement. Settling in Wilmslow, he died in October 2007.

JOHN HOLD

Young striker John Hold was Cherries' leading marksman in 1967-68. Initially with Fareham Town, he turned professional with Bournemouth in November 1964 and made his League debut in the 1-0 defeat at Watford in April 1966. He scored the winner against Sheffield Wednesday in the 1969-70 League Cup second round replay, netting 25 goals in 85 League games before joining Northampton in August 1971, then Margate, Ashford and Canadian sides London City and Toronto Portuguese. Settling in Lincoln, he was a food hall manager for Asda, then a salesman at Golfers World and lawn operative for Green Thumb.

PHIL HOLDER

Ex-England Youth midfielder Phil Holder skippered AFC Bournemouth during Alec Stock's reign at Dean Court. Starting with Tottenham Hotspur, he featured in the 1974 UEFA Cup final and reunited with Terry Venables at Crystal Palace in February 1975. He helped them reach the FA Cup semi-finals in 1975-76 and win promotion in 1976-77, then had a spell with Memphis Rogues before joining Cherries in March 1979. Scoring four goals in 58 League games until injury ended his career in November 1980, he has since held various coaching, managerial and scouting posts including a spell assisting Steve Perryman at Hiroshima.

KEN HOLLAND

Versatile inside-forward Ken Holland briefly appeared for Cherries during the 1948-49 campaign. A former Wolves amateur, he turned professional with Bury in September 1944 but failed to secure a first-team slot and moved to Dean Court in September 1948. He made his League debut in that month's 1-0 victory at Watford and also deputised for Ken Bennett in Bournemouth's next two Third Division (South) matches at home to Exeter City and Brighton. Joining Leslie Knighton's Shrewsbury Town in February 1949, then in the Midland League, he later played for Brush Sports. He died in Basford in December 1972.

MATT HOLLAND

Influential midfielder Matt Holland was AFC Bournemouth's 'Player of the Season' in 1995-96. Starting with West Ham, he moved to Dean Court initially on loan in January 1995 and made his League debut in that month's 2-0 defeat at Huddersfield Town. He became Cherries' captain and netted 18 goals in 104 League games before being sold to Ipswich Town for £800,000 in July 1997. Ever-present five times, the Republic of Ireland international skippered Ipswich's 1999-2000 promotion success and joined Charlton Athletic for £750,000 in June 2003. He gained 49 caps and has since become a TV football pundit.

PAT HOLLAND

Young winger Pat Holland helped Cherries clinch promotion in 1970-71. Signing professional for West Ham in April 1969, he made his First Division debut in that month's 2-1 defeat at home to Arsenal. 'Patsy' was loaned to Bournemouth in March 1971 and played ten League games while at Dean Court. Featuring in the Hammers' 1975 FA Cup final triumph, he also appeared in the 1976 ECWC final and 1980-81 Second Division title campaign before hanging up his boots. He coached at Orient, QPR and Spurs, then became Millwall's chief scout and assistant-manager. Later MK Dons' chief scout, he briefly coached at Arsenal.

DANNY HOLLANDS

Midfielder Danny Hollands had a spell as captain during Cherries' 2009-10 promotion campaign. He turned professional with Chelsea in November 2003 but failed to make an impact and made his League debut while on loan to Torquay United in March 2006, featuring in their relegation escape. Moving to Dean Court in July 2006, he was 'Player of the Year' in 2007-08 and also starred as AFC Bournemouth qualified for the League One play-offs in 2010-11, netting 24 goals in 193 League games before joining Charlton Athletic in May 2011. He was loaned to Swindon and Gillingham, moving to Portsmouth in March 2014.

DANNY HOLMES

Teenage midfielder Danny Holmes made his only League appearance as a substitute in Cherries' 2-0 defeat at Blackpool in September 1992. A former Middlesbrough trainee under his uncle Bruce Rioch, he joined his elder brother Matty at Dean Court in July 1991. He was loaned to Farnborough Town for the 1991-92 campaign, helping take West Ham to an FA Cup third round replay, moving permanently in January 1993. Later with Aldershot, Salisbury, Bognor Regis, Andover, Poole Town, Lymington & New Milton, Poppies and Holt United, he assisted Matty at Cherries' Centre of Excellence, also working as a window cleaner.

DEREK HOLMES

Scottish striker Derek Holmes appeared in AFC Bournemouth's 2002-03 Second Division play-off final triumph. Signing professional for Hearts in January 1995, he joined Ross County in October 1999 and moved to Cherries for £40,000 in September 2001. He regularly featured as a substitute, netting 16 goals in 115 League games before joining Carlisle United in February 2005. Appearing in their 2004-05 Conference play-off final success, he also helped win the League Two title in 2005-06. He moved to Rotherham United in July 2007, since playing for St Johnstone, Queen of the South, Airdrie United, Arbroath and East Fife.

MATTY HOLMES

Midfielder Matty Holmes featured in Cherries' 1991-92 FA Cup third round replay win at Newcastle United. A nephew of Bruce Rioch, the former Luton Town junior turned professional at Dean Court in August 1988 and netted eight goals in 114 League games before following Harry Redknapp to West Ham for £40,000 in August 1992. He helped win promotion in 1992-93 and moved to Blackburn Rovers for £1,200,000 in August 1995, then played for Charlton Athletic until injury curtailed his League career. Later with Dorchester Town, he has since coached at Cherries' Centre of Excellence and run a coaching school.

ALEC HOOTON

Right-half Alec Hooton briefly appeared for Cherries during the closing weeks of the 1935-36 campaign. Christened Alfred Alexander, he played for Southampton and Howard's Athletic before moving to Dean Court. He was given his League debut in Cherries' 4-1 defeat at Watford in March 1936 and made four Third Division (South) appearances before joining Poole Town in July 1936. Later trainer, he became general manager of Pender Plating in Creekmoor, then was briefly a park-keeper for Poole Corporation and worked at a home for disabled children in Canford Heath until suffering a fatal heart-attack in March 1970.

TREVOR HOWARD

Versatile midfielder Trevor Howard was AFC Bournemouth's top scorer in 1974-75. Signing professional for Norwich City in July 1967, he helped win the Second Division title in 1971-72 and was a League Cup finalist in 1973. He joined Cherries in a £50,000 deal involving Tony Powell in August 1974 and netted 11 goals in 86 League outings prior to joining Cambridge United in July 1976. Ever-present in their 1976-77 Fourth Division title triumph, he also starred in their 1977-78 promotion success before a knee injury ended his career. He spent 17 years as a meter inspector for British Gas, becoming a taxi driver in Cambridge.

JACK HOWARTH

Centre-forward Jack Howarth was an experienced member of John Benson's squad. Initially with Stanley United, he had spells at Chelsea and Swindon Town prior to joining Aldershot in July 1965. He was top scorer five times and reunited with Dick Conner at Rochdale in January 1972. Rejoining Shots ten months later, he helped clinch promotion in 1972-73, netting a record 171 League goals before joining Cherries for £6,000 in January 1977. Scoring six times in 42 Fourth Division games, he moved to Southport in March 1978, then Farnborough Town, Andover, Basingstoke Town, Salisbury and Romsey, becoming a postman.

BOBBY HOWE

Versatile left-back Bobby Howe partnered Mel Machin in Cherries' defence. Signing professional for West Ham in January 1963, he was an FA Youth Cup winner that season and gained considerable top-flight experience before reuniting with John Bond at Dean Court for £33,000 in January 1972. He netted six goals in 100 League games for Cherries until injury ended his career, then assisted brother-in-law Trevor Hartley for a year until January 1975. Briefly Plymouth Argyle's youth coach, he has since held various coaching posts in the United States including senior director of coaching and education for USA Soccer Federation.

EDDIE HOWE

England U-21 central defender Eddie Howe was twice AFC Bournemouth's 'Player of the Season'. He made his League debut in Cherries' 2-0 victory at home to Hull City seven months before turning professional in July 1996. Featuring in the 1998 Auto Windscreens Shield final, he followed his half-brother Steve Lovell to Portsmouth for £400,000 in March 2002 but was plagued by injuries. He rejoined Cherries in August 2004 and netted 12 goals in 270 League games overall. After a spell as coach, he became manager in January 2009, returning from a spell at Burnley to guide Cherries to the Premier League for the first time.

GARY HOWLETT

Former Republic of Ireland international midfielder Gary Howlett featured in AFC Bournemouth's 1986-87 Third Division title triumph. Initially with Home Farm, he moved via Coventry City to Brighton in August 1982 and scored on his First Division debut at home to Liverpool seven months later. He played in the 1983 FA Cup final and joined Cherries for

£15,000 in December 1984, netting seven goals in 60 League games before joining York City for £8,000 in January 1988. Later with Shelbourne, he coached Malahide United, Shelbourne, Monaghan United and Drumcondra, working for Aer Lingus at Dublin Airport.

WILLIE HUCK

French winger Willie Huck featured as AFC Bournemouth narrowly failed to qualify for the Second Division play-offs in 1998-99. The son of former French international Jean-Noel Huck, he moved from Monaco to Arsenal in November 1998 and joined Cherries for £50,000 in March 1999. He made his League debut in that month's 2-1 win at home to Colchester and regularly featured as a substitute, playing 40 Second Division games while at Dean Court. Returning to France with Angers in July 2002, he moved to Montlucon in July 2006 and has since played for Toulon and Vendee Poire Sur Vie in his native country.

KIRK HUDSON

Teenage striker Kirk Hudson made his only League appearance as a substitute in AFC Bournemouth's 2-1 victory at home to Swindon Town in September 2005. A former Ipswich Town junior, he joined Celtic in July 2003 but failed to make an impact. He moved to Cherries in July 2005, scoring in a pre-season match against Southampton and featuring in the 1-0 League Cup second round defeat at finalists Wigan Athletic. Joining Aldershot Town in January 2006, he helped win the Conference 'double' in 2007-08 and reach the League Two play-offs in 2009-10, then had spells with Brentford, AFC Wimbledon and Canvey Island.

BILLY HUGHES

Former Northern Ireland international outside-right Billy Hughes played for Cherries during the 1953-54 campaign. Initially with Larne, he moved to Bolton Wanderers in August 1948 and made his First Division debut at Birmingham seven months later. He joined Bournemouth in June 1953, scoring once in 16 League outings before moving to Northwich Victoria in July 1954. A key figure as Rhyl reached the FA Cup fourth round in 1956-57, he then played for Bangor City and Mossley while running an off-licence in Bolton. Later working for Chloride, Royal Ordnance and Lansing Linde, he died in Swinton in June 2005.

HARRY HUGHES

Centre-half Harry Hughes skippered Cherries to the FA Cup sixth round in 1956-57. He played for Symingtons and Southport before moving to Chelsea in February 1951, making his First Division debut against Liverpool six months later. Joining Cherries in June 1952, he scored twice in 77 League games before moving to Gillingham in July 1958. Twice ever-present, he joined Guildford City in July 1963, then managed Woking and Guildford. He settled near Guildford and managed the Tottenham Hotspur club shop for 11 years. Later devoting his time to the Christians in Sport organisation, he died in October 2013.

RICHARD HUGHES

Former Scotland international midfielder Richard Hughes had two spells at Dean Court. Born in Glasgow, he developed with Italian side Atalanta while his parents were living there and joined Arsenal in August 1997. Mel Machin paid £20,000 for him in July 1998 and he starred as Cherries narrowly failed to qualify for the Second Division play-offs in 2000-01. Sold to Portsmouth for £100,000 in July 2002, he was capped five times, becoming their longest-serving player. He revived his career with Eddie Howe back at Cherries in July 2012, netting 15 goals in 157 League games overall before appointed first-team technical director.

RALPH HUNT

Young centre-forward Ralph Hunt played alongside Stan Newsham in Cherries' attack. A nephew of former Spurs star Doug Hunt, he turned professional with hometown Portsmouth in August 1950 but had few top-flight chances and joined Bournemouth in February 1954. He netted seven goals in 33 League outings prior to joining Norwich City in July 1955. Scoring a club record 31 League goals for the Canaries in 1955-56, he played for Derby County, Grimsby Town, Swindon Town, Port Vale, Newport County and Chesterfield until his death in a car crash in December 1964. His brother Dennis played over 300 games for Gillingham.

STEVE HUTCHINGS

Teenage striker Steve Hutchings briefly appeared for AFC Bournemouth during the 2007-08 campaign. Born in Portsmouth, he was a trainee at Brockenhurst College and appeared regularly for Cherries' reserves before being handed a place on the bench. His solitary League appearance for the club came during an injury crisis and was as a substitute for Sam Vokes in the 2-0 victory at home to Millwall in March 2008. Following a loan spell at Dorchester Town a year later, he joined Havant & Waterlooville in July 2009 and has since played for Gosport Borough, Moneyfields, Australian side Shepparton and Moneyfields again.

BILLY HUTCHINSON

Outside-left Billy Hutchinson briefly appeared for Bournemouth early in the 1930-31 season. Starting with hometown Chester-le-Street, he moved via Birmingham to Cherries in August 1930 and made his League debut in the following month's 0-0 draw at home to Southend. He contested a first-team slot with Willie Webb and also played in Bournemouth's 1-1 draw at home to Watford a week later. Moving to Leeds United in July 1931, he was a fringe member of their 1931-32 promotion squad and joined Darlington in July 1932, then appeared for Halifax Town. He settled back in his native North-East and died in June 1975.

JIMMY HUTCHINSON

Inside-forward Jimmy Hutchinson scored Cherries' first post-war League goal against QPR in September 1946. Signing professional for Sheffield United in September 1937, he guested for several clubs during wartime service in the Royal Navy and joined Bournemouth in June 1946. He netted three times in eight League outings before joining Lincoln City in November 1946 and starred in their 1947-48 Third Division (North) title triumph. Moving to Oldham Athletic in February 1949, he later played for Denaby United. He died in Sheffield in November 1997. His son Barry played for Chesterfield, Derby County and Lincoln.

DAVID HUTCHISON

Scottish forward David Hutchison briefly played for Cherries at the start of the 1936-37 campaign. He had spells with Dykehead and Albion Rovers before helping Motherwell to finish Scottish League runners-up in 1926-27. Moving to Carlisle United in August 1928, he featured in their first-ever Football League match and formed a lethal partnership with Jimmy McConnell. He joined Luton Town in May 1932 and moved via Airdrie and Stenhousemuir to Bournemouth in August 1936, Scoring on his debut in the 3-1 win at Aldershot on the opening day, he also featured in the following week's 1-0 victory over Gillingham.

SAMMY IGOE

Diminutive midfielder Sammy Igoe was an experienced figure in AFC Bournemouth's 2009-10 promotion success. He turned professional with Portsmouth in February 1994 and was sold to Reading for £100,000 in March 2000. Helping them win promotion in 2001-02, he joined Swindon Town in July

2003 and moved via Millwall to Bristol Rovers initially on loan in January 2006. He scored in their 2006-07 League Two play-off final success and joined Cherries in August 2008. Netting three goals in 49 League outings, he moved to Havant & Waterlooville in June 2010, then helped Gosport Borough win promotion in 2012-13.

JOHN IMPEY

Ex-England Youth central defender John Impey skippered AFC Bournemouth's 1981-82 promotion success. Signing professional for Cardiff City in August 1972, he made his League debut at home to Portsmouth four months later. He moved to Cherries in July 1975 and netted seven goals in 284 League games prior to joining Torquay United in August 1983. Joining Exeter City in August 1985, he then played for Torquay again and Weymouth before joining Torquay's coaching staff. Managing their 1990-91 Fourth Division play-off final triumph, he has become a self-employed builder/property developer in Torquay.

DANNY INGS

Young striker Danny Ings helped AFC Bournemouth to reach the League One play-offs in 2010-11. A former trainee at Dean Court, he was given his first-team debut as a substitute in the Johnstone's Paint Trophy defeat at Northampton in October 2009. He made his League debut in Cherries' 2-0 defeat at MK Dons in December 2010 and netted seven goals in 27 League One games before following Eddie Howe to Burnley in August 2011. Leading marksman alongside Sam Vokes as they regained Premier League status in 2013-14, the England U-21 star was top scorer again in 2014-15 and moved to Liverpool in June 2015.

HARRY ISHERWOOD

Stocky left-back Harry Isherwood helped Cherries take West Ham to an FA Cup fifth round replay in 1928-29. Initially with Fleetwood, he had a spell with Sunderland prior to joining Birmingham in May 1927 and made his First Division debut in that month's 3-2 defeat by Sheffield United. He moved to Bournemouth in June 1928 and played 18 League games before reuniting with Joe Smith at Worcester City in August 1929. Helping retain the Birmingham League title in 1929-30, he was ever-present in 1933-34, joining Hereford United in July 1934. He was a delivery driver for Bulmer's and died in Whitchurch in December 1966.

SHWAN JALAL

Former England Semi-Pro goalkeeper Shwan Jalal missed just two matches in AFC Bournemouth's 2009-10 promotion success. Born in Baghdad, he had spells with Hastings Town, Tottenham Hotspur, Woking and Peterborough United, then was loaned to Morecambe before moving to Dean Court in August 2008. He also starred as Cherries qualified for the League One play-offs in 2010-11 but was then displaced by Darryl Flahavan. Featuring in the 2012-13 promotion campaign, he made 148 League appearances and was loaned to Leyton Orient prior to joining Bury in June 2014, helping them to win promotion in 2014-15.

DAVID JAMES

Ex-England international goalkeeper David James appeared in AFC Bournemouth's 2012-13 promotion campaign. Initially with Watford, he was ever-present in 1990-91. He joined Liverpool in June 1992 and featured in their 1995 League Cup final success, moving to Aston Villa in June 1999. An FA Cup finalist in 2000, he moved via West Ham and Manchester City to Portsmouth in August 2006. He helped win the FA Cup in 2008 and was a finalist again in 2010. Capped 53 times, he moved via Bristol City to Cherries in September 2012, making 19 League appearances. Later with IBV, he is player-boss of Kerala Blasters.

JAMIE JENKINS

Welsh midfielder Jamie Jenkins was a young member of Mel Machin's squad at AFC Bournemouth. A former trainee at Dean Court, he turned professional in July 1997 and made his only League appearance as a substitute in Cherries' 4-0 victory at home to Stoke City in February 1999. He joined Barry Town in July 1999 and helped them to win the League of Wales title and Welsh Cup 'double' in three successive seasons, also beat Porto in the 2001-02 European Cup second qualifying round second-leg. Gaining Welsh Semi-Pro international honours, his younger brother Jody was also an AFC Bournemouth trainee.

JACK JOHNSON

Outside-right Jack Johnson appeared for Cherries during the 1928-29 campaign. Initially with Denaby United, he moved via Sheffield Wednesday to Bournemouth in June 1928 and made his League debut in the 2-1 defeat at Luton three months later. He scored four times in 12 Third Division (South) games before joining Rotherham United in November 1930. Moving to Barnsley in September 1933, he featured in their 1933-34 Third Division (North) title campaign. He joined Carlisle United in June 1934 and was ever-present in 1936-37, then appeared for Accrington Stanley. He died in Preston in December 1991.

PETER JOHNSON

Winger Peter Johnson was a popular member of John Benson's squad at Dean Court. Signing professional for Orient in August 1971, he made his League debut at Swindon eight months later and moved to

Crystal Palace in August 1974. He joined Cherries in exchange for Mark Nightingale in August 1976, scoring 11 goals in 107 League games before reuniting with Stuart Morgan at Weymouth in July 1979. Helping them to finish Conference runners-up in 1979-80, he then had spells playing for Barnet, Weymouth again, Parley Sports and Poole Town. He became a financial planning consultant for Allied Dunbar in Bournemouth.

ANDY JONES

Former Welsh international striker Andy Jones partnered Luther Blissett in AFC Bournemouth's attack. Initially with Wrexham, he starred for Rhyl before joining Port Vale in May 1985 and was top scorer in their 1985-86 promotion success. Sold to Charlton Athletic for £350,000 in September 1987, he joined Cherries for £80,000 in October 1990 and netted eight goals in 40 Third Division games before moving to Leyton Orient for £90,000 in October 1991. Later with Poole Town, Havant and Ringwood, he has settled in Ringwood and was a product manager for Mizuno soccer boots, since working for British Telecom.

BRYN JONES

Hard-tackling left-back Bryn Jones starred in Cherries' 1961-62 promotion near-miss. From a notable footballing family, including Mickey below, he turned professional with Swansea in September 1951 and played alongside his Welsh international brother Cliff before moving to Newport County in June 1958. He joined Cherries for £5,000 in February 1960 and scored five goals in 118 League games prior to joining Northampton Town for £7,000 in October 1963. Later with Watford, Chelmsford and Folkestone, he was a sports teacher at Holloway Boys Comprehensive (including Charlie George) and died in October 1990.

DAVID JONES

Young central defender David Jones featured in Cherries' 1970-71 promotion success. A former apprentice at Dean Court, he helped Bournemouth reach the FA Youth Cup semi-finals in 1968-69 and turned professional in January 1970. He starred in Cherries' 1971-72 promotion near-miss, netting five goals in 134 League outings before being sold to Nottingham Forest for £80,000 in August 1974. Reuniting with John Bond at Norwich City in September 1975, he was capped eight times by Wales before injury ended his career. He settled back in Highcliffe, working locally in the printing trade and as a delivery driver.

GARETH JONES

Welsh winger Gareth Jones was a young member of Trevor Hartley's squad at AFC Bournemouth. Signing professional for Torquay United in October 1972, he made his League debut in that month's 1-0 victory at home to Doncaster Rovers and moved to Dean Court in an exchange deal involving Jim De Garis in March 1974. He appeared as a substitute in Cherries' last two matches that season at home to Halifax Town and Wrexham, playing four Third Division games overall. Following a brief spell at Weymouth, he joined Bridgend Town in July 1975 and played for several Welsh League clubs, settling back in his native Cardiff.

GLANVILLE JONES

Welsh outside-left Glan Jones contested a first-team slot with Wally Hanlon as Bournemouth finished third in the Third Division (South) in 1948-49. Initially with Merthyr Tydfil, he joined Hull City in June 1946 and made his League debut in their 2-2 draw at home to Crewe three months later. He moved to Dean Court in May 1947, netting three goals in nine League games for Cherries prior to joining Crewe Alexandra in March 1949. Reuniting with Paddy Gallacher at Weymouth in June 1949, he starred in their 1949-50 FA Cup run, then worked for Kennedy's builders merchants until his death in a car crash in December 1956.

JACK JONES

Welsh wing-half Jack Jones contested a first-team slot with Peter Monaghan during the 1937-38 season. He played for Pentwyn Albion and Penrhiwceiber before joining Swansea Town in August 1931. Scoring on his League debut in a 5-1 win over Burnley, he helped win the Welsh Cup in 1932. He moved to Torquay United in May 1934 and missed just one match in 1934-35, joining Bournemouth in exchange for Arthur Rhodes in June 1938. His solitary goal in 12 Third Division (South) games came in the Cherries' 5-2 defeat by Torquay seven months later and he joined Chester in June 1939. He died in Bristol in September 2002.

KENWYNE JONES

Trinidad & Tobago international striker Kenwyne Jones helped Cherries to clinch the Championship title in 2014-15. He played for Joe Public and W Connection before joining Southampton in July 2004. Loaned to Sheffield Wednesday and Stoke City, he starred as Saints reached the Championship play-offs in 2006-07. He joined Sunderland in £6,000,000 deal involving Stern John in August 2007, then Stoke for £8,000,000 in August 2010, playing in the 2011 FA Cup final. Swapped for Cardiff City's Peter Odemwingle in January 2014, he was loaned to Cherries in March 2015 and scored once in six substitute appearances.

MICKEY JONES

Stylish inside-right Mickey Jones impressed with Bournemouth during the 1927-28 campaign. From a notable football family, he was christened Emlyn and played for Dowlais and hometown Merthyr Tydfil before joining Cherries in August 1927. He scored twice in six consecutive League games while at Dean Court, moving to Everton in March 1928. Failing to make an impact with the Toffees, he joined Southend United in June 1929. He was ever-present in his first three seasons and moved to Northwich Victoria in August 1936, then Solihull Town, Nuneaton Borough and Barrow. He died in Margate in April 1973.

ROGER JONES

England U-23 goalkeeper Roger Jones helped Cherries take Liverpool to an FA Cup third round replay in 1967-68. Initially with Portsmouth, he moved to Bournemouth in May 1965 and played 160 League games before sold to Blackburn Rovers for £30,000 in January 1970. He was ever-present in their 1974-75 Third Division title triumph and followed Gordon Lee to Newcastle United for £100,000 in March 1976. Later with Stoke City and Derby County, he captained York City's 1983-84 Fourth Division title triumph and coached under Denis Smith at Sunderland. He was a painter and decorator, then Swindon Town's kit man.

STEVE JONES

Striker Steve Jones was AFC Bournemouth's leading marksman in two consecutive seasons. Initially with Billericay Town, he joined West Ham in November 1992 and helped win promotion that season. He moved to Cherries for £150,000 in October 1994 and netted 26 goals in 74 League games before rejoining Harry Redknapp's West Ham in a deal involving Mark Watson in May 1996. Sold to Charlton Athletic for £400,000 in February 1997, he was loaned back to Cherries before featuring in their 1997-98 First Division play-off final triumph. Later with Bristol City and Hornchurch, he then ran a memorabilia shop in London.

CLAUS JORGENSEN

Danish midfielder Claus Jorgensen was AFC Bournemouth's 'Player of the Year' in 1999-2000. Previously with AC Horsens, he moved to Dean Court in July 1999 and starred as Cherries narrowly failed to qualify for the Second Division play-offs in 2000-01. Joining Bradford City in July 2001, he moved to Coventry City in August 2003 and rejoined Cherries on loan in January 2004, netting 14 goals in 103 League games overall. Capped by the Faroe Islands, he joined Blackpool in January 2006, helping win promotion in 2006-07, then Port Vale and Fleetwood. He has since run Unique Floorcare and coaches at Coventry's Academy.

TRESOR KANDOL

Tall striker Tresor Kandol played for AFC Bournemouth during the 2001-02 campaign. Initially with Luton Town, he was briefly with Cambridge United before Sean O'Driscoll signed him in October 2001. He made 12 Second Division appearances for Cherries prior to joining Chesham United in July 2002, then had spells with Purfleet, Thurrock, Dagenham & Redbridge and Darlington. Sold to Barnet for £50,000 in January 2006, he moved to Leeds United for £200,000 in November 2006 and helped win promotion in 2009-10. He was loaned to Millwall and Charlton, then played for Spanish side Albacete and Hampton & Richmond.

JEM KARACAN

Turkish Youth midfielder Jem Karacan had a loan spell at AFC Bournemouth in 2007-08. Born in Catford of a Turkish Cypriot father and English mother, he turned professional with Reading in July 2007 and was loaned to Cherries in October 2007. His solitary goal in 13 consecutive League games was a stunning strike in the following month's 3-1 defeat at home to Leeds United. He also had a loan spell at Millwall before securing a regular first-team slot with Reading and gaining Turkish U-21 honours. Starring in the Royals' 2011-12 Championship title triumph, he became club captain and moved to Galatasaray in June 2015.

TOMMY KEANE

Republic of Ireland Youth midfielder Tommy Keane was a fringe member of AFC Bournemouth's 1986-87 Third Division championship squad. A former apprentice at Dean Court, he was given his League debut as substitute in Cherries' 1-0 defeat at home to Walsall four months before turning professional in September 1986. He also appeared against West Brom and Plymouth Argyle early in the 1987-88 season, then followed Roger Brown to Colchester United in December 1987. Later playing for Galway United, Sligo Rovers, Galway again, Finn Harps and Athlone Town, he died in his native Galway in December 2012.

REG KEATING

Much-travelled winger Reg Keating helped Bournemouth to finish sixth in the Third Division (South) in 1936-37. He had spells with Halton Grange, Annfield Plain, Scotswood, Newcastle United, Lincoln City, Gainsborough Trinity, Scarborough, Stockport County, Birmingham, Norwich City, North Shields and Bath City before joining Cardiff City in January 1934. Twice leading marksman, he moved via Doncaster Rovers to Dean Court in November 1936. He scored five times in 11 League outings for Cherries prior to joining Carlisle United in July 1937, then Blyth Spartans. He died in North Walbottle in October 1961.

JUSTIN KEELER

Young midfielder Justin Keeler briefly played for AFC Bournemouth during the closing weeks of the 1999-2000 season. Previously with Christchurch, he joined Cherries in January 2000 and was given his debut in that month's Auto Windscreens Shield defeat at Bristol City. He impressed in the reserves but made only four substitute appearances for AFC Bournemouth in the Second Division prior to joining Dorchester Town in March 2001 after a loan spell. Scoring in the Magpies' 2002 Southern League Cup final triumph, he moved to Bashley in May 2007, then Brockenhurst and Poppies before Brockenhurst and Bashley again.

ARTHUR KEELEY

Outside-right Arthur Keeley understudied Bob Redfern during the 1937-38 season. Initially with Ellesmere Port, he joined Wolves in July 1936 and made his First Division debut in their 5-2 win over Grimsby nine months later. He failed to secure a regular first-team slot and followed the well-worn trail to Bournemouth in May 1937. Making two League appearances, he joined Chester in June 1938 and was switched to centre-forward, starring alongside Bill Pendergast in their 1938-39 FA Cup run. He joined Portsmouth in July 1939 and served in the Royal Sussex Regiment but was sadly killed in action in France in August 1944.

JAMES KEENE

Young striker James Keene had a loan spell at AFC Bournemouth during the 2005-06 campaign. A former Portsmouth scholar, he had few top-flight chances and was loaned to Cherries in September 2005, scoring twice in 11 League One games while at Dean Court, including a superb individual effort in the 2-0 win at Brentford. Also loaned to Kidderminster, Boston United and Swedish side GAIS, he joined Elfsborg in January 2007. He had further loan spells at Fredrikstad, Djurgardens and Pompey, then played for Indian sides Bnei Yehuda and North East United before returning to Sweden with Halmstad in April 2015.

ALBERT KEETLEY

Versatile full-back Albert Keetley was a member of Jack Bruton's squad at Dean Court. Signing professional for Bury in March 1950, he was given his League debut at Birmingham City ten months later but failed to secure a regular first-team slot and joined Bournemouth in July 1952. He provided reliable defensive cover for Laurie Cunningham and Ian Drummond, making 86 League appearances before a knee injury curtailed his career in July 1959. Later trainer-coach with Weymouth, Bradford City and Exeter City, he spent 23 years with various branches of Bournemouth Social Services until retiring in June 1993.

DICK KEITH

Ex-Northern Ireland international full-back Dick Keith featured in Cherries' 1963-64 promotion near-miss. He starred as Linfield won the Northern Irish Cup in 1953 and Northern Ireland League title three times. Northern Ireland 'Player of the Year' in 1955-56, he joined Newcastle United in September 1956. Forming a notable partnership with Alf McMichael for club and country, he moved to Bournemouth in February 1964 and played 47 League games prior to joining Weymouth in August 1966. He was a warehouse supervisor at Kennedy's builder merchants until his tragic death in an accident at work in February 1967.

EDDIE KELLY

Former Scotland U-23 midfielder Eddie Kelly featured in Cherries' 1981-82 promotion campaign. Signing professional for Arsenal in February 1968, he starred as they won the Fairs Cup in 1970 and 'double' in 1970-71. He moved to QPR for £60,000 in September 1976, then won promotion with Leicester City in 1979-80 and Notts County in 1980-81. Reuniting with David Webb at Dean Court in August 1981, he made 13 League appearances before rejoining Leicester in November 1981, then linked up with Webb again at Torquay United. He has since been a publican and worked in double-glazing, settling in Paignton.

YANN KERMORGANT

French striker Yann Kermorgant starred in AFC Bournemouth's 2014-15 Championship title triumph. He played for Vannes, Chatellerault, Grenoble and Stade Reims in his native country before joining Leicester City in August 2009. Infamously missing a penalty in the 2010 Championship play-off semi-final defeat by Cardiff City, he was loaned to Arles-Avignon for the 2010-11 season, then reunited with Chris Powell at Charlton Athletic in September 2011. He helped them win the League One title in 2011-12 and moved to Cherries in January 2014, grabbing a hat-trick on his full debut in the 5-0 win over Doncaster Rovers.

DAVE KEVAN

Loan midfielder Dave Kevan made his only League appearance as a substitute in AFC Bournemouth's 2-1 defeat at home to Wrexham in April 1994. Signing professional for Notts County in August 1986, he helped them qualify for the Third Division play-offs in 1987-88. He joined Stoke City for £75,000 in January 1990, featuring in their 1992 Autoglass Trophy final success and 1992-93 Second Division title triumph. Injury ended his career in January 1995 and he has since coached at Stoke, Burnley, Notts County, Stockport County, Hereford, Stoke again, Cheltenham Town, Forest Green Rovers and Notts County again.

STEVE KILCAR

Scottish inside-right Steve Kilcar understudied Ernie Whittam as Cherries finished sixth in the Third Division (South) in 1936-37. Starting with Linlithgow Rose, he moved via East Stirlingshire to Bradford Park Avenue in May 1929. He helped their reserves to win the Midland League title in 1931-32, then had spells playing for Coventry City, Mansfield Town, Chester and Burnley before joining Bournemouth in September 1936. Making five League appearances while at Dean Court, he moved to Watford in July 1937 but a knee injury curtailed his career soon afterwards. He died in Uphall, West Lothian, in June 1963.

JOHN KING

Fearless wing-half John King was a member of Don Welsh's squad at Dean Court. Initially with Everton, he moved to Bournemouth in July 1960 and his solitary goal in 21 Third Division games came in the 2-1 win at home to Tranmere Rovers six months later. He was sold to Tranmere for £2,000 in February 1961 and helped them win promotion in 1966-67, then repeated the feat with Port Vale in 1969-70. Briefly with Wigan Athletic, he rejoined Tranmere as manager, plotting promotion in 1975-76. He achieved managerial success with Northwich, Caernarvon and Tranmere again, becoming their director of football in April 1995.

TOM KING

Hard-tackling right-back Tom King partnered George Bellis in Bournemouth's defence. He impressed with Sneinton prior to joining Notts County in August 1934 and moved to Dean Court in August 1935. Making 66 League appearances for Cherries, he joined Luton Town in February 1937 and helped clinch the Third Division (South) title. He worked as a lathe operator for George Kent Ltd engineering firm in Luton before rejoining the Hatters as groundsman for ten years in July 1954. Employed by Hydrosteeer Engineering until retiring in June 1974, he then lived near his sister-in-law in Scarborough until his death in June 1993.

HARRY KINGHORN

One of Cherries' finest servants, Harry Kinghorn had two spells as manager during 24 years at Dean Court. He was a goalkeeper with Arniston Rovers, Alloa, Leith and Sheffield Wednesday, then scouted for Arsenal and became Bournemouth's trainer-manager in July 1925. Appointed trainer on Leslie Knighton's arrival as manager in July 1925, he made an emergency appearance in Cherries' 0-0 draw at Brentford in March 1929. He took charge again in June 1939 and plotted Bournemouth's 1946 Third Division (South) Cup final triumph. Leaving in May 1947, he scouted for Portsmouth and died in Montrose in April 1955.

JACK KIRKHAM

Centre-forward Jack Kirkham played for Cherries either side of the Second World War. Initially with Ellesmere Port, he joined Wolves in March 1936 and understudied Dennis Westcott, helping twice finish League Championship runners-up before moving to Dean Court in October 1938. He was Cherries' leading marksman that season and guested for Clapton Orient and Notts County during the war. Featuring in the 1946 Third Division (South) Cup final success, he netted 27 goals in 48 League games, joining Wellington Town (later Telford United) in July 1948. He resided in Wolverhampton until his death in December 1982.

ERNIE KIRKPATRICK

Versatile wing-half Ernie Kirkpatrick briefly deputised for Cliff Halliwell during the 1929-30 season. He helped Fleetwood to win the Lancashire Combination title in 1923-24 before joining Oldham Athletic in September 1925, Returning to Fleetwood in July 1927, he joined Chorley in February 1928 and was a Lancashire Combination winner again in 1927-28 and 1928-29. He moved to Bournemouth in May 1929 and played two consecutive League games, at home to Watford and at Newport County, prior to rejoining Chorley in June 1930. Later Fleetwood's coach and groundsman, he died in Heywood in March 1971.

BILL KITCHENER

Versatile left-back Bill Kitchener featured in AFC Bournemouth's 1971-72 promotion near-miss. He appeared alongside Bobby Howe and Harry Redknapp in West Ham's 1963 FA Youth Cup final triumph, gaining top-flight experience before reuniting with John Bond at Torquay United for £10,000 in December 1967 after a loan spell. Following Bond to Cherries for £15,000 in July 1971, he scored twice in 36 League games while at Dean Court until injury curtailed his League career in February 1973. He later played for Cambridge City, Wealdstone, Christchurch and New Milton, then joined Hampshire Constabulary.

PHIL KITE

Ex-England Youth goalkeeper Phil Kite understudied Gerry Peyton while at AFC Bournemouth. Signing professional for Bristol Rovers in October 1980, he was ever-present in 1982-83 and joined Southampton in August 1984. He moved to Gillingham in February 1987 and helped them reach the Third Division play-off final that season, joining Cherries in August 1989. Making seven League appearances while at Dean Court, he moved to Sheffield United in August 1990 and later played for Cardiff and Bristol City. He was Bristol Rovers' physiotherapist for 19 years and had a testimonial match against West Brom in July 2015.

JO KUFFOUR

Striker Jo Kuffour was AFC Bournemouth's leading marksman in 2007-08. Full name Osei-Kuffour, he was an Arsenal trainee and helped win the FA Youth Cup shortly before turning professional in July 2000. He made his League debut while on loan to Swindon Town and joined Torquay United in October 2002, starring in their 2003-04 promotion success. Following Leroy Rosenior to Brentford in July 2006, he joined Cherries in July 2007, netting 12 goals in 44 League games prior to joining Bristol Rovers in August 2008. He was top scorer in 2009-10, since playing for Gillingham, Wycombe Wanderers and Sutton United.

ADAM LALLANA

England Youth midfielder Adam Lallana had a loan spell at AFC Bournemouth in 2007-08. Initially with Cherries' Centre of Excellence, he turned professional with Southampton in December 2005. Loaned back to Cherries in October 2007, he made three League appearances while at Dean Court. He scored in Saints' 2010 Johnstone's Paint Trophy final triumph and starred as they won promotion in two consecutive seasons. Gaining England U-21 honours, he made his full international debut against Chile in November 2013. He moved to Liverpool for £25,000,000 in July 2014, with a reported £4,000,000 paid to Cherries.

JAMES LAMB

Left-back James Lamb was ever-present in Bournemouth's 1923-24 Football League debut campaign. Previously in the Army, he moved to Dean Court as Boscombe stepped up from the Hampshire League in 1920, missing just one match in each of Cherries' three seasons in the Southern League. He helped to finish runners-up in 1922-23, shortly before the club was elected to the Football League in June 1923. Featuring in Cherries' first-ever Football League match at Swindon Town, he made 63 Third Division (South) appearances while at Dean Court before hanging up his boots. He died in Bournemouth in September 1945.

JIM LAMPARD

Goalkeeper Jim Lampard understudied Peter McSevich whilst at Dean Court. Christened Alfred James, he was previously with Forest Green Rovers and joined Bournemouth in August 1929. He made his League debut in the 1-1 draw at home to Brighton seven months later, also helping to win 4-2 at home to Merthyr. Moving to Barnsley in June 1930, he also made two League appearances for the Tykes. He worked for Pye distribution in Cambridge, then ran the Crosskeys pub in Cottenham, also coach/groundsman of Cottenham United. Later the handyman at Churchill College in Cambridge, he died in Cottenham in November 1969.

DAVE LANGAN

Former Republic of Ireland international right-back Dave Langan played for Cherries during the 1987-88 campaign. Initially with Derby County, he joined Birmingham for £350,000 in July 1980 and reunited with Jim Smith at Oxford United in August 1984. He starred in their 1984-85 Second Division title triumph and 1986 League Cup final success, moving to Cherries in December 1987. Making 20 League appearances, he joined Peterborough in August 1988, then Ramsey, Holbeach and Rothwell. He worked in the security industry but is now registered disabled. His autobiography 'Running Through Walls' came out in 2012.

EVERALD LA RONDE

Young full-back Everald La Ronde helped AFC Bournemouth beat holders Manchester United in the 1983-84 FA Cup third round. A former West Ham apprentice, he turned professional in January 1981 and captained that year's FA Youth Cup final triumph but had few top-flight chances before moving to Cherries in September 1983. He made 24 Third Division appearances and was loaned to Peterborough United prior to joining Swedish side Kalmar in May 1985. Later playing for Woodford Town, Walthamstow Avenue, Dagenham and Wealdstone, he became a special systems technician for Canary Wharf Management.

EDDIE LAWRENCE

Former Welsh international left-half Eddie Lawrence starred as Cherries finished in their highest pre-war position in 1936-37. Initially with Druids, he joined Wrexham in February 1926 and moved to Clapton Orient in August 1928. He toured Canada with the Welsh FA before joining Notts County in May 1931. Capped twice, he moved to Bournemouth in August 1936 and his only goal in 39 League games clinched the 2-1 victory over Reading in April 1937, rejoining Clapton Orient the following month. He worked for the John Player cigarette company in Nottingham, then scouted for Notts County and died in July 1989.

GEORGE LAWRENCE

Winger George Lawrence helped AFC Bournemouth reach the FA Cup fourth round in 1990-91. Initially with Southampton, 'Chicken George' joined Oxford United in November 1982 and starred in their 1983-84 Third Division title triumph. He had another spell with Saints and joined Millwall in July 1987, featuring in their 1987-88 Second Division title campaign. Moving to Cherries for £100,000 in August 1989, he netted five goals in 75 League games, joining Finnish side Mikkelin Pallo in June 1992. Later with Weymouth, Portsmouth, Maltese side Hibernians and Hednesford, he has been a sports therapist and London bus driver.

HERBERT LAWSON

Centre-forward Herbert Lawson briefly appeared for Bournemouth during the 1934-35 season. He turned professional with Reading in August 1934 and made his League debut in the following month's 1-1 draw at Swindon. Moving to Dean Court in an exchange deal involving Tommy Tait in November 1934, he played three Third Division (South) games for Cherries prior to joining Barrow in August 1935. Despite scoring five goals in his first six matches, he was displaced by Tommy Reid and finished leading marksman for their reserves, moving to Frickley Colliery in June 1937. He settled in Barrow and died in May 1975.

JAMES LAWSON

Young striker James Lawson had a loan spell at AFC Bournemouth in 2006-07. A former Southend United trainee, he scored on his full League debut in a 2-1 win over Oldham shortly before turning professional in October 2005 and helped them to win the League One title in 2005-06. He was loaned to Grimsby Town prior to joining Cherries on loan in January 2007, making four League appearances while at Dean Court. Also loaned to Dagenham & Redbridge, appearing in their 2006-07 Conference title campaign, he joined Grays Athletic in August 2007 and has since played for Chelmsford, Welling United and Concord Rangers.

GEORGE LAX

Stocky wing-half George Lax failed to prevent Cherries having to seek re-election in 1933-34. Starting with Frickley Colliery, he joined Wolves in June 1929, featuring in their 1930-31 FA Cup run and 1931-32 Second Division title campaign. He moved via Barnsley to Bournemouth in July 1933 and his solitary goal in seven League games came in the 4-1 defeat at Coventry City nine months later. Joining Worcester City in July 1934, he had a spell as Evesham's player-manager, then coached Bohemians. He briefly managed Scunthorpe United, then reunited with Major Buckley as Hull City's trainer before other coaching posts.

CHRIS LEADBITTER

Midfielder Chris Leadbitter was a versatile member of Tony Pulis' squad. Initially with Grimsby Town, he moved via Hereford to Cambridge United in August 1988 and starred in their meteoric rise under John Beck. He moved to Dean Court for £25,000 in August 1993 and featured in Cherries' 1994-95 relegation escape, scoring three goals in 54

League games prior to joining Plymouth Argyle in July 1995. Helping win promotion in 1995-96, he moved via Dorchester Town to Torquay United, featuring in the 1997-98 Third Division play-off final, then Plymouth again and Guisborough. He works in a chemical plant on Teesside.

DEREK LEAVER

Inside-forward Derek Leaver played for Cherries during the 1955-56 season. A former Burnley amateur, he represented the RAF and turned professional with Blackburn Rovers in May 1949, scoring on his League debut in their 4-1 victory over Manchester City in November 1950. He reunited with Jack Bruton at Bournemouth in July 1955, netting five goals in 29 Third Division (South) outings prior to joining Crewe Alexandra in March 1956. Later with Macclesfield Town and Wigan Athletic, he spent 35 years running the family firm D&C Leaver bakers and confectioners in Blackburn until retiring in November 1995.

JOHN LEDWIDGE

Irish inside-right John Ledwidge played for Bournemouth during the 1932-33 season. Born in Dublin, he began with Richmond Rovers before joining Shelbourne in July 1929 and topped their goalscoring charts as they finished Irish League runners-up in 1929-30. He moved via Bray Unknowns to Dean Court in July 1932 and scored on his League debut to clinch Cherries' 1-1 draw at Bristol City two months later. Briefly playing alongside record scorer Ron Eyre in attack, he netted seven goals in 17 Third Division (South) games for Cherries before returning to Dublin with Dolphin in July 1933, settling back in his native city.

TREVOR LEE

Striker Trevor Lee played alongside Trevor Morgan in Cherries' attack. He impressed with Epsom & Ewell prior to joining Millwall with Phil Walker in October 1975, helping them win promotion in 1975-76 and reach the FA Cup sixth round in 1977-78. After spells with Colchester United and Gillingham, he moved to Dean Court for £5,000 in November 1982 and scored nine times in 34 League games for Cherries before joining Cardiff City for £2,000 in December 1983. He later played for Northampton Town, Fulham, Bromley and ended his career back at Epsom & Ewell. Settling in London, he became a care worker.

IAN LEIGH

Goalkeeper Ian Leigh starred in AFC Bournemouth's 1981-82 promotion success. Moving to Dean Court from Swaythling in October 1979, he displaced Kenny Allen in goal and was a key figure as Cherries beat holders Manchester United in the 1983-84 FA Cup third round. He also featured in that season's Associate Members Cup final triumph and made 123 League appearances prior to joining Hamrun Spartans in May 1986. Starring in two Maltese League and Cup 'double' triumphs, he later played for Poole Town, Bashley and Salisbury. He became an insurance salesman and has since run IT firm Logcom, based in Texas.

BILLY LEITCH

Scottish left-half Billy Leitch featured prominently in Cherries' 1923-24 Football League debut campaign. Initially with Greenock Overton, he moved via Port Glasgow to Partick Thistle in July 1915 and joined Coventry City in September 1920. He was given his League debut in the following month's 1-0 defeat at home to West Ham and joined Bournemouth in July 1923. Missing just two League matches in 1924-25, his solitary goal in 81 Third Division (South) games came in the 2-0 win at home to Brentford in October 1924. 'Sticker' joined Helensburgh in July 1927 and later resided in Peterhead until his death in 1971.

DAVE LENNARD

Midfielder Dave Lennard was an experienced member of John Benson's squad at Dean Court. Initially with Bolton Wanderers, he joined Halifax in July 1969, then Blackpool and Cambridge United, before helping Chester win promotion and reach the League Cup semi-finals in 1974-75. Moving via Stockport to Cherries in September 1977, he scored four times in 59 League games before becoming Salisbury's player-boss in July 1979. He had a spell as Cherries' youth team boss, then managed Bashley to the Wessex League title in 1986-87. A science teacher at several local schools, then a postman, he now lives in Spain in retirement.

JACK LEWIS

Experienced left-half Jack Lewis contested a first-team slot with Tommy Casey while at Dean Court. A former West Brom amateur, he joined Crystal Palace in July 1938 and was ever-present in 1946-47. Harry Lowe paid £7,500 for him in November 1949 and his solitary goal in 45 League outings for Bournemouth clinched the following month's 2-1 victory at home to Reading. He moved to Reading in July 1951 and was ever-present as they were Third Division (South) runners-up in 1951-52, then played for Kettering Town and was Worcester City's trainer. Later a publican in his native Walsall, he died on Christmas Day 2002.

MORGAN LEWIS

Young midfielder Morgan Lewis featured in AFC Bournemouth's 1986-87 Third Division title campaign. Born locally, the former Bournemouth School for Boys pupil was given his League debut in Cherries' 4-1 victory at home to Bradford City two months before turning professional in July 1984. He helped to beat champions elect Bradford City 4-1 again in April 1985 made 12 League appearances while at Dean Court prior to joining Weymouth in July 1987 where an ankle injury curtailed his career. Settling in Brighton, he taught English as a foreign language and has since been a production editor in medical marketing.

TOMMY LIDDLE

Left-back Tommy Liddle understudied Joe Sanaghan as Bournemouth finished Third Division (South) runners-up in 1947-48. Initially with Kirkby Stephen, he served in the RAF before joining Cherries in February 1947 and made his solitary League appearance in the 3-0 defeat at Reading seven months later. He played in the 1948 Combination Cup final, then had spells with Yeovil Town, Chippenham United, Portland United and Parley Sports. Settling locally, he spent 35 years as a plumber for Christchurch Council and died in October 1994. His son Geoff was a compositor with the 'Daily Echo' for 37 years.

CRAIG LINDFIELD

England Youth striker Craig Lindfield had a loan spell at AFC Bournemouth at the start of the 2008-09 season. A former Liverpool trainee, he turned professional in August 2006 and helped to win the FA Youth Cup in two consecutive years. He was loaned to Notts County and Chester City before joining Cherries on loan in August 2008. His solitary goal in three League games came in that month's 3-1 defeat at Port Vale. He was then loaned to Accrington Stanley prior to joining Macclesfield in December 2009 and has since played for Accrington again, Chester and FC United of Manchester, helping win promotion in 2014-15.

JIM LISTER

Scottish inside-forward Jim Lister scored Cherries' first-ever goal in the Football League at Swindon Town in August 1923. Starting with Glasgow Perthshire, he had spells with Kilmarnock, Glasgow Rangers, Renton, Armadale, Dumbarton and Morton before joining Bury in July 1919. He then played for Hartlepool United and Llanelly, moving to

Football League new-boys Bournemouth in July 1923. Scoring seven times in 28 Third Division (South) games while at Dean Court, he joined Aberdare Athletic in July 1924. He later appeared for Ebbw Vale and resided back in his native Glasgow until his death in September 1978.

ROY LITTLEJOHN

Outside-right Roy Littlejohn gained England Amateur international honours while with Cherries. Born locally, he attended Bournemouth Grammar School and progressed through the ranks at Dean Court, making his League debut in Bournemouth's 2-1 win at Swindon in September 1952. He scored twice in 22 Third Division (South) games before moving to Portsmouth in July 1956, then featured in Woking's 1958 Amateur Cup final triumph. Later playing for Poole Town, Salisbury, Bridport and Christchurch, he spent 33 years with Leslie Jones Architects in Poole and was senior partner when he retired in June 1992.

STEWART LITTLEWOOD

Centre-forward Stewart Littlewood played for Cherries in 1933-34. He had spells with Hardwick Colliery, Chesterfield, Matlock, Sheffield Wednesday and Luton Town before joining Port Vale in November 1926. Swapped for Oldham Athletic's Albert Pynegar in January 1929, he was top scorer in 1929-30 and rejoined Port Vale in March 1931. He scored a club record six goals in a 9-1 win over Chesterfield in September 1932. Moving to Bournemouth in July 1933, he netted 11 goals in 18 League games before joining Altrincham in July 1934, then Northwich Victoria. He died in his native Rotherham in January 1977.

DOUG LIVERMORE

Midfielder Doug Livermore had a loan spell at AFC Bournemouth during the 1974-75 campaign. Signing professional for Liverpool in November 1965, he moved to Norwich City in November 1970, starring as they won the Second Division title in 1971-72 and were League Cup finalists in 1973. He was loaned to Cherries in March 1975 and made ten League appearances while at Dean Court. Joining Cardiff City in August 1975, he helped win promotion in 1975-76, then played for Chester before coaching at Cardiff, Norwich, Swansea City, Spurs, Liverpool, Nottingham Forest, Norwich again and Leicester City.

BERT LOCK

Veteran goalkeeper Bert Lock featured in Bournemouth's 1923-24 Football League debut campaign. He played for St Mary's Guild before joining Southampton in January 1907 and moved to Glasgow Rangers in May 1909. Helping them win the Scottish League title on four occasions, he joined QPR in July 1921 and returned to Saints in September 1922 as cover for Tommy Allen. He was an FA Cup quarter-finalist that season and joined Cherries in January 1924, making 13 Third Division (South) appearances. Settling in his native Southampton, he was later a carpenter and joiner with Southern Railway and died in March 1957.

BILLY LONGDON

Centre-forward Billy Longdon played for Cherries during the 1946-47 season. A former Mansfield Town amateur, he had spells with Folkestone and Brentford prior to joining Brighton in July 1939. He guested for several clubs, including Cherries, during wartime service in the RAF and played over 100 wartime games for Brighton before returning to Dean Court in May 1946. His only goal in nine League outings came in the 2-0 win over Leyton Orient in April 1947. He moved to

Rochdale in July 1947, then joined newly-formed Tonbridge the following summer and later played for King's Lynn. He died in Truro in November 1986.

DENNIS LONGHORN

Midfielder Dennis Longhorn featured in Cherries' 1970-71 promotion campaign. A former apprentice at Dean Court, he made his League debut in Bournemouth's 1-1 draw at home to Torquay five months before turning professional in August 1968. He scored once in 30 League games before joining Mansfield Town for £5,000 in December 1971. He moved to Sunderland in February 1974, helping win the Second Division title in 1975-76, then played for Sheffield United, Aldershot, Colchester United and Chelmsford City. Later manager/coach of Halstead, Wivenhoe and Braintree, he became football coach at Center Parcs in Thetford.

BRIAN LOUGHNANE

Winger Brian Loughnane was a member of Freddie Cox's squad at Dean Court. A former Manchester City amateur, he had a spell with Witton Albion before joining Leeds United in August 1952. He moved to Shrewsbury in July 1953, then Bournemouth in July 1956. Unlucky not to feature in the epic 1956-57 FA Cup run as Nelson Stiffle kept him out of the side, he netted six goals in 43 League games for Cherries prior to joining Wellington Town in July 1959. He played for GKN Sankey where he worked as a metal finisher, then spent 23 years as a maintenance worker at Rolls Royce and died in Shrewsbury in July 2014.

STEVE LOVELL (1)

Former Welsh international striker Steve Lovell briefly played for Cherries during the 1992-93 season. Initially with Crystal Palace, he reunited with George Graham at Millwall in March 1983 and was leading marksman in their 1984-85 promotion success. He joined Gillingham for £20,000 in February 1987 and was top scorer four times. Loaned to Cherries in November 1992, he made three League appearances. Later playing for Kent non-League clubs while Gillingham's community officer, he was an FA Vase finalist with Deal in 2000. He has managed Sittingbourne, Gravesend & Northfleet, Hastings United and Ashford Town.

STEVE LOVELL (2)

Young striker Steve Lovell featured as AFC Bournemouth narrowly failed to qualify for the Second Division play-offs in 1998-99. The half-brother of Eddie Howe, he was a trainee at Dean Court and made his League debut in Cherries' 1-0 victory at home to Macclesfield three months before turning professional in July 1999. He joined Portsmouth for £250,000 in August 1999 and followed Jim Duffy to Dundee in June 2002. Later with Aberdeen, Falkirk and Partick Thistle, he returned to Cherries in July 2010 but had injury problems, scoring once in 17 League games overall before hanging up his boots in September 2011.

JIM LOVERY

Outside-left Jim Lovery scored in Cherries' 7-1 victory at home to Southend United on New Year's Day 1938. Previously with Wolves, failing to make an impact, he followed the well-worn trail to Bournemouth in October 1937 and was given his League debut in that month's 2-1 defeat at Bristol City. He maintained a regular first-team slot that season, on the opposite flank to Bob Redfern, but was displaced by the arrival of Bill Tunnicliffe, scoring nine goals in 30 Third Division (South) games before moving to Bradford City in July 1939. His career was ended by the Second World War and he died in East Devon in September 2004.

JIMMY LOVIE

Scottish wing-half Jimmy Lovie appeared for Cherries during the 1960-61 season. Initially with hometown Peterhead, he then played in Army football prior to joining Dundee United in March 1953, then appeared for Peterhead again before moving to Bury in January 1957. He was given his League debut in their 2-1 defeat at York City eight months later and moved to Dean Court in July 1960. Making nine Third Division appearances for Bournemouth, he joined Chesterfield in July 1961, then played for Alfreton Town. He settled in Chesterfield and was a partner in a betting shop on Newbold Moor until retiring in June 1996.

EDMUND LOWSON

Versatile wing-half Edmund Lowson provided reliable cover while at Dean Court. Starting with Crook Town, he moved via Cuckfield Albion to Blackpool and made his League debut in their 1-1 draw at Stoke in April 1922. He had a spell with Doncaster Rovers before moving to Bournemouth in June 1924, making four Third Division (South) appearances prior to joining Poole Town in May 1926. Returning to his native North East with Durham City in June 1927, he was ever-present in 1927-28, their final Football League campaign, then finished his playing career with Halifax Town. He settled in Halifax and died in June 1955.

JIMMY LUMSDEN

Scottish inside-right Jimmy Lumsden briefly played for Bournemouth at the start of the 1928-29 campaign. Initially with West Calder Swifts, he had a spell with Preston but failed to secure a first-team slot, moving to Dean Court in July 1928. He was given his League debut in Cherries' 2-0 defeat at Northampton on the opening day of the season and also appeared in the 3-3 Third Division (South) draw at Fulham two days later. Moving to Bo'ness in January 1931, he was unable to prevent them finishing bottom of the Scottish League Second Division that season. He died in Dalkeith in 1986. His brother Bob played for Luton Town.

BILLY LUNN

Popular inside-left Billy Lunn featured in Cherries' 1947-48 promotion near-miss. A former Northern Ireland Schoolboy international, he had spells with Distillery and Glenavon before moving to West Brom in February 1946. He joined Bournemouth in February 1948 and scored 19 times in 47 League outings before joining Newport County in July 1950, then reunited with Harry Lowe at Yeovil Town in June 1952. Featuring in their 1954-55 Southern League 'double' triumph, he became a local sales rep for household goods and died in January 2000. His younger brother Harry played over 200 games for Swindon Town.

MICK LYNNE

Goalkeeper Mick Lynne understudied Republic of Ireland international Tommy Godwin while at Dean Court. He turned professional with Preston NE in March 1956 and made his First Division debut in place of Fred Else in their 4-2 defeat at home to West Brom in January 1959. Helping them take FA Cup holders Bolton to a fifth round replay that season, he moved to Bournemouth in June 1959 and made 17 League appearances prior to joining Brighton in July 1961, then played for Dorchester Town and Poole Town. Now living in Wisbech, he taught at Neale-Wade Community College and is a part-time care worker.

MIKE LYONS

Hard-tackling right-back Mike Lyons helped Cherries reach the FA Cup sixth round in 1956-57. Initially a centre-forward with Bristol City, he joined rivals Bristol Rovers in July 1953 and switched to a defensive role, moving to Bournemouth in July 1956. He played alongside Arnold Woollard and made 105 League appearances prior to joining Swindon Town in October 1959, then played for Yeovil Town. Later Bristol Rovers' reserve team trainer for 17 years while an insurance broker, he then assisted Bath City and Forest Green Rovers. He was briefly Almondsbury Town chairman and now owns several properties in Bristol.

BOBBY McALINDEN

Winger Bobby McAlinden made his only League appearance for Cherries in the 0-0 draw with Colchester in September 1976. A former Manchester City apprentice, he made his League debut in their 3-2 defeat at home to Preston seven months before turning professional in May 1964. He then moved via Port Vale to Glentoran, helping win the Irish Cup in 1966. Later with Stalybridge, he followed his friend George Best to Los Angeles Aztecs in April 1976. Briefly reuniting with John Benson at Dean Court, he then played for Memphis Rogues. He ran Besties bar in Hermosa Beach for 20 years and now lives in Portland, Oregon.

KIERAN McANESPIE

Scotland U-21 defender Kieran McAnespie had a loan spell at AFC Bournemouth during the 2001-02 campaign. Initially with St Johnstone, he helped clinch the Scottish First Division title in 1996-97 and joined Fulham for £80,000 in August 2000 but failed to make an impact at Craven Cottage. After a loan spell at Hearts, he was loaned to Cherries in February 2002 and scored once in seven League games while at Dean Court. He joined Plymouth Argyle in March 2003 and has since played back in Scotland for Falkirk, Ayr United, Alloa Athletic, Greenock Morton, Arbroath, Stirling Albion and Kilbirnie Ladeside.

BOB McCULLOCH

Scottish outside-left Bob McCulloch missed just four matches for Bournemouth in 1924-25. He began with Auckinleck Talbot and joined Kilmarnock in October 1922, appearing in the Scottish First Division, then had a loan spell with Arbroath before making the long move to Dean Court in May 1924. Given his League debut in Cherries' 3-1 defeat at Millwall on the opening day of the season, he helped to avoid having to seek re-election for the second consecutive year and netted four goals in 38 Third Division (South) games prior to joining Watford in June 1925. He settled back in his native Glasgow and died in April 1964.

MIKE McCULLOCH

Scottish inside-left Mike McCulloch played for Bournemouth during the 1924-25 campaign. Starting with hometown Denny Hibernians, he joined Falkirk in July 1913 and moved via Hearts to Nelson in June 1922. He captained their 1922-23 Third Division (North) title triumph and joined Chesterfield in June 1924 but lost his place after injury and joined Cherries in March 1925. Partnering Ron Eyre in attack, his solitary goal in ten League games came in the following month's 3-1 victory at home to Aberdare and he returned to Scotland with Second Division side St Bernard's in June 1925. He died in Edinburgh in August 1973.

DONAL McDERMOTT

Republic of Ireland Youth winger Donal McDermott had two spells at AFC Bournemouth. He turned professional with Manchester City in October 2007 and featured in their 2008 FA Youth Cup success. Loaned to MK Dons, Chesterfield and Scunthorpe before Cherries in March 2011, he helped to reach the League One play-offs. He joined Huddersfield in August 2011 and returned to Cherries in January 2012. Helping win promotion in 2012-13, he scored twice in 29 League games overall prior to joining Dundalk in July 2014, featuring in their 2014-15 League of Ireland title triumph. He moved to Rochdale in May 2015.

BOB MacDONALD

Bob Macdonald was one of seven different players who appeared at left-back for Cherries during the 1963-64 season. Starting with Vale of Leven, he moved to Manchester City in September 1956 and made his First Division debut in their 3-0 victory at home to Nottingham Forest in October 1961. He failed to secure a regular slot and moved to Dean Court in August 1963. His solitary League appearance for Bournemouth was in the 1-0 defeat at home to Bristol City two months later and he briefly played for Weymouth before joining Falkirk. He provided reliable defensive cover in the Scottish First Division for three seasons.

JACK McDONALD

Outside-left Jack McDonald was ever-present in Cherries' 1947-48 promotion near-miss. Initially with Wolves, he moved to Dean Court in May 1939 and featured in Bournemouth's 1946 Third Division (South) Cup final success. He was top scorer in 1946-47, netting 35 goals in 80 League outings before being sold to Fulham for £12,000 in June 1948. Starring in their 1948-49 Second Division title triumph, he then played for Southampton, Southend, Weymouth and Poole. He was licensee of the 'Royal Oak' in Bere Regis and 'Tatnum Hotel' in Poole. Later working for Pearl Assurance in Wimborne, he died in Ryde in June 2007.

MARTIN MacDONALD

Versatile right-half Martin Macdonald was a member of Jack Bruton's squad at Dean Court. Signing professional for Portsmouth in November 1948, he joined Cherries in November 1951 and his solitary goal in 51 Third Division (South) games came in the 3-1 victory at Norwich City in December 1953. He moved to Weymouth in July 1956, then reunited with Ken Bird at Dorchester Town in June 1957 and later had a spell playing for Portland United. After 14 years as caretaker at the Covent of the Cross in Bournemouth, he spent 20 years as a machinist at Wellworthy/AE Goetze in Ringwood until retiring in September 1996.

SCOTT McDONALD

Australian international striker Scott McDonald featured in Cherries' 2002-03 promotion campaign. Born in Melbourne of Scottish/Australian parentage, he played for Eastern Pride, joining Southampton in August 2001. He joined Cherries in March 2003, scoring once in seven League outings. Moving via Wimbledon to Motherwell in January 2004, he was top scorer three times and joined Celtic for £700,000 in July 2007. Leading marksman in their 2007-08 Scottish League title triumph, he reunited with Gordon Strachan at Middlesbrough for £3,500,000 in February 2010, since playing for Millwall and Motherwell again.

SHAUN MACDONALD

Welsh international midfielder Shaun MacDonald helped AFC Bournemouth to win promotion in 2012-13. A former Swansea City trainee, he helped them to win the Football League Trophy shortly before turning professional in April 2006. He failed to secure a regular first-team slot with his hometown club and spent five loan spells with Yeovil Town. Gaining a record 25 Welsh U-21 caps, he made his full international debut in the 4-1 defeat by Switzerland in October 2010. He moved to Dean Court for £125,000 in August 2011, scoring once in 81 League games by the end of Cherries' 2014-15 Championship title campaign.

TED MacDOUGALL

Striker Ted MacDougall scored a record 42 goals in Cherries' 1970-71 promotion success. Initially with Liverpool, he moved via York City to Dean Court in July 1969 and was top scorer three times, netting nine goals in the 1971-72 FA Cup win over Margate. Sold to Manchester United for £220,000 in September 1972, the Scotland international moved via West Ham to Norwich City and helped win promotion in 1974-75. He repeated that with Southampton in 1977-78, rejoining Cherries in November 1978 and scoring 119 goals in 198 League games overall. Later with Blackpool, he coaches youth soccer in the United States.

MIKE McELHATTON

Young, versatile midfielder Mike McElhatton featured in AFC Bournemouth's 1994-95 relegation escape. A former trainee at Dean Court, he made his League debut in Cherries' 0-0 draw at home to Wigan Athletic two months before turning professional in July 1993. He scored twice in 42 League games prior to joining Scarborough for £15,000 in September 1996. Starring as they reached the Third Division play-offs in 1997-98, he joined Rushden & Diamonds in June 1998, featuring in their 1998-99 FA Cup run and 2000-01 Conference title campaign. Injury ended his career and he has since worked locally in the building trade.

BILL McGARRY

Ex-England international right-half Bill McGarry had a successful spell as Cherries' player-manager. He impressed with Port Vale before moving to Huddersfield Town in March 1951, starring in their 1952-53 promotion success and 1953-54 FA Cup run. Appointed Bournemouth's player-boss in March 1961, he plotted the 1961-62 promotion near-miss, scoring twice in 78 League outings. He became Watford's boss in July 1963, then managed Ipswich to the Second Division title in 1967-68, Wolves to League Cup glory in 1974, Saudi Arabia, Newcastle, Zambia and Wolves again. He died in South Africa in March 2005.

DOUG McGIBBON

Centre-forward Doug McGibbon was Cherries' leading marksman in three successive seasons. The son of former Southampton forward Charlie McGibbon, he turned professional with Saints in December 1938 and made his League debut at Plymouth five months later. He moved to Fulham in January 1947 and Harry Lowe paid £5,000 for him in September 1948. Scoring 65 goals in 103 League outings for Cherries, he joined Lovell's Athletic in August 1951 where a head injury ended his career. He spent 24 years as an engineer with Sperry/Honeywells aircraft instruments in Brentford and died in Aylesbury in October 2002.

DAVID McGOLDRICK

Young striker David McGoldrick impressed during his loan spell with AFC Bournemouth in 2006-07. Initially with Notts County, he followed Leon Best to Southampton in August 2004 and was loaned back to the Magpies before joining Cherries on loan in February 2007. He netted six goals in 12 League games while at Dean Court. Also loaned to Port Vale, he was ever-present leading marksman for

Saints in 2008-09 and returned to his native Nottingham with Forest in June 2009. He then had further loan spells at Sheffield Wednesday and Coventry City before joining Ipswich Town initially on loan in January 2013.

BRIAN McGORRY

Midfielder Brian McGorry was AFC Bournemouth's top scorer in 1992-93. Previously with Weymouth, he moved to Cherries for £30,000 in August 1991 and netted 11 goals in 61 League games before sold to Peterborough United for £60,000 in February 1994. He joined Wycombe Wanderers in August 1995, then played for Cardiff City, Hereford United, Torquay United, Telford United, Southport and Chester City. Helping Tamworth to win the Southern League title and reach the FA Trophy final in 2002-03, he then played for Nuneaton Borough and coached Vauxhall Motors, becoming a personal trainer in Liverpool.

BOB McGOWAN

Much-travelled Scottish centre-forward Bob McGowan briefly succeeded record goalscorer Ron Eyre in Bournemouth's attack. He had spells with Nithsdale Wanderers, Kello Rovers, Carlisle United, Crewe Alexandra, Nithsdale again and Glasgow Rangers, then was Kilmarnock's top scorer in 1929-30. Later at Ballymena United and Dunfermline Athletic, he moved to Dean Court in August 1932. His only goal in six League games came in Cherries' 2-1 defeat at Southend four months later and he joined Queen of the South in May 1933, then played again for Dunfermline and Kilmarnock. He died in Dunfermline in May 1984.

MARTIN McGRATH

Ex-England Schoolboy midfielder Martin McGrath played for AFC Bournemouth during the 1980-81 campaign. A former Southampton apprentice, he turned professional in October 1978 and made his solitary First Division appearance in their 2-0 defeat at Leeds United in March 1980. He moved to Cherries in June 1980, playing 22 Fourth Division games before joining Oxford City in March 1981 Quitting football, he became a croupier in London's Ritz Club then worked for British Airways Special Services at Heathrow Airport and now lives in a small village in Normandy, running a website selling designer toothbrushes.

TOM McINALLY

Ex-Scotland international forward Tom McInally was one of Cherries' most notable pre-war signings. Starting with St Anthony's, he joined Celtic in May 1919, starring in their 1921-22 Scottish League title triumph. He moved to Third Lanark in September 1922 and was top scorer before rejoining Celtic in May 1925. A key figure as they won the Scottish League title in 1925-26 and Scottish Cup in 1927, he moved via Sunderland to Bournemouth in November 1929. He scored once in ten League games, joining Morton in May 1930, then Derry City, Armadale and Nithsdale. Later a Celtic scout, he died in September 1955.

NORMAN MACKAY

Scottish forward Norman Mackay played on trial in Cherries' 1-0 victory at home to Brentford in January 1928. He played for Leith Amateurs, Gala Fairydean, Hibernian, St Bernard's, Edinburgh Royal, Lochgelly United and Broxburn before joining Aston Villa in December 1923. Briefly appearing in the top-flight, he then had spells with Bathgate, Broxburn again and Lovell's Athletic. He moved via Cherries to Plymouth Argyle and scored a hat-trick on his debut, starring in their 1929-30 Third Division (South) title triumph. Later appearing for Southend United, Clydebank and Llanelly, he became a civil servant in Edinburgh.

TOM McKECHNIE

Striker Tom McKechnie played for Cherries during the 1966-67 campaign. Initially with Glasgow Rangers, he moved via Kirkintilloch Rob Roy to Luton Town in May 1961 and scored twice on his home debut in a 4-2 win over Derby County three months later. He was leading marksman in 1964-65, moving to Dean Court in July 1966 and netting twice in 14 League games for Bournemouth prior to joining Colchester United in September 1967. Later with Bury Town, he played against

Cherries in the 1968-69 FA Cup first round. He settled back in his native Milngavie and spent 20 years with Barr Stroud instrument makers.

JOHNNY MacKENZIE

Scottish outside-right Johnny MacKenzie starred in Cherries' 1947-48 promotion near-miss. He played for Partick Thistle and was serving with Jim Stirling in the Scots Guards at Victoria Barracks, Windsor, when Harry Lowe signed him on loan in August 1947. Scoring nine goals in 38 Third Division (South) outings while at Dean Court, he rejoined Partick in July 1948 and appeared in three Scottish League Cup finals. He gained nine Scotland caps, moving to Dumbarton in July 1960, then playing for Derry City. Later a sales rep for Dowly Haudralics/Dunlop, he settled on the remote Isle of Tiree in the Hebrides in retirement.

BILL McKINNEY

Tough-tackling right-back Bill McKinney played for Cherries during the 1965-66 season. He impressed with Wallsend St Lukes prior to joining Newcastle United in May 1956 and made his First Division debut in their 3-3 draw at Spurs in December 1957. Featuring in their 1964-65 Second Division title campaign, he followed Dick Keith to Bournemouth in August 1965. He made 17 League appearances before moving to Mansfield Town in June 1966, then played for Wellington Town (later Telford United). Settling near his son and daughter in Telford, he spent 26 years as a panel beater with GKN Sankey until August 1997.

EDDIE McMANUS

Outside-right Eddie McManus understudied Tommy Southren while at Dean Court. Previously with Dover, he joined Bournemouth in August 1954 and made his League debut in the 4-0 defeat at Tranmere Rovers in February 1959. He played four Third Division games for Cherries prior to joining Gillingham in August 1960. Following spells with Gravesend & Northfleet and Canterbury City, he moved to Salisbury in July 1962, then gave Parley Sports lengthy service. He has since been manager and chairman of Wareham Rangers, settling in Wareham.

DON McPHAIL

Scottish winger Don McPhail played for Bournemouth during the 1932-33 campaign. Starting with hometown Dumbarton, he joined Middlesbrough in April 1928 and was given his First Division debut in their 5-1 win over Blackpool in January 1931. He moved to Dean Court in September 1932 and contested a first-team slot with Len Williams, making 14 League appearances for Cherries before joining Barnsley in August 1933. Later with Carlisle United, Burton Town, Nuneaton Town, Swindon Town, Dunfermline Athletic, Dartford and Burton again, he settled back in Scotland and died in Helensburgh in June 1997.

JOSH McQUOID

Northern Ireland international striker Josh McQuoid had two spells at AFC Bournemouth. A former trainee at Dean Court, he made his League debut in Cherries' 2-0 victory at home to Doncaster in March 2007 and helped win promotion in 2009-10. Sold to Millwall for £550,000 in January 2011, following a loan spell, he then reunited with Eddie Howe on loan at Burnley, rejoining Cherries in exchange for Scott Malone in July 2012. He was a promotion winner in 2012-13, then loaned to Peterborough (2014 Johnstone's Paint Trophy triumph) and Coventry. Scoring 13 times in 106 League games overall, he joined Luton in June 2015.

PETER McSEVICH

Popular goalkeeper Peter McSevich was ever-present for Bournemouth in 1930-31. A Scottish Junior international, he impressed with Shieldmuir prior to joining Celtic in August 1924. He moved via Aberdeen to Dean Court in July 1928 and starred as Cherries took West Ham to an FA Cup fifth round replay in 1928-29. Scoring in the 4-1 defeat at Brighton in October 1931 when switched to outside-right after being injured in the match, he made 142 League appearances prior to joining Coventry City in February 1932, then Walsall and Wellington. He spent 28 years as caretaker at Walsall Library and died in January 1979.

MEL MACHIN

Mel Machin achieved success as both a player and manager at AFC Bournemouth. Initially with Port Vale, the right-back moved via Gillingham to Cherries in December 1970. He helped clinch promotion that season and netted seven goals in 110 League games, following John Bond to Norwich City in December 1973. Later Norwich's chief coach, he managed Manchester City and Barnsley, returning to Dean Court as boss in August 1994. He led Cherries to the 1998 Auto Windscreens Shield final, then was director of football for two years until August 2002 and had a spell as Huddersfield Town's caretaker-manager.

DAVID MADDEN

Young midfielder David Madden had a loan spell at AFC Bournemouth during the 1982-83 campaign. Signing professional for Southampton in January 1981, he failed to secure a first-team slot and was loaned to Cherries in January 1983, making five League appearances while at Dean Court. He joined Arsenal in August 1983, then had spells with Charlton Athletic, Los Angeles Razors and Reading prior to joining Crystal Palace in August 1988. Helping them to win promotion in 1988-89, he also appeared in the 1990 FA Cup final. He later played for Maidstone United and now runs a property investment company.

SHAUN MAHER

Irish central defender Shaun Maher starred as AFC Bournemouth narrowly failed to qualify for the League One play-offs in 2004-05. Initially with Bohemians, he joined Fulham in December 1997 but soon returned to Bohemians and starred in their 2000-01 Irish 'double' success. He moved to Cherries in August 2001 and overcame a serious knee injury to score five goals in 98 League games until released in May 2007 after further injury problems. Joining Drogheda United in January 2008, he helped Sporting Fingal win the FAI Cup in 2009 and has since played for Galway United, Limerick, Monaghan United and Ballymena United.

HARRY MAIDMENT

Outside-left Harry Maidment created numerous goalscoring chances for Ron Eyre. Born locally, he played for Guildford before moving to Dean Court in June 1924. He made his League debut in Cherries' 6-3 defeat at Norwich four months later and secured a regular first-team slot during the 1925-26 campaign, netting 16 goals in 71 Third Division (South) games prior to joining Thames in July 1928. Later playing for Woking and Cowes, he worked for Bournemouth fire service, then was a labourer for the local council and a beer cellarman at the Bournemouth Pavilion until his retirement. He died in Bournemouth in September 1971.

SCOTT MALONE

Former England Youth left-back Scott Malone played for AFC Bournemouth in 2011-12. He was Wolves' Academy 'Player of the Year' in 2008-09 and turned professional at Molineux in February 2009. Loaned to Hungarian First Division side Ujpest Dosza, he also had loan spells at Southend United and Burton Albion before moving from Wolves to Dean Court initially on loan in August 2011. He joined on a permanent basis for £150,000 five months later and scored five times in 32 League games for Cherries. Moving to Millwall in an exchange deal with Josh McQuoid in May 2012, he joined Cardiff City in January 2015.

HARRY MARDON

Centre-forward Harry Mardon was Cherries' leading marksman in 1937-38. Born in Cardiff, he grew up in Bristol and played for Victoria Albion and Hereford United before joining Notts County in July 1936. He moved to Dean Court in exchange for Joe Riley in December 1937 and netting four goals in Cherries' then record 7-1 win over Southend on New Year's Day 1938, scoring 14 times in 25 League games prior to joining Bristol City in September 1938. Settling in Bristol, he spent 30 years as a boilermaker at Charles Hill Shipyard in Hotwells and died in July 1981. His grandson Paul Mardon was a Welsh international.

FRED MARSDEN

Long-serving right-back Fred Marsden was ever-present in Cherries' 1947-48 promotion near-miss. A former Blackburn Rovers junior, he had spells with Clitheroe, Manchester Central, Accrington Stanley and gained top-flight experience with Wolves before moving to Bournemouth in July 1936. Captaining the 1946 Third Division (South) Cup final triumph, he scored once in 194 League games for Cherries before following Paddy Gallacher to Weymouth in June 1949, featuring in their 1949-50 FA Cup run. He was later Cherries' A team player-coach and a delivery driver, residing locally until his death in November 1989.

CLIFF MARSH

Inside-forward Cliff Marsh partnered Doug McGibbon and Jack Cross in Cherries' attack. Initially with Tyldesley United, he moved via Winsford United to Leeds United in September 1948 and scored on his League debut at home to West Brom a month later. He joined Bournemouth in May 1949 and netted twice in 39 Third Division (South) games prior to joining Worcester City with Bill Gripton in June 1952. Moving to Yeovil Town in June 1953, he starred in their 1954-55 Southern League 'double' triumph. He worked for Vigar & Co timber merchants in Winton and died at Queen's Park Golf Club on Christmas Eve 1990.

ANDY MARSHALL

England U-21 goalkeeper Andy Marshall had a loan spell at AFC Bournemouth during the 1996-97 season. He turned professional with Norwich City in July 1993 and was loaned to Cherries in September 1996, making 11 League appearances in place of Jimmy Glass. Succeeding Bryan Gunn as Norwich's first-choice keeper, he joined rivals Ipswich Town in July 2001 and had a loan spell at Wolves, moving to Millwall in January 2004. He was an FA Cup finalist in 2004, joining Coventry City in July 2006 and voted their 'Player of the Season' in 2006-07. Moving to Aston Villa in June 2009, he is now their goalkeeping coach.

GEORGE MARSHALL

Experienced left-back George Marshall played alongside Edgar Saxton in Bournemouth's defence. Initially with Shankhouse in his native North-East, he had a period with Southend United prior to joining Wolves in August 1919. He made his League debut in a 2-0 defeat at Fulham a year later and featured in the 1921 FA Cup final, missing just four Second Division games that season. Displaced by Harry Shaw, he had spells with Walsall and Reading, moving to Dean Court in July 1924. He made 20 consecutive Third Division (South) appearances for Cherries prior to joining Darlaston in July 1925, where injury ended his career.

KEN MARSHALL

Goalkeeper Ken Marshall briefly appeared in Cherries' 1923-24 Football League debut campaign. Born locally, he understudied Alec Heron during Boscombe's three seasons in the Southern League, helping to finish runners-up in 1922-23. He faced further competition after the arrival of Bert Lock from Southampton and had to wait until March 1924 to make his Third Division (South) debut in Cherries' 3-1 victory at home to QPR, also appearing in the 0-0 draw at home to Plymouth Argyle a week later. Moving to Poole Town in July 1924, helping to win the Western League title in 1925-26, he died in Christchurch in February 1957.

DENNIS MARTIN

Wing-half Dennis Martin was a valuable member of Cherries' squad over seven seasons at Dean Court. He turned professional under Harry Lowe in August 1947 and was given his League debut in Bournemouth's 2-1 victory at home to Notts County in April 1949. Making 23 Third Division (South) appearances for Cherries, he joined Poole Town in July 1954 and helped win the Western League title in 1956-57, then had spells playing for Tunbridge Wells, Yiewsley and Folkestone, becoming their chairman. He later settled back in Bournemouth, becoming chairman of Allnatt Centres, school journey centres in Swanage.

BOB MASSEY

Young full-back Bob Massey understudied Arnold Woollard while at Dean Court. Signing professional for Bournemouth in May 1958, he made his League debut in the 2-2 draw at Reading in April 1960. He played five Third Division games for Cherries, including a 4-4 draw with Colchester United in February 1961, moving to Guildford City in July 1961. Starring as they won the Southern League Cup in 1963 and 1967, he joined Andover in July 1969 and helped them step up to the Southern League in 1971, then assisted Salisbury. He went into business partnership with his brother Ray and now lives in New Milton.

STEVE MASSEY

Fast, skilful striker Steve Massey played alongside Mick Butler in AFC Bournemouth's attack. Initially with Stockport County, scoring on his League debut as a 16 year old against Darlington in February 1975, he moved to Dean Court for £5,000 in July 1978 and netted 19 goals in 97 Fourth Division games for Cherries, joining Peterborough United with Geoff Butler in August 1981. He moved via Northampton to Hull City in July 1983 and starred in their 1984-85 promotion success, then played for Cambridge United, Wrexham and was Truro City's player-boss. He has since run holiday parks in Devon and Cornwall.

NEIL MASTERS

Versatile left-back Neil Masters played for AFC Bournemouth at Blackburn Rovers in the 1992-93 FA Cup third round. A Northern Ireland Youth international, he turned professional at Dean Court in August 1990 and made his League debut in Cherries' 0-0 draw at Wigan Athletic in October 1992, scoring twice in 38 Second Division games before being sold to Wolves for £300,000 in December 1993. He helped them qualify for the First Division play-offs in 1994-95 but successive injuries hindered his progress. Reunited with Tony Pulis at Gillingham in March 1997, he later briefly appeared for Norwegian side Moss.

RON MEADOWS

Goalkeeper Ron Meadows provided reliable cover for Ken Bird while at Dean Court. Initially with Morecambe, he represented the RAF during wartime service in the Middle East and turned professional with Burnley in September 1946. Unable to make an impact as Jimmy Strong made a club record 220 consecutive appearances, he moved to Bournemouth with Gordon Haigh in April 1950. He played 16 Third Division (South) games for Cherries prior to joining Accrington Stanley in July 1952, then coached Lancaster City and Morecambe. Settling in Lancaster, he spent 27 years with Storey Brothers plastics firm.

SCOTT MEAN

Stylish midfielder Scott Mean had two spells at AFC Bournemouth. A former trainee at Dean Court, he signed professional for Cherries in August 1992 and made his League debut in that month's 1-1 draw at Preston. He featured in the 1994-95 relegation escape, moving to West Ham for £100,000 in July 1996. Unlucky to suffer a knee injury while on loan to Port Vale, he rejoined Cherries in July 1999 and netted 12 goals in 106 League games overall. He was briefly with Kingstonian, joining hometown Crawley Town in October 2000. He became an actor in Sky One's Dream Team, also appearing in The Bill and EastEnders.

JJ MELLIGAN

Republic of Ireland U-21 midfielder JJ Melligan had a loan spell at AFC Bournemouth during the 2001-02 season. Christened John Joseph, he began with Wolves and was loaned to Cherries in November 2001, making eight

League appearances. He also had loan spells at Kidderminster Harriers and Doncaster Rovers, helping the latter to win the Third Division title in 2003-04. Moving to Cheltenham Town for £25,000 in July 2004, he was a promotion winner again in 2005-06 and joined Leyton Orient in June 2007. He has since played for Dundalk, Cheltenham again, Solihull Moors, Wolverhampton Casuals and Hinckley AFC.

DICK MELLORS

Goalkeeper Dick Mellors was ever-present for Cherries in 1936-37. A former amateur with Chesterfield and Mansfield, he turned professional with Sheffield Wednesday in December 1925 and understudied England international John Brown in two League Championship campaigns. He joined Reading in July 1931 and starred as they were Third Division (South) runners-up in 1931-32. Moving to Bournemouth in June 1934, he made 117 League appearances before joining Queen of the South in December 1937. He rejoined Cherries as trainer after the war, then emigrated to Australia and died in Sydney in October 1960.

LES MELVILLE

Ex-England Youth left-half Les Melville was a member of Freddie Cox's squad at Dean Court. Signing professional for Everton in April 1950, he moved to Bournemouth for £1,000 in July 1956 and was given his League debut in the 3-0 defeat at Southampton a month later., making 25 League appearances prior to joining Oldham Athletic in March 1958. He joined Worcester City four months later and starred in their epic 1958-59 FA Cup third round defeat of Liverpool, then played for Macclesfield Town. Settling in Stockport, he spent 25 years as a design engineer for heating ventilation firms and died in February 2009.

MICKAEL MENETRIER

Mickael Menetrier started the 2000-01 season as AFC Bournemouth's first-choice goalkeeper. Previously with Metz in his native France, he moved to Dean Court in August 2000 and made his League debut in the 1-1 draw at Bristol Rovers on the opening day of the campaign. He helped Cherries draw 0-0 at Norwich City in the League Cup first round first-leg but lost his place to Gareth Stewart, making 13 Second Division appearances for Cherries prior to joining Belgian side Virton in July 2002. After four seasons with US Bologne, he moved to Cherbourg and has since played for Istres and Luxembourg side F91 Dudelange.

JOHN MEREDITH

Winger John Meredith was ever-present for Cherries in 1969-70. He had spells with Doncaster Rovers, Sheffield Wednesday and Chesterfield before moving to Gillingham in March 1964. Ever-present three times, he reunited with Freddie Cox at Dean Court in an exchange deal involving Ken Pound in August 1969 and helped Bournemouth to beat Sheffield Wednesday in the 1969-70 League Cup second round. He scored once in 51 League games, becoming Hastings United's player-boss in August 1972. Now living in York, he spent 30 years as a divisional administrator with Combined Insurance Company of America.

NEIL MERRICK

England Semi-Pro international central defender Neil Merrick featured in AFC Bournemouth's 1974-75 relegation battle. The son of former Birmingham City and England goalkeeper Gil Merrick, he played for Bromsgrove Rovers and Worcester City before moving to Dean Court in September 1974. He made 15 League appearances for Cherries prior to joining South African side Germiston Callies in June 1975, then moved via Maidstone United to Weymouth and helped finish Conference runners-up in 1979-80. Later with Trowbridge, Poole and Basingstoke, he settled in Iford, becoming a self-employed stationery salesman.

ALF MESSER

Experienced centre-half Alf Messer had a spell as Bournemouth's player-coach. He had spells with Sutton Town, Mansfield Town and Nottingham Forest before joining Reading in June 1923. Ever-present three times, he starred as they won the Third Division (South) title in 1925-26 and were FA Cup semi-finalists in 1926-27. He was unlucky not to gain England honours and joined Spurs for £2,000 in July 1930. Starring in their 1930-31 promotion near-miss, he moved to Cherries in May 1934 but played only ten League games due to a knee injury, then coached Thornycroft Athletic and Oxford City. He died in Reading in July 1947.

HARRY MEYER

Experienced inside-right Harry Meyer briefly appeared for Cherries during the 1924-25 campaign. Born locally, 'Porky' was a regular scorer for his works team Bournemouth Trams and featured in Cherries' three Southern League campaigns, helping to finish runners-up in 1922-23, shortly before the club was elected to the Football League. He made his Third Division (South) debut in Bournemouth's 3-1 victory at Merthyr in November 1924, also appearing in the 2-1 defeat at Bristol City three months later. Returning to Bournemouth Trams, he continued to play local football for many years. He died in Poole in January 1947.

DOSSIE MILES

Versatile centre-half 'Dossie' Miles was an influential figure as Cherries took Liverpool to an FA Cup third round replay in 1926-27. Real name William, he was born locally and a prolific scorer during four seasons with Bournemouth Trams. He represented Hampshire as a centre-forward before moving to Dean Court in May 1924. Given his League debut in Cherries' 2-1 defeat at Millwall three months later, he switched to a defensive role in his third season at the club and netted ten goals in 94 Third Division (South) games prior to joining Watford in July 1929, then rejoined Bournemouth Trams. He died in Weymouth in March 1971.

SID MILES

Centre-half Sid Miles made his solitary League appearance in Cherries' 2-0 defeat at Southend United in February 1958. Born locally, he won the Military Medal and represented the Combined Services whilst serving in the RASC in Malaya, joining Cherries in July 1955. He understudied Harry Hughes and Mike Burgess and moved to Peterborough United with Dennis Bushby in July 1958, then played for Salisbury. Later Poole Town's manager, he became head of PE during 23 years at Homefield School, working with fellow ex-Cherries Peter Rushworth and Eric Wilkinson. He died in Bournemouth in February 2014.

NORMAN MILLAR

Irish right-back Norman Millar succeeded Eric Sibley in Bournemouth's defence. He played for Linfield and Glentoran before moving to Dean Court in July 1937 and made his League debut in Cherries' 2-1 defeat at Bristol City three months later. His solitary goal in 22 Third Division (South) games came in the 3-0 victory at home to Aldershot in December 1937. Displaced by the emergence of the notable Fred Marsden and Joe Sanaghan defensive partnership, he returned to Irish football with Dundalk in July 1939. He settled back in Bournemouth after the Second World War and died in Poole in August 1998.

JIMMY MILLER

Experienced outside-right Jimmy Miller featured prominently in Bournemouth's 1923-24 Football League debut campaign. He had spells with South Shields Albion, Wallsend Park Villa, Newcastle United and Grimsby Town before joining Everton in June 1919. Moving via Coventry City to Preston in January 1920, he then played for Pontypridd and Chesterfield prior to joining Cherries in June 1923. He made 38 Third Division (South) appearances while at Dean Court, moving to Swansea in May 1924 and helping win the Third Division (South) title in 1924-25. Later with Luton Town, he died in Tynemouth in December 1957.

JOE MILLER

Former Northern Ireland international right-half Joe Miller missed just two matches for Bournemouth in 1932-33. He played for Largs Thistle, Port Glasgow, Morton, Arthurlie, Johnstone, Nuneaton Town and Aberdare before joining Middlesbrough in April 1926. Starring as they won the Second Division title in 1926-27 and 1928-29, he was capped three times including against England in October 1929, moving to Hibernian in November 1930. He moved via Ards to Dean Court in March 1932 and made 75 Third Division (South) appearances for Cherries prior to joining Ballymena in July 1934, then Ross County.

KEITH MILLER

Versatile midfielder Keith Miller was ever-present in Cherries' 1970-71 promotion success. Initially with Walthamstow Avenue, he joined West Ham in September 1965 and made his First Division debut at Ipswich Town in November 1968, reuniting with John Bond at Dean Court for £10,000 in July 1970. He was also ever-present in AFC Bournemouth's 1971-72 promotion near-miss and became captain, scoring 19 goals in 383 League games prior to joining Dorchester Town in July 1980. Later their player-boss, he also managed Fareham and Poole Town. He settled locally and became sales manager of Compass Publications.

PAUL MILLER

Hard-tackling central defender Paul Miller was an experienced member of Harry Redknapp's squad at Dean Court. Signing professional for Spurs in May 1977, he made his First Division debut at local rivals Arsenal in April 1979, starring in two FA Cup final successes and scoring in their 1984 UEFA Cup final triumph. He joined Charlton Athletic for £130,000 in February 1987 and moved via Watford to AFC Bournemouth for £50,000 in August 1989. Scoring once in 47 League outings, he moved to Swansea City in January 1991. He has since worked as a business development manager in the City and been a football agent.

RALPH MILLER

Versatile defender Ralph Miller missed just one match for Cherries in 1968-69. Initially with Slough Town, he joined Charlton Athletic in September 1963 and moved to Gillingham with David Stocks in May 1965, following Stocks to Dean Court in July 1968. He scored once in 72 League games for Bournemouth before joining Weymouth initially on loan in November 1970, featuring in their 1973 Southern League Cup final triumph. Reuniting with Tony Nelson at Poole Town in May 1976, he later played for Tony Priscott's Ringwood Town. He became a building labourer, then a painter and decorator, and died locally in 2014.

DUDLEY MILLIGAN

Bustling centre-forward Dudley Milligan was leading marksman as Cherries were Third Division (South) runners-up in 1947-48. Capped three times by South Africa while with Johannesburg Rangers, he joined Clyde following a trial in December 1937 and moved to Chesterfield in November 1938. He scored on his international debut for Northern Ireland against Wales four months later and joined Bournemouth in August 1947. Netting 26 goals in 45 League games while at Dean Court, he moved to Walsall in October 1948, then played for Ballymena United. He was a welder in Belfast before returning to South Africa.

MATT MILLS

Ex-England Youth central defender Matt Mills had a loan spell at AFC Bournemouth during the 2004-05 campaign. Starting with Southampton, he was loaned to Cherries in February 2005 and netted three goals in 12 League games. He joined Manchester City for £750,000 in January 2006 and reunited with Sean O'Driscoll at Doncaster Rovers for £300,000 in August 2007. Voted 'Player of the Year' in their 2007-08 promotion success, he was sold to Reading for £2,000,000 in August 2009. He then had spells at Bolton Wanderers and Leicester City before following Dougie Freedman to Nottingham Forest in July 2015.

ALEX MILNE

Young Scottish inside-left Alex Milne briefly appeared for Bournemouth in 1937-38. Initially with Dunoon Athletic, he joined Third Lanark in July 1935 and played regularly in the Scottish League First Division. He had a spell with French side Lille before moving to Dean Court in August 1937. Making his League debut in the following month's 1-0 victory at home to Crystal Palace, he also appeared in Cherries' next two matches against Cardiff City and Walsall. Returning to Scotland with Cowdenbeath in October 1937, he helped win the Scottish League Second Division title in 1938-39 and had a loan spell with East Fife.

GRAHAM MITCHELL

Central defender Graham Mitchell briefly played for AFC Bournemouth during the 1993-94 season. He began with Huddersfield Town and was ever-present in 1990-91, then 'Player of the Year' in 1991-92. Loaned to Cherries in December 1993, he made four League appearances while at Dean Court. He played for Huddersfield in the 1994 Autoglass Trophy final, moving to Bradford City in exchange for Lee Sinnott in December 1994. Helping them win promotion in 1995-96, he later appeared for Raith Rovers, Cardiff City, Halifax Town, Bradford PA and Farsley Celtic before returning to Huddersfield as youth coach.

PAUL MITCHELL

Versatile England Youth right-back Paul Mitchell had two spells at AFC Bournemouth. Born locally, he signed professional at Dean Court in August 1989 and made his League debut in Cherries' 0-0 draw at Brentford a year later. Together with Keith Rowland, he reunited with Harry Redknapp at West Ham for £40,000 in August 1993 but had injury problems and returned to Cherries in March 1996. He made 16 League appearances overall before joining Torquay United in August 1996. Later playing for Barry Town, Llanelli, Salisbury and Wimborne Town, he has since been a Cherries match analyst for Opta Sports.

TOMMY MITCHINSON

Stylish midfielder Tommy Mitchinson featured in Cherries' 1971-72 promotion near-miss. Initially with Sunderland, he was a member of their 1963-64 promotion squad, appearing in the top-flight before joining Mansfield Town in January 1966. He was ever-present in 1966-67, then moved via Aston Villa to Torquay United in May 1969. Reunited with John Bond at Dean Court for £23,000 in December 1971, his solitary goal in 32 League games came in the 3-0 victory at home to Bradford City three months later. His career was ended by meningitis and he spent over 30 years as a self-employed milkman in his native Sunderland.

MARK MOLESLEY

Former England Semi-Pro midfielder Mark Molesley featured in AFC Bournemouth's 2009-10 promotion success before sidelined with a foot problem. Initially with Hayes, he captained Great Britain Colleges and joined Cambridge City in June 2005. He reunited with Terry Brown at Aldershot in May 2006 and starred in their 2006-07 FA Cup run. Moving to Stevenage in May 2007, he had a spell with Grays Athletic prior to joining Cherries in October 2008. He scored five goals in 52 League games and was loaned to Aldershot and Plymouth, moving to Exeter City in January 2013, then Aldershot again and Weymouth in July 2015.

PETER MONAGHAN

Scottish left-half Peter Monaghan was a young member of Charlie Bell's squad at Dean Court. Initially with St John's Boys Guild in his native Stevenston, he impressed with Ardeer Recreation before moving to Bournemouth in June 1937 and was given his League debut in the 1-1 draw at home to QPR three months later. His solitary goal in 63 Third Division (South) games came in Cherries' 5-2 win at home to Bristol Rovers in March 1939 and he featured in the 10-0 win over Northampton in September 1939, expunged from official records on the outbreak of war. He was killed in action in the Netherlands in January 1945.

DEAN MOONEY

Striker Dean Mooney was AFC Bournemouth's joint top scorer in 1980-81. Signing professional for Orient in July 1974, he had spells with SK Haugar, Dulwich Hamlet, Walthamstow Avenue, Oxford City and GAIS before moving to Dean Court for £15,000 in December 1980. He featured in Cherries' 1981-82 promotion campaign and netted ten goals in 27 League outings. Later playing for Vasalund, Trowbridge Town and RS Southampton, he briefly reunited with David Webb at Torquay United in August 1984. He gave Bournemouth Electric lengthy service in various capacities and has since been a local taxi driver.

JON MOORE

Former Welsh Youth left-back Jon Moore was a member of Alec Stock's squad at Dean Court. Initially with Bristol Rovers, he moved to Millwall for £20,000 in December 1974, featuring in their 1975-76 promotion success and 1977-78 FA Cup run. He joined AFC Bournemouth in May 1979 and scored twice in 36 League games before moving to Poole Town in March 1981. Joining Maidstone five months later, he starred in their 1983-84 Conference title triumph, then played for Gravesend & Northfleet and helped to win the Bob Lord Trophy in 1985. He became a foreign exchange broker for Tullett & Tokyo in the City.

TOMMY MOORE

Much-travelled inside-left Tommy Moore contested a first-team slot with Willie Chalmers while at Dean Court. A grandson of former Aston Villa star Ike Moore, the England Junior international impressed with Stourbridge before joining Aston Villa in February 1932. He scored on his First Division debut against Huddersfield Town three months later but never fully recovered from a broken leg and moved via another spell at Stourbridge to Bournemouth in July 1934. Scoring twice in six League games, he returned to Stourbridge, then played for Birmingham, Swansea, Stourbridge again, Dudley Town and Vono Sports.

BILL MORALEE

Long-serving left-half Bill Moralee was ever-present for Cherries in 1931-32. Initially an inside-forward with Crook Town, he joined Huddersfield Town in July 1927 but failed to secure a first-team slot and moved to Dean Court with Tommy Duff in June 1928. He starred as Bournemouth took West Ham to an FA Cup fifth round replay in 1928=29 and scored six goals in 189 Third Division (South) games before following Billy Birrell to QPR in June 1936. Featuring in their 1937-38 promotion challenge, he settled in Bournemouth after the war and worked as a bookmaker until suffering a fatal heart-attack in August 1967.

MATTHEW MORGAN

Scottish outside-right Matthew Morgan briefly appeared for Cherries at the start of the 1930-31 campaign. Initially with Renfrew Juniors, he joined St Mirren in July 1924 and played regularly in the Scottish First Division for six seasons. He was an early Billy Birrell signing for Bournemouth in July 1930, featuring in the first six Third Division (South) games of the season, before returning to the Scottish First Division with Ayr United in October 1930. Briefly with fellow strugglers Hibernian, he then played in Irish football for Glentoran, Linfield, Coleraine and Shelbourne. He later settled in Stockport and died in July 1985.

NICKY MORGAN

Striker Nicky Morgan had a loan spell at AFC Bournemouth during the 1992-93 season. Starting with West Ham, he featured in their 1980-81 Second Division title campaign and was loaned to Den Haag before joining Portsmouth in March 1983. He was leading marksman in 1985-86 and moved to Stoke City in November 1986. Joining Bristol City in March 1990, he helped clinch promotion and was top scorer in 1990-91. Loaned to Cherries in October 1992, his solitary goal in six League outings clinched that month's 1-0 victory at home to Stockport County. He later played for Exeter City, Dorchester Town and Salisbury.

RON MORGAN

Welsh inside-forward Ron Morgan understudied Willie Smith during the 1935-36 campaign. A former Wolves amateur, he moved to Dean Court in June 1935 and made his League debut in Cherries' 2-1 defeat at Northampton seven months later. He also appeared in that season's 1-1 draw at Clapton Orient, joining Northfleet United in June 1936. After helping Doncaster Rovers to finish Third Division (North) runners-up in two consecutive seasons, he joined Accrington Stanley in June 1939 and appeared for them either side of the war. Moving to Worcester City in January 1947, he died in Wolverhampton in May 1990.

STUART MORGAN

Central defender Stuart Morgan served AFC Bournemouth in several capacities. Initially with West Ham, he had spells with Torquay United and Reading before joining Colchester United in August 1972. He helped them win promotion in 1973-74 and moved to Dean Court in March 1975, netting five goals in 81 League outings for Cherries prior to joining Weymouth in June 1977. Later their manager, he rejoined Cherries as assistant-boss, then managed Torquay, Weymouth again and was Cherries' YDO. He managed Dorchester for six years before scouting for Harry Redknapp at West Ham, Portsmouth and Southampton.

TREVOR MORGAN

Much-travelled striker Trevor Morgan was twice AFC Bournemouth's top scorer. He played for Tonbridge, Dartford and Leytonstone/Ilford prior to joining Cherries in September 1980. Returning from a spell at Mansfield, he helped clinch promotion in 1981-82 and beat Manchester United in the 1983-84 FA Cup third round. He netted 46 goals in 141 League games overall, moving to Bristol City in March 1984, then Exeter City, Bristol Rovers, Bristol City again, Bolton, Colchester and South China, assisting Terry Cooper at Birmingham and Exeter. He has coached clubs in Australia and India, notably Sorrento and East Bengal.

PAUL MORRELL

Long-serving left-back Paul Morrell was a key figure in AFC Bournemouth's 1986-87 Third Division title triumph. Initially with Poole Town, he moved via Bath City to Weymouth in July 1981 and featured in their 1982-83 FA Cup run. He moved to Dean Court in June 1983 and scored in Cherries' 1984 Associate Members Cup final triumph, also helping take Manchester United to an FA Cup fifth round replay in 1988-89. Netting eight goals in 343 League games until released after his testimonial in May 1993, he helped Salisbury win promotion in 1994-95 and assisted various local clubs while working as a probation officer.

DAVID MORRIS

Young utility player David Morris briefly appeared for AFC Bournemouth during the 1990-91 campaign. A former trainee at Dean Court, he turned professional in July 1990 and made his only League appearance for Cherries as a substitute for Sean O'Driscoll during the 1-1 draw at Mansfield Town in March 1991. He played in the Football League again after moving to Hereford United in February 1993, then joined Yeovil Town in July 1994 and moved via Weymouth to Bashley in August 1995. Later with Lymington & New Milton, then Bashley again, he has since worked locally as manager of a water distribution company.

MARK MORRIS

Central defender Mark Morris was AFC Bournemouth's 'Player of the Season' in 1992-93. Signing professional for Wimbledon in September 1980, he featured in the Dons' meteoric rise and followed Dave Bassett to Watford in July 1987, then Sheffield United in July 1989. He starred in their 1989-90 promotion triumph and moved to Cherries for £95,000 in July 1991. Scoring eight goals in 194 League games, he reunited with Jimmy Case at Brighton in October 1996, then had a spell with Hastings Town. He was later Dorchester's manager, plotting their 2002 Southern League Cup final triumph, becoming a local publican.

BOB MORTIMER

Stocky, flame-haired forward Bob Mortimer played for Bournemouth during the 1934-35 campaign. He had spells with Connah's Quay & Shotton, Barrow, Bolton Wanderers, Northampton Town and Brentford before moving to Cherries in May 1934 and netted three goals in 18 League games. Joining Accrington Stanley in June 1935, he moved to top-flight Portsmouth with Billy Harker in February 1936 but rejoined Accrington and scored a club record 33 League goals in 1936-37. He moved to York City in June 1938 and was top scorer in 1938-39. Later with Horwich RMI, he became a grocer in Bolton and died in April 1965.

NEIL MOSS

Goalkeeper Neil Moss starred in AFC Bournemouth's 2002-03 Third Division play-off final triumph. Born locally, he was a trainee at Dean Court and turned professional in January 1993, making his League debut in Cherries' 2-1 defeat at Swansea three months later. He moved to Southampton for £250,000 in December 1995 and provided cover in the Premier League. Loaned to Gillingham, he rejoined Cherries in

September 2002 and made 115 consecutive League appearances until sidelined by a broken leg. He played 184 League games overall for Cherries before retiring in July 2008 and has since become the club's goalkeeping coach.

RYAN MOSS

Teenage striker Ryan Moss had the shortest League career of any AFC Bournemouth player. He was a trainee at Dean Court when given a surprise first-team call-up due to an injury crisis, making his only League appearance as a late substitute in Cherries' 1-0 defeat at Luton in August 2004. Never featuring in the first-team again, he moved to Dorchester Town in June 2005. He joined Bashley in July 2006 and starred in their 2006-07 Southern League South & West title triumph, since playing for Dorchester, Bashley, Dorchester for a third spell, AFC Totton, Havant & Waterlooville, Kingstonian and Margate.

PAUL MOULDEN

Ex-England Youth striker Paul Moulden partnered Luther Blissett in Cherries' attack. In the Guinness Book of Records for his goalscoring feats in junior football in 1981-82, he turned professional with Manchester City in September 1984 and was leading marksman in their 1988-89 promotion success. He joined Cherries as part of the Ian Bishop deal in July 1989 and netted 13 goals in 32 League games before being sold to Oldham Athletic for £225,000 in March 1990. Later playing for Birmingham City, Huddersfield Town, Rochdale, Accrington Stanley and Bacup Borough, he has since run a fish and chip shop in Bolton.

BRIAN MUNDEE

Versatile left-back Brian Mundee briefly appeared for AFC Bournemouth during the 1982-83 campaign. Previously with Hungerford Town, he moved to Dean Court in January 1982 and made his League debut in Cherries' 0-0 draw at home to Sheffield United eight months later. He played four League games before joining Northampton Town in October 1983. Moving to Cambridge United in March 1986, he had spells with Maidstone United, Weymouth, Salisbury, Basingstoke Town, Bashley, Salisbury again, Downton, Basingstoke again and was Poppies' player-boss. He became a wall-coating specialist for Mastex Coatings.

DENNY MUNDEE

Utility player Denny Mundee featured in AFC Bournemouth's 1991-92 FA Cup third round replay win at Newcastle United. A former QPR apprentice, he had a spell with Swindon Town and was Salisbury's top scorer in 1987-88. Harry Redknapp signed him in May 1988 and he netted six goals in 100 League games for Cherries before joining David Webb's Brentford in August 1993. He starred as they qualified for the play-offs in 1994-95, then played for Brighton, Dorchester, Salisbury and Bath City until a back injury. Settling locally, he became a wall-coating specialist for Mastex Coatings with his older brother Brian.

VINCE MURPHY

Irish winger Vince Murphy briefly played for Bournemouth at the start of the 1928-29 campaign. Initially with Jarrow, he moved via Grimsby Town to Cherries in July 1928 and made his League debut in the following month's 2-2 draw at home to Southend United. He appeared in the first six matches of the season before being displaced by Bob Bryce, moving to Walsall in December 1928. Later with Notts County, Wigan Athletic, Gateshead, Ayr United and Crook Town, he went into partnership with former Jarrow team-mate Alf Maitland in a Newcastle tailoring business. He died in Birkenhead in September 1972.

ROB MURRAY

Versatile central defender Rob Murray was an influential figure in AFC Bournemouth's 1994-95 relegation escape. A former trainee at Dean Court, he was given his League debut in Cherries' 2-0 defeat at Blackpool four months before turning professional in January 1993. The Scotland U-21 international secured a regular first-team slot midway through the 1994-95 campaign and partnered Mark Morris in the heart of defence, scoring 12 goals in 147 Second Division games until released in May 1998. He had a spell in the United States with Colin Clarke's Richmond Kickers, then played for Dorchester Town and Bournemouth Poppies.

TERRY MURRAY

Former Republic of Ireland international inside-left Terry Murray was a Jack Bruton signing for Cherries. Initially with Dundalk, he represented the League of Ireland and made his only international appearance in the 5-1 defeat by Belgium in May 1950. He joined Hull City in September 1951, moving to Bournemouth in March 1954. His solitary goal in 13 Third Division (South) games clinched the following month's 1-1 draw at Shrewsbury Town and he moved to King's Lynn in July 1955. Later playing for Bedford Town, Hastings United and Rushden Town, he spent 35 years with Britannic Assurance, settling in Bedford.

TOMMY NAYLOR

Versatile defender Tommy Naylor helped Cherries take Liverpool to an FA Cup third round replay in 1967-68. Signing professional at Dean Court in October 1963, he made his League debut in Bournemouth's 4-3 defeat at Colchester United in October 1964. He was a member of the 1970-71 promotion squad and scored three times in 142 League games before joining Football League new-boys Hereford United in August 1972. Helping win promotion in 1972-73, he later played for Dorchester and Ringwood. He was a taxi driver, then a night support worker for the Hesley Group and died in Bournemouth in May 2010.

GEORGE NDAH

Former England Youth striker George Ndah had a loan spell at AFC Bournemouth during the 1995-96 campaign. He turned professional with Crystal Palace in August 1992 and was loaned to Cherries in October 1995, scoring twice in 12 League outings while at Dean Court. Helping Palace regain top-flight status in 1996-97, he was sold to Swindon Town for £500,000 in November 1997. He joined Wolves for £1,000,000 in October 1999 and was a promotion winner again in 2002-03 but successive injury problems curtailed his career in April 2006. His older brother Jamie played for Torquay United and Barnet.

GORDON NEAVE

Scottish left-half Gordon Neave was ever-present for Cherries in 1952-53. The son of former Kilmarnock star Bobby Neave, he impressed with Pollok Juniors prior to joining Portsmouth in March 1947. He failed to secure a first-team slot and moved to Dean Court with Ian Drummond in June 1949. Making 85 League appearances for Bournemouth, he joined Aldershot in July 1955 and returned to Pompey as youth team coach in September 1958. He was later trainer, physio and kit man with two testimonial matches during a 41 year period at Fratton Park before retiring in May 1999. Settling in Copnor, he died in August 2003.

JIMMY NEIGHBOUR

Experienced winger Jimmy Neighbour had a loan spell at AFC Bournemouth during the 1982-83 season. He turned professional with Tottenham Hotspur in November 1968 and featured in their 1971 League Cup final triumph. Moving to Norwich City in September 1976, then West Ham in September 1979, he helped reach the FA Cup final in 1980 and played in the 1981 League Cup final. Loaned to Cherries in January 1983, he made six League appearances while at Dean Court. He later held coaching posts at Enfield, West Ham, Doncaster Rovers, St Albans City and Spurs. Settling in Woodford Green, he died in April 2009.

TONY NELSON

Central defender Tony Nelson gave Cherries lengthy service in various capacities. The son of former Scotland international Jimmy Nelson, he had spells as a centre-forward with Newport County and Bristol City before moving to Dean Court in June 1956. He was switched to a defensive role and starred in Bournemouth's 1961-62 promotion near-miss. Scoring once in 195 League games prior to assisting Freddie Cox, he then was Cherries' chief scout until January 1975. Later manager of Poole Town and Poppies, he became Winton branch manager of Morris Dibben estate agents and still lives locally in retirement.

STAN NEWSHAM

Fast inside-forward Stan Newsham was Cherries' leading marksman in three successive seasons. A former Bolton Wanderers amateur, he moved to Dean Court in June 1952 and starred in Bournemouth's 1956-57 FA Cup run, netting 74 goals in 142 Third Division (South) games prior to joining Notts County for £10,000 in August 1957. He was top scorer in their 1959-60 promotion success, then played for Wellington Town and Burton Albion. After being a fruiterer in Pokesdown, he was licensee of the 'Good Companion' pub in Portsmouth, then the 'Fisherman's Rest' in Titchfield and died in Portsmouth in May 2001.

MARK NEWSON

Ex-England Semi-Pro right-back Mark Newson skippered AFC Bournemouth's 1986-87 Third Division title triumph. Initially with Charlton Athletic, he moved to Maidstone United in February 1980 and joined Cherries in May 1985. He was twice ever-present, helping take Manchester United to an FA Cup fifth round replay in 1988-89. Scoring 23 goals in 177 League games, he was sold to Fulham for £125,000 in February 1990, then Barnet, Aylesbury United, Gravesend & Northfleet, Fisher and Romford. He has since coached at West Ham, VCD Athletic, Chatham, Stevenage, Dover Athletic and Crystal Palace's Academy.

GRAHAM NEWTON

Popular wing-half Graham Newton helped Cherries take Burnley to an FA Cup third round replay in 1965-66. A former Wolves amateur, he played for Blackpool and Walsall before joining Coventry City in January 1964, helping to clinch the Third Division title. Moving to Dean Court in December 1964, he netted three goals in 28 League games for Bournemouth prior to joining Atlanta Chiefs in April 1967, starring in their 1968 NASL Soccer Bowl triumph. Later with Port Vale, Reading, Hednesford, Worcester and Stourbridge, he managed Willenhall and Stourbridge, since running International Soccer Camps UK.

BILLY NICHOL

Scottish inside-left Billy Nichol played for Cherries in the opening two games of the 1928-29 campaign. Previously with hometown Lochgelly Celtic, he moved to Bournemouth in August 1928 and made his League debut in that month's 2-2 draw at home to Southend United. He also featured in the 5-1 defeat at

Norwich City two days later before losing his place. One of five different players who appeared in the inside-left position that season, he failed to make any further first-team appearances prior to joining Gillingham in July 1929. Later with Scottish Second Division side St Bernard's, he settled in Scotland.

SID NICHOLSON

Young centre-half Sid Nicholson understudied Jack Coxford while at Dean Court. Previously with Cardiff City and Merthyr Town, he joined Bournemouth in July 1931 and made his League debut in the 1-1 draw at Crystal Palace six months later. He played eight Third Division (South) games for Cherries, including the 6-1 victory at home to Bristol City in January 1933, before moving to Midland League side Scunthorpe United in July 1933. Returning to the Football League with Barnsley in July 1935, he later played for Aberdeen until the Second World War. He settled back in his native Shildon and died in May 1959.

MARK NIGHTINGALE

Ex-England Youth defender Mark Nightingale featured in Cherries' 1984 Associate Members Cup final triumph. Signing professional at Dean Court in July 1974, he was swapped for Crystal Palace's Peter Johnson in July 1976, then moved via Norwich City and Bulova back to Cherries in August 1982. Twice ever-present, he featured in the 1983-84 FA Cup third round win over holders Manchester United and scored eight times in 199 League games overall, moving to Peterborough United in July 1986. He played for Kettering Town, King's Lynn, Wisbech and Warboys, since working for Hotpoint in Peterborough.

OLLIE NORRIS

Colourful Irish inside-forward Ollie Norris starred as Cherries reached the FA Cup sixth round in 1956-57. Initially with Middlesbrough, he had a spell with Worcester City, moving to Dean Court in July 1955. He scored 34 goals in 96 League games for Bournemouth prior to joining Northampton Town in September 1958, then played for Gloucester City, Ashford Town, Rochdale and Sligo Rovers. Emigrating to Australia in January 1962, he assisted several sides in Melbourne and was a PE teacher at various colleges until December 1983. He then ran his own party fun bags business and died in Melbourne in June 2011.

PETER NORTON

Right-back Peter Norton was a young member of Freddie Cox's squad at Dean Court. The son-in-law of former Cherries favourite Laurie Cunningham, he turned professional with Bournemouth in November 1966 and made his League debut in the 3-1 defeat at Middlesbrough four months later. He contested a first-team slot with Terry Gulliver and his only goal in 19 Third Division games came in the 2-2 draw at home to Reading in April 1967. Moving to Crewe Alexandra in July 1968, he then gave Parley Sports lengthy service. Settling in Creekmoor, he became a sergeant during 30 years with Dorset Police until June 1999.

RALPH NORTON

Versatile forward Ralph Norton played alongside the likes of John Hold and Chris Weller while at Dean Court. Signing professional for Reading in October 1959, he helped them take top-flight Burnley to an FA Cup fourth round replay in 1964-65. He joined Cherries in July 1966 and made a significant contribution in the 1966-67 relegation battle, scoring four goals in 48 League games before joining Poole Town in July 1968. Later playing for Cheltenham Town, Salisbury, Cheltenham again and Welton Rovers, he settled in Keynsham and became a senior buyer for engine components over 30 years with Rolls Royce in Filton.

ROY O'BRIEN

Republic of Ireland Youth central defender Roy O'Brien made his only League appearance for Cherries in the 1-1 draw at Gillingham in October 1996. A former Arsenal trainee, he captained their youth team and moved to AFC Bournemouth in August 1996. He was sidelined by a knee injury while at Dean Court and joined Dorchester Town in July 1997. Joining Yeovil Town in August 2000, he helped win the Conference title in 2002-03, then appeared for Weymouth and Dorchester again, succeeding Shaun Brooks as player-boss in March 2009. He then managed Yeovil Ladies team and worked in their community scheme.

WILLIE O'BRIEN

Scottish inside-left Willie O'Brien secured a regular first-team slot during the closing weeks of the 1937-38 campaign. Previously with Celtic's nursery club St Anthony's in his native Glasgow, he moved to Dean Court in June 1936 and made his League debut in central defence in Cherries' 2-1 win at home to Reading ten months later. He scored three goals in his first two matches after switched to the attack in February 1938, netting five times in 16 Third Division (South) games. Moving to Port Vale in May 1938, he failed to hold a regular first-team slot and joined Watford in May 1939 but the Second World War ended his career.

GARRETH O'CONNOR

Irish midfielder Garreth O'Connor scored in AFC Bournemouth's 2002-03 Third Division play-off final triumph. He impressed with Bohemians prior to joining Cherries in June 2000 and was given his League debut in the 3-1 defeat at Colchester three months later. Moving to Steve Cotterill's Burnley with Wade Elliott in July 2005, he rejoined Cherries on loan in August 2007 and netted 24 goals in 174 League games overall. He joined Luton in October 2008, helping win the Johnstone's Paint Trophy in 2009, then played for St Patrick's Athletic, Drogheda, St Patrick's again, Stirling Lions, Monaghan United and Shelbourne.

JAMES O'CONNOR

Versatile full-back James O'Connor was an influential figure for AFC Bournemouth during the 2005-06 campaign. A former Aston Villa trainee, he helped win the FA Youth Cup in 2002 and turned professional in April 2004. He was loaned to Port Vale before joining Cherries in February 2005. Scoring once in 45 League games while at Dean Court, he moved to Doncaster Rovers for £130,000 in May 2006. He helped them win the Johnstone's Paint Trophy in 2007 and promotion in 2007-08. Moving to Derby County in July 2012, he briefly reunited with Sean O'Driscoll on loan at Bristol City and joined Walsall in June 2014.

MARK O'CONNOR

Republic of Ireland U-21 midfielder Mark O'Connor featured in AFC Bournemouth's 1986-87 Third Division title triumph. Initially with QPR, he played for Exeter City on loan and Bristol Rovers before moving to Cherries in March 1986. He helped take Manchester United to an FA Cup fifth round replay in 1988-89 and followed Tony Pulis to Gillingham in December 1989. Reuniting with him at Cherries in July 1993, he scored 15 goals in 186 League games overall before following Pulis back to Gillingham in August 1995. He has since assisted him at Gillingham, Portsmouth, Plymouth Argyle, Stoke City and West Brom.

BRIAN O'DONNELL

Midfielder Brian O'Donnell helped AFC Bournemouth clinch promotion in 1981-82. A former Cherries apprentice, he joined Bristol Rovers in May 1976 and played for Australian side Blacktown City before returning to Dean Court in January 1982. He made 14 League appearances for Cherries prior to joining Torquay United in October 1982. Later with Yeovil Town, Blacktown again, Poole Town, Bath City, Weymouth, Yeovil again, Farnborough, Basingstoke, Bashley and Salisbury, he managed Bournemouth Sports, Poppies, Poole and was Cherries' youth coach. He has scouted for West Brom and Middlesbrough.

SEAN O'DRISCOLL

Ex-Republic of Ireland international midfielder Sean O'Driscoll was ever-present in AFC Bournemouth's 1986-87 Third Division title triumph. Moving from Alvechurch to Fulham in November 1979, he helped win promotion in 1981-82, joining Cherries in February 1984. He starred in the 1984 Associate Members Cup final success, scoring 19 goals in a then club record 423 League games. Appointed manager in August 2000, he guided Cherries to promotion in 2002-03 and became Doncaster Rovers' boss in September 2006. He has since managed Crawley, Forest, Bristol City, England U-19s and is now Liverpool's assistant-boss.

EUNAN O'KANE

Republic of Ireland U-21 midfielder Eunan O'Kane starred in AFC Bournemouth's 2012-13 promotion success. Starting with Maiden City Soccer Academy, he joined Everton in August 2007 and moved to Coleraine in July 2009. He joined Torquay United in January 2010 and helped twice qualify for the League Two play-offs. Having represented Northern Ireland at underage levels, he switched allegiance to Eire in October 2011. He moved to Cherries in July 2012 and scored as they took eventual winners Wigan Athletic to an FA Cup third round replay in 2012-13, also featuring in the 2014-15 Championship title campaign.

MARCUS OLDBURY

Young midfielder Marcus Oldbury played for AFC Bournemouth during the 1995-96 season. A former Norwich City trainee, he turned professional in July 1994 but failed to make an impact with the Canaries and moved to Dean Court in July 1995. He was given his League debut in Cherries' 3-1 defeat at Stockport County two months later and often featured as a substitute, making 13 Second Division appearances prior to joining Bashley in September 1996. Moving to Lymington & New Milton in November 1998, he then played for Dorchester Town, Wimborne Town and Hamworthy United, settling in Bournemouth.

KEN OLIVER

Centre-forward Ken Oliver was an experienced member of Freddie Cox's squad at Dean Court. After spells with Sunderland and South Shields, he joined Barnsley in February 1960 and starred in their 1960-61 FA Cup run. He played for Watford and Workington before moving to Bournemouth in January 1967. Scoring four goals in 14 League games for

Cherries until a knee injury ended his career in January 1968, he later coached at Bradford City, Newcastle United, Birmingham City, Walsall, Spurs and in the Middle East. He became a consultant for KAM Sports International and a self-employed taxi driver based in Tamworth.

MANNY OMOYINMI

Ex-England Schoolboy winger Manny Omoyinmi had a loan spell at AFC Bournemouth during the 1996-97 campaign. Born in Lagos, Nigeria, he turned professional with West Ham in May 1995 and was loaned to Cherries in September 1996, making seven League appearances while at Dean Court. Inexplicably featuring in West Ham's 1999-2000 League Cup quarter-final victory when Cup-tied, leading to a replay defeat, he was also loaned to Leyton Orient, Gillingham Scunthorpe United and Barnet before joining Oxford United in July 2000. He had spells playing for Gravesend & Northfleet, Lewes and Worthing.

ALAN O'NEILL

Inside-forward Alan O'Neill played alongside Denis Coughlin and Ken Hodgson in Cherries' attack. Initially with Sunderland, he was top scorer in 1957-58 and joined Aston Villa in October 1960. He scored in their 1961 League Cup final triumph and moved via Plymouth Argyle to Cherries in February 1964. Scoring eight goals in 37 League outings, he joined Cambridge United in June 1966, then had spells with Southern Suburbs, Chelmsford City, Drumcondra, Toronto Hellas, New York Cosmos and Vancouver Whitecaps, managing South Shields and Blyth Spartans. He ran a hotel, then a rest home in Bournemouth.

JOHN O'NEILL

Utility player John O'Neill appeared for AFC Bournemouth in the 1998 Auto Windscreens Shield final. Starting with Queen's Park, he was leading marksman in 1993-94 and moved to Celtic in May 1994. He joined Cherries initially on loan in March 1996 and netted ten goals in 124 League games prior to joining Ross County in October 2000. Moving to Queen of the South in January 2001, he starred in their 2001-02 Scottish League Second Division title triumph, then played for St Mirren and Queen of the South again, appearing in the 2008 Scottish Cup final. He has since been with Stirling Albion and Auchinleck Talbot.

JOHN O'ROURKE

Former England U-23 striker John O'Rourke was a Trevor Hartley signing for AFC Bournemouth. Initially with Arsenal, he moved via Chelsea to Luton Town in December 1963 and was top scorer three times. He joined Middlesbrough in July 1966 and starred in their 1966-67 promotion success, then had spells with Ipswich Town, Coventry City and QPR prior to joining Cherries for £35,000 in January 1974. Scoring four times in 22 League outings, he later played for Poole Town, Johannesburg Rangers, Weymouth, Dorchester and Poole again before running Lakewood News in Highcliffe. He then worked at Bournemouth Airport.

JOHN O'SHEA

Republic of Ireland international defender John O'Shea had a loan spell at AFC Bournemouth during the 1999-2000 campaign. Initially with hometown Waterford, he joined Manchester United in September 1998 and was loaned to Cherries in January 2000. He made his League debut in that month's 2-1 defeat at Colchester and scored once in ten Second Division games while at Dean Court. Helping United win the FA Cup in 2004, League Cup twice and Premier League title on five occasions, he moved to Sunderland in July 2011 and was a League Cup finalist in 2014. He has now gained over 100 caps for his country.

MARK OVENDALE

Goalkeeper Mark Ovendale was ever-present for AFC Bournemouth in 1998-99. He played for Wisbech Town, then had a season with Northampton Town before moving to Barry Town in July 1995. Starring as they won the League of Wales title in three successive seasons and Welsh Cup in 1997, he moved to Dean Court for £30,000 in May 1998. He made 89 League appearances for Cherries before sold to Luton Town for £425,000 in August 2000. Helping win promotion in 2001-02, he then played for Barry, York City, Tiverton, Carmarthen, Newport County and Wimborne. He tragically died from cancer in August 2011.

MARCOS PAINTER

Republic of Ireland U-21 defender Marcos Painter briefly featured in AFC Bournemouth's 2012-13 promotion campaign. He turned professional with Birmingham City in July 2005 and made his Premier League debut in their 1-0 win at home to Fulham five months later. Sold to Swansea City for £50,000 in November 2006, he helped win the League One title in 2007-08 but lost his place after a knee injury and joined Brighton in January 2010. He was ever-present in their 2010-11 League One title triumph. Loaned to Cherries in February 2013, he made two League appearances. He moved to Portsmouth in August 2013.

EDDIE PARKER

Outside-left Eddie Parker contested a first-team slot with Eddie Parris as Cherries finished sixth in the Third Division (South) in 1936-37. Initially with Croydon-based Anerley Argyle, he moved to Crystal Palace in November 1932 and made his League debut in their 1-0 win at Bristol Rovers nine months later. He joined Mansfield Town in June 1934, scoring twice in their 8-2 win over Rotherham three months before joining Bournemouth in August 1936. Making 12 Third Division (South) appearances while at Dean Court, he moved to Bristol Rovers in July 1937, then Dartford. He died in Brighton in February 1983.

REG PARKER

Tall left-back Reg Parker helped Bournemouth to beat Bristol City 6-1 in January 1933. Born in Reading, he impressed with Tilehurst before moving to Dean Court in October 1931. He was given his League debut in Cherries' 0-0 draw at Cardiff City five months later and secured a regular first-team slot midway through the 1932-33 season after Jack Whitehouse switched to the inside-left position. Making 49 Third Division (South) appearances for Cherries before moving to West Ham in March 1935, he failed to secure a regular first-team slot at Upton Park, joining Torquay United in 1936. He died in Bury St Edmunds in April 1979.

JOE PARKINSON

Versatile midfielder Joe Parkinson was an influential member of Tony Pulis' squad at Dean Court. Signing professional for Wigan Athletic in March 1989, he helped them take top-flight Coventry to an FA Cup third round replay in 1990-91 and moved to Dean Court for £35,000 in July 1993. He scored once in 30 League games for Cherries before following David Williams to Everton for £800,000 in March 1994. Starring in their 1995 FA Cup final triumph, his career was ended by a knee injury in November 1999 and he became Everton's fans liaison officer. He has since been a forklift driver for Smith Bateson and coached at Wigan.

LES PARODI

Young left-back Les Parodi helped AFC Bournemouth win the Football Combination title in 1973-74. A former Charlton Athletic junior, he moved via Staines Town to Dean Court in September 1972 and made his League debut in Cherries' 1-1 draw at Tranmere Rovers in February 1974. He scored twice in 49 Third Division games until a pelvic injury curtailed his League career in April 1975, then had spells playing for Christchurch, AP Leamington, Salisbury, Poole Town, Dorchester Town, Oxford City, Dagenham and Seattle Sounders and Columbus Magic in the United States. He has local business and property interests.

EDDIE PARRIS

Ex-Welsh international winger Eddie Parris featured in Bournemouth's 8-1 FA Cup first round replay win over Walthamstow in 1935-36. Born in Pwllmeyric of West Indian parents, he impressed with Chepstow Town prior to joining Bradford PA in August 1928. He was leading marksman as they reached the FA Cup fifth round in 1931-32. Billy Birrell signed him in June 1934 and he netted 23 goals in 104 League games for Cherries before moving to Luton Town in February 1937, helping to clinch the Third Division (South) title. Later with Northampton Town and Cheltenham Town, he died in Gloucester in February 1971.

ALEX PARSONS

Teenage striker Alex Parsons briefly played for AFC Bournemouth during the 2011-12 season. A former trainee, he turned professional at Dean Court in July 2011 and had a loan spell at Wimborne Town with Dan Strugnell before making his solitary League appearance as a substitute in Cherries' 2-0 victory at home to Wycombe Wanderers in January 2012. He was then loaned to Bashley before being released by new AFC Bournemouth manager Paul Groves in May 2012. Following an unsuccessful trial with Brighton, he trained with the Nike Football Academy and has since appeared for Whitehawk and Bognor Regis.

JOHN PARSONS

Former Welsh Schoolboy striker John Parsons helped AFC Bournemouth win the Football Combination title in 1973-74. Signing professional for Cardiff City in December 1968, he netted the winner on his League debut at home to Oxford United in February 1971 and was a prolific goalscorer in their reserves. He moved to Dean Court in February 1973 and his only goal in seven League games came on his debut in Cherries' 1-1 draw at home to Grimsby two months later. Moving to Newport County in March 1975, he later played for Bridgend, Barry Town, Sully, Maesteg and Lydney, working for Cardiff City Council.

JOE PARTINGTON

Welsh U-21 striker Joe Partington featured in AFC Bournemouth's 2009-10 and 2012-13 promotion campaigns. A former youth player with hometown Portsmouth, he joined Cherries as a trainee and made his League debut in the 4-1 victory at Luton Town four months before turning professional in August 2008. He captained the reserves on a number of occasions and scored twice in 52 League outings for Cherries. Following loan spells at Eastbourne Borough and Aldershot, where sidelined by a serious knee injury, he joined Eastleigh initially on loan in January 2015 and helped them to qualify for the Conference play-offs.

TOMMY PATERSON

Striker Tommy Paterson was a popular member of John Benson's squad at Dean Court. Initially with Leicester City, he joined Middlesbrough in September 1974 and made his First Division debut three months later. He moved to AFC Bournemouth in April 1976, scoring ten goals in 57 League outings before joining Darlington in June 1978. Reuniting with Stuart Morgan at Weymouth in June 1979, he later played for Poole, Dorchester and Salisbury, then coached Wimborne. He settled locally, with his own industrial cleaning business. His father-in-law Ken 'Nimbus' Sullivan gave Cherries lengthy back-room service.

TOMMY PATON

Scottish inside-forward Tommy Paton played for Cherries either side of the Second World War. He had spells with Ardeer Recreation, Wolves and Swansea before moving to Dean Court in February 1939. Scoring in Bournemouth's 10-0 win at home to Northampton seven months later, he was a wartime guest for several clubs and featured in Cherries' 1946 Third Division (South) Cup final triumph, netting eight times in 46 League games prior to joining Watford in January 1948. He later played for Folkestone and became a clerk with HM Customs & Excise, residing in Folkestone until his death in December 1991.

CLIVE PAYNE

Influential right-back Clive Payne featured in AFC Bournemouth's 1975-76 promotion challenge. Signing professional for Norwich City in March 1968, he was ever-present in their 1971-72 Second Division title triumph and played alongside Geoff Butler in the 1973 League Cup final. He moved to Dean Court in a multi-player exchange deal involving Mel Machin, John Benson and Fred Davies in December 1973 and scored three times in 101 League games for Cherries until a recurring ankle injury ended his career in April 1976. Settling back in his native Aylsham, he ran a sports shop for five years, then Aylsham Windows.

GAVIN PEACOCK

Former England Youth midfielder Gavin Peacock was once AFC Bournemouth's most expensive signing. Initially with QPR, his father Keith signed him for Gillingham in October 1987 and he moved to Cherries for £250,000 in August 1989. He netted eight goals in 56 League games, joining Newcastle United in exchange for Wayne Fereday plus £150,000 in November 1990. Starring in their 1992-93 First Division title triumph, he joined Chelsea for £1,250,000 in August 1993 and played in the 1994 FA Cup final. Later rejoining QPR, he worked in the media and is now a Christian minister in the Rocky Mountains, Canada.

ALEX PEARCE

Scotland U-21 central defender Alex Pearce had a loan spell at AFC Bournemouth in 2007-08. A former Reading trainee, he turned professional in October 2006 and was loaned to Northampton before joining Cherries on loan in November 2007. He made 11 League appearances while at Dean Court. Also loaned to Norwich and Southampton, he was captain and 'Player of the Year' in Reading's 2011-12 Championship title triumph. He represented Scotland at underage levels before switching allegiance to Republic of Ireland and scored on his international debut against Oman in September 2012. He joined Derby in June 2015.

JASON PEARCE

Commanding central defender Jason Pearce captained AFC Bournemouth to promotion in 2009-10. He turned professional with Portsmouth in July 2006 and was loaned to Bognor Regis and Woking before joining Cherries in August 2007. Given his League debut in that month's 0-0 draw at Nottingham Forest, he was ever-present 'Player of the Year' as Cherries qualified for the League One play-offs in 2010-11, netting seven goals in 162 League games prior to rejoining Portsmouth in July 2011. He was their 'Player of the Year' in 2011-12 and moved to Leeds United in May 2012, then Wigan Athletic in January 2015.

FRANK PEED

Centre-forward Frank Peed understudied Ron Eyre during the 1930-31 campaign. Born in Argentina of a Wolverhampton mother, he played for Brereton Social before joining Aston Villa in October 1928 but failed to make an impact and moved to Dean Court in June 1930. He made his League debut in Cherries' 2-0 defeat at home to Walsall three months later and also appeared in the next match, lost 2-0 at Notts County. Moving to Norwich City in October 1930, he then had spells playing for Newport County, Barrow and Bath City. He later worked as a checker at Swansea docks and died in Birmingham in May 1969.

ADRIAN PENNOCK

Versatile defender Adrian Pennock was an early Tony Pulis signing for AFC Bournemouth. He turned professional with Norwich City in July 1989 and moved to Cherries for £30,000 in August 1992. Starring in the 1994-95 relegation escape, he scored nine goals in 131 League games and overcame a knee injury, reuniting with Pulis at Gillingham for £30,000 in October 1996. He helped win promotion in 1999-2000, then was Gravesend & Northfleet's player-coach before managing Welling United. Later reunited with Pulis as Stoke City's youth team boss, he became Forest Green Rovers' manager in November 2013.

JACK PERCIVAL

Left-half Jack Percival was an experienced figure as Cherries were Third Division (South) runners-up in 1947-48. Initially with Low Pittington, he moved from Durham City to Manchester City in October 1932, skippering their 1936-37 League Championship success and helping win the Second Division title in 1946-47. He joined Bournemouth in May 1947 and his solitary goal in 52 League outings clinched the 2-1 win at Newport County in August 1948. Appointed Murton's player-boss in June 1949, he rejoined Durham as manager, then worked at Lambton Colliery and was an HGV driver until a fatal accident in January 1976.

RUSS PERRETT

Experienced central defender Russ Perrett played for AFC Bournemouth in 2007-08. A former Portsmouth youth player with Darren Anderton, Andy Awford and Kit Symons, he had a spell with Lymington before rejoining

Pompey in September 1995. He appeared in their 1996-97 FA Cup run and moved to Cardiff City for £10,000 in July 1999, helping them win promotion in 2000-01. Moving to Luton Town in August 2001, he featured in their 2001-02 and 2004-05 promotion triumphs. He joined Cherries in July 2007 and made ten League One appearances before hanging up his boots in May 2008 after suffering a bout of pleurisy.

JAIME PETERS

Canadian international midfielder Jaime Peters had a loan spell at AFC Bournemouth during the 2011-12 season. Initially with Kaiserslautern, he joined Ipswich Town in August 2005 on the recommendation of Frank Yallop. He had loan spells at Yeovil Town and Gillingham before helping Ipswich to reach the League Cup semi-finals in 2010-11. Capped 26 times by Canada, he was loaned to Cherries in September 2011 and made eight League appearances while at Dean Court. He was released by Ipswich in August 2012 and had an extended trial back at Yeovil prior to joining Vancouver Whitecaps in his native country.

LOU PETERS

Ex-England Youth winger Lou Peters helped Cherries to finish fourth in the Third Division in 1968-69. Christened Roger, he turned professional with Bristol City in March 1961 and featured alongside John Atyeo in their 1964-65 promotion success. He was top scorer in 1966-67 and moved to Dean Court for £5,000 in June 1968, netting three goals in 37 League games for Bournemouth before following Tommy Taylor to Bath City in January 1970 after displaced by John Meredith. Later a senior consultant during 30 years with Sun Life of Canada, he became an independent financial adviser in Weston-in-Gordano.

CARL PETTEFER

Midfielder Carl Pettefer briefly played for AFC Bournemouth at the start of the 2008-09 campaign. He turned professional with Portsmouth in November 1998 and was loaned to Exeter City before joining Southend United in February 2004. Featuring in two consecutive LDV Vans Trophy finals, he was ever-present as they won promotion in 2004-05. He helped win the League One title in 2005-06, then spent two seasons with Oxford United. Moving to Cherries on trial in August 2008, he appeared as a substitute in the 1-1 draw at Aldershot. He joined Bognor Regis in September 2008, then AFC Totton and Poole Town.

GERRY PEYTON

Republic of Ireland international goalkeeper Gerry Peyton was ever-present 'Player of the Year' in AFC Bournemouth's 1986-87 Third Division title triumph. Initially with Atherstone, he moved via Burnley to Fulham in December 1976 and was a key figure in their 1981-82 promotion success. He moved to Dean Court in July 1986 and starred as Cherries took Manchester United to an FA Cup fifth round replay in 1988-89. Gaining a club record seven caps, he made 202 League appearances before following Jimmy Gabriel to Everton in July 1991. Later with Brentford, he became Arsenal's goalkeeping coach.

FORBES PHILLIPSON-MASTERS

Central defender Forbes Phillipson-Masters had a loan spell at AFC Bournemouth during the 1977-78 campaign. Signing professional for Southampton in June 1974, he was loaned to Cherries in September 1977 and scored twice in seven League games for his hometown club. He helped Saints win promotion to the top-flight that season and joined Plymouth Argyle in August 1979. Moving to Bristol City in November 1982, he helped them win promotion in 1983-84, then played for Yeovil Town. He became a painter and decorator and has a building business in Verwood, also coaching the Dorset County representative side.

HENRY PICTON

Welsh left-half Henry Picton understudied Eddie Lawrence as Cherries finished sixth in the Third Division (South) in 1936-37. Moving to Bournemouth in December 1936, 'Taffy' was given his League debut in the 3-2 victory at home to Northampton Town four months later and made seven Third Division (South) appearances before moving to Crewe Alexandra in August 1938, helping win the Cheshire Bowl in 1941. He featured as Troedyrhiw won the South Wales & Monmouthshire Senior Cup in 1947, then played for Ton Pentre and Ton Corinthians and was a miner at Tymawr Colliery until his death aged 59 in July 1974.

TOT PIKE

Outside-left Tot Pike appeared for Bournemouth during the 1927-28 season. Real name Theo, he began with Sunderland Co-op and had a spell with Southend United before turning professional with Fulham in July 1925. He joined Cherries in June 1927 and netted three goals in 16 Third Division (South) games. Moving to Birmingham in February 1928, he then played for Southend again, helping to finish third in the Third Division (South) in 1931-32 and reach the FA Cup fourth round in 1932-33. Later with Norwich City, he was Bury Town's player-coach, then a publican in Bury St Edmunds. He died in October 1967.

FRED PINCOTT

Big centre-half Fred Pincott was ever-present for Cherries in 1937-38. Starting with Bristol Royal Victoria, he joined Wolves in November 1931 and gained top-flight experience before moving to Bournemouth in May 1934. He made 196 Third Division (South) appearances prior to joining Dartford in June 1939. A wartime guest for Bournemouth, Bristol City and Chester, he joined Gravesend & Northfleet in June 1946, then Newport County and became Bideford's player-coach. Later settling near his eldest daughter in Eastleigh, he was a labourer for Pirelli group and the local council. He died in Eastleigh in February 2000.

BRETT PITMAN

Striker Brett Pitman had two spells at AFC Bournemouth. Born in Jersey, he played for St Paul's before turning professional at Dean Court in July 2005. He made his League debut in the following month's 2-1 defeat at Bradford City and was top scorer in Cherries' 2008-09 'Greatest Escape' and 2009-10 promotion success. Sold to Bristol City for £800,000 in August 2010, he returned initially on loan in November 2012. He was leading marksman in Cherries' 2012-13 promotion success and helped to win the Championship title in 2014-15, netting 96 goals in 268 League games overall before joining Ipswich Town in June 2015.

KEN POUND

Winger Ken Pound starred as Cherries took Liverpool to an FA Cup third round replay in 1967-68. A former Portsmouth amateur, he joined Yeovil in July 1963 and featured in their 1963-64 Southern League title triumph before moving to Swansea in July 1964. He joined Bournemouth in exchange for Denis Coughlin in August 1966, scoring 24 goals in 102 League outings prior to being swapped for Gillingham's John Meredith in July 1969. Later with Weymouth, he worked in the commercial departments of several clubs including Cherries, then became a financial adviser for Britannic Assurance in Southampton.

TONY POWELL

Hard-tackling central defender Tony Powell starred in Cherries' 1970-71 promotion success. Previously with Bath City, he moved to Dean Court in April 1968 and was ever-present for AFC Bournemouth in 1973-74. He scored ten goals in 219 League games before following John Bond to Norwich City in exchange for Trevor Howard in August 1974. Helping them win promotion and reach the League Cup final in 1974-75, he was ever-present in three consecutive seasons prior to reuniting with Jimmy Gabriel at San Jose Earthquakes in March 1981. Later at Seattle Sounders, he became a hotel receptionist in Hollywood.

CARL PRESTON

Teenage midfielder Carl Preston briefly appeared for AFC Bournemouth in 2008-09. He was a trainee at Dean Court and had not been involved with the first-team before making his League debut in Cherries' 2-0 win at home to Bury in December 2008. Also playing in the 2-0 defeat at Brentford six days later, he was loaned to Poole Town during the second half of that season. He was released by Eddie Howe that summer and briefly joined Weymouth. Rejoining hometown Poole in August 2009, he has since featured in their rise under Tommy Killick, including the Southern League First Division South & West title in 2012-13.

TONY PRISCOTT

Winger Tony Priscott was Cherries' joint top scorer in 1966-67. Signing professional for Portsmouth in July 1959, he featured in their 1961-62 Third Division title campaign, moving to Aldershot in August 1962. He was leading marksman in 1964-65 and reunited with Freddie Cox at Bournemouth for £5,000 in January 1966, netting six goals in 61 League games before rejoining Aldershot for £3,000 in August 1967. Later with Poole Town, then Ringwood's player-boss, he was a builder with team-mate Rod Taylor until August 1982. He studied at Moorlands College in Sopley and became joint pastor at King's Church in Ringwood.

JACK PROCTOR

Hard-tackling right-back Jack Proctor displaced long-serving Jack Hayward in Bournemouth's defence. Starting with New Delaval Villa, he joined Huddersfield Town in November 1930 but was unable to secure a first-team slot behind England international Roy Goodall before moving to Dean Court in May 1932. He was given his League debut in Cherries' 3-0 defeat at Cardiff City three months later and played 53 Third Division (South) games prior to joining Hartlepool United in July 1934. Later playing for Blyth Spartans, he became a labourer in a timber yard and resided in his native New Delaval until his death in April 1978.

NEIL PROSSER

Striker Neil Prosser briefly played for AFC Bournemouth during the 1980-81 season. He starred as Harlow Town reached the FA Cup fourth round in 1979-80, scoring their late equaliser at Leicester City in the third round and helping to win the replay. Joining Cherries in July 1980, he was given his League debut in the following month's 1-0 victory at home to

Hereford United and also featured in the 2-0 defeat at Lincoln. He briefly revived his League career with Tranmere Rovers in September 1982, then was Swanage's player-boss and later managed Christchurch, Swanage again and New Milton, becoming a Dorset FA coach.

EDDIE PRUDHAM

Experienced striker Eddie Prudham appeared for AFC Bournemouth during the 1980-81 campaign. Signing professional for Sheffield Wednesday in July 1969, he struggled to impress and was loaned to Partick Thistle before being sold to Carlisle United for £35,000 in November 1974. He appeared for the Cumbrians in the top-flight and had loan spells at Hartlepool and Workington, moving to Stockport County in July 1977. Alec Stock signed him in May 1980 and he played four League games for Cherries until hanging up his boots in April 1981. He has since been a prison officer at HMP Wakefield, Albany and Camphill.

RYAN PRYCE

Teenager Ryan Pryce was one of five different goalkeepers who appeared in the League for Cherries in 2007-08. The trainee was given his League debut when Gareth Stewart was forced off during the 4-1 defeat at home to Southend in January 2008. He gained further opportunities with Neil Moss also out of action and turned professional in August 2008. Understudying Shwan Jalal the following season, he played five League games for AFC Bournemouth until leaving in September 2009. After providing goalkeeper cover at Salisbury City, he joined Gosport Borough initially on loan and moved to Fleet Town in November 2011.

DAVID PUCKETT

Striker David Puckett featured in AFC Bournemouth's 1986-87 Third Division title triumph. Initially with Southampton, he helped them finish League Championship runners-up in 1983-84. He moved to Dean Court with Mark Whitlock as part of the Colin Clarke deal in July 1986 and overcame a knee injury to join Aldershot in January 1989. Top scorer four times, he rejoined Cherries in March 1992 and netted 14 goals in 39 League games overall. He later played for Woking, Weymouth, Newport IW, Salisbury, Havant, Wokingham, Bashley, Eastleigh and BAT, coaching at Saints' Academy, Lymington and Totton & Eling.

GARY PUGH

Tall striker Gary Pugh briefly played for AFC Bournemouth at the end of the 1980-81 season. He turned professional with West Ham in February 1978 but failed to make an impact and had a spell with Dover before moving to Dean Court for £1,800 in January 1981. His solitary goal in three substitute appearances clinched Cherries' 2-2 draw at home to Bury three months later and he was sold to Gravesend & Northfleet for £1,500 in August 1981. He appeared for Thanet United, then briefly reunited with David Webb at Torquay United in November 1984 before spells at Canterbury City and Whitstable, settling in Margate.

MARC PUGH

Winger Marc Pugh was top scorer as AFC Bournemouth qualified for the League One play-offs in 2010-11. A former Burnley trainee, he was loaned to Kidderminster before turning professional with Bury in July 2006. He joined Shrewsbury Town in July 2007 and had a loan spell at Luton, moving to Hereford United initially on loan in March 2009. Joining Cherries in June 2010, he was an important figure in the 2012-13 promotion success and 2014-15 Championship title triumph. He grabbed a hat-trick in the record 8-0 win at Birmingham in October 2014, netting 40 goals in 207 League games by the end of 2014-15.

TONY PULIS

Hard-tackling midfielder Tony Pulis featured in Cherries' 1986-87 Third Division title triumph. He played for Bristol Rovers, Happy Valley, Bristol Rovers again and Newport County before moving to Dean Court in August 1986. Sold to Gillingham for £10,000 in July 1989, he rejoined AFC Bournemouth as player-coach in August 1990 and netted four goals in 90 League games overall. He was manager between June 1992 and August 1994, since managing Gillingham (promotion in 1995-96), Bristol City, Portsmouth, Stoke City, Plymouth Argyle, Stoke again (promotion in 2007-08 and 2011 FA Cup final) and West Brom.

STEPHEN PURCHES

Versatile favourite Stephen Purches scored a spectacular goal in AFC Bournemouth's 2002-03 Third Division play-off final triumph. He turned professional with West Ham in July 1998 and joined Cherries in July 2000. Given his League debut in the following month's 1-1 draw at Bristol Rovers, he moved to Leyton Orient in June 2007. He rejoined Cherries in June 2010 and helped reach the League One play-offs in 2010-11, netting ten goals in 277 League games overall before injury ended his career in May 2014. The brother-in-law of Warren Feeney, he had a testimonial against West Ham and joined the coaching staff.

JIMMY QUINN

Northern Ireland international striker Jimmy Quinn was AFC Bournemouth's leading marksman in 1991-92. He played for Oswestry, Swindon, Blackburn Rovers, Swindon again, Leicester, Bradford City and West Ham prior to joining Cherries for £40,000 in August 1991. Scoring 19 times in 43 League games while at Dean Court, he joined Reading for

£55,000 in July 1992. He became their joint player-boss, then Peterborough United's player-coach before managing Swindon Town, Northwich Victoria, Shrewsbury Town, Cambridge United, briefly Cherries from October 2008 until January 2009, then Nantwich Town.

BILLY RAFFERTY

Striker Billy Rafferty was AFC Bournemouth's top scorer in 1984-85. Initially with Port Glasgow, he joined Coventry City in September 1969 and moved via Blackpool to Plymouth Argyle in March 1974. He was leading marksman in their 1974-75 promotion success and joined Carlisle United in May 1976. Twice top scorer, he then played for Wolves, Newcastle United and Portsmouth. He starred in their 1982-83 Third Division title triumph, then joined Cherries in February 1984 and netted 19 goals in 58 League outings. Later with Portuguese sides Farense and Loultanos, he runs Shapers health and beauty salon in Carlisle.

DENNIS RAMPLING

Outside-right Dennis Rampling featured in Cherries' 1949 Combination Cup final triumph. Signing professional for Fulham in November 1942, he served in the RAF and made his League debut at home to Coventry in April 1948. He moved to Dean Court as part of the Jack McDonald deal two months later, netting four goals in 24 Third Division (South) games for Bournemouth before joining Brentford in May 1949. Later playing for Weymouth and Ashford Town, he was a fitter for EMI and Fairey Aviation in Hayes, then a publican in Aldershot and Chobham until August 1977, settling in Woking in retirement.

NEIL RAMSBOTTOM

Experienced goalkeeper Neil Ramsbottom briefly played for AFC Bournemouth at the start of the 1983-84 campaign. Initially with Bury, he was a key figure in their 1967-68 promotion success and reunited with Bob Stokoe at Blackpool in February 1971. He joined Coventry City in March 1972, then had spells with Sheffield Wednesday, Plymouth Argyle ('Player of the Year' in 1976-77),

Blackburn Rovers, Sheffield United and Bradford City before moving to Cherries on a non-contract basis in August 1983. Making four League appearances in place of Ian Leigh, he later played for Chorley and became a financial consultant.

ADRIAN RANDALL

England Youth midfielder Adrian Randall was a fringe member of AFC Bournemouth's 1986-87 Third Division championship squad. A former trainee, he was given his League debut in the 1-1 draw at home to Doncaster five months before turning professional in September 1986 and made three League appearances, moving to Aldershot in September 1988. He joined Burnley in December 1991 and was twice a promotion winner. Sold to York City for £140,000 in December 1995, he joined Bury in December 1996, helping win the Second Division title. He later played for Salisbury and Forest Green Rovers, becoming a lorry driver.

JACKIE RANDLE

Experienced left-back Jackie Randle was unable to prevent Cherries having to seek re-election in 1933-34. He played for Exhall Colliery prior to joining Coventry City in February 1922 and was ever-present in 1925-26. Scoring a unique hat-trick of own goals in their 3-0 defeat at Bristol City in September 1926, he moved to Birmingham in November 1927 and was unlucky not to play in the 1931 FA Cup final. Billy Birrell signed him in October 1933 and he made 28 League appearances for Bournemouth before joining Guildford City in July 1934. Later groundsman at Newdigate Colliery, he died in Hove in February 1990.

MICHAEL RANKINE

Big striker Michael Rankine had a loan spell at AFC Bournemouth in 2008-09. A nephew of Mark Rankine and cousin of Danny Rose, he began with hometown Doncaster and had spells with Armthorpe Welfare and Barrow before joining Scunthorpe United in

September 2004. Helping them win promotion in 2004-05, he moved via Alfreton to Rushden & Diamonds in July 2006. He was loaned to Cherries in October 2008 and made three League appearances. Moving to York City in June 2009, he featured in the 2010 Conference play-off final and has since had spells with Aldershot, Hereford United, Gateshead and Altrincham.

RONNIE RANSON

Left-back Ronnie Ranson understudied Joe Sanaghan during the 1938-39 campaign. Starting with Birtley, he had a spell with Portsmouth before joining Bournemouth in June 1938 and made his solitary League appearance in the 5-2 defeat at Torquay seven months later. He moved to Clapton Orient in May 1939, then joined Guildford City after wartime service in India. Ever-present as they were Southern League runners-up in 1946-47, he reunited with Paddy Gallacher at Weymouth in July 1949, playing at Manchester United in the 1949-50 FA Cup third round. Later with Alton Town, he died in Portsmouth in February 1983.

TOKELO RANTIE

South African international striker Tokelo Rantie was a member of AFC Bournemouth's 2014-15 Championship title squad. He graduated from the Stars of Africa Academy and was loaned to Ferroviario De Beira, Mozambique side CD Maxaquene, Swedish side IFK Hassleholm, Orlando Pirates and Malmo FF. Scoring on his international debut against Gabon in June 2012, he appeared for his country in the 2013 Africa Cup of Nations. He joined Malmo on a permanent basis in April 2013, helping win the Swedish title before moving to Cherries for an undisclosed fee reported to be a club record £2,500,000 in August 2013.

HARDIE RATTRAY

Scottish inside-right Hardie Rattray played for Bournemouth during the 1924-25 season. Initially with Benburb in his native Glasgow, he appeared in the Scottish First Division with Kilmarnock before moving to Dean Court in June 1924. He made his League debut in Cherries' 3-1 defeat at Millwall on the opening day and his only goal in 11 Third Division (South) games clinched the 1-0 victory at home to Southend United the following month. Displaced by the mid-season arrival of Les Roberts and Ron Eyre, he returned to Scotland with Second Division side Arthurlie. He settled back in Glasgow and died in September 1990.

MARK RAWLINSON

Versatile midfielder Mark Rawlinson was an early Mel Machin signing for AFC Bournemouth. A former Manchester United trainee, he featured in the same youth team as Paul Scholes, David Beckham and the Neville brothers, turning professional in July 1993 and helping their reserves win the Pontins League title in 1993-94. He joined Cherries in July 1995 and was given his League debut in the following month's 2-1 win at Wycombe, scoring twice in 79 Second Division games before moving to Exeter City in July 2000. Later with Weymouth, Dorchester and FC United, he has since run his own personal training business.

JOE READMAN

Versatile forward Joe Readman played alongside record scorer Ron Eyre while at Dean Court. He began with Wheatley Hill Alliance and moved via top-flight Bolton Wanderers to Bournemouth in May 1924. Featuring in the upturn in the club's fortunes under Leslie Knighton, he netted 20 goals in 49 League games prior to joining Brighton in August 1927. He moved via Millwall to Mansfield Town in July 1931 and scored their first-ever goal in the Football League, then joined Ramsgate in August 1933. Later playing for his works team Ramsgate Press Wanderers, he resided in Ramsgate until his death in January 1973.

BOB REDFERN

Outside-right Bob Redfern played for Cherries either side of the Second World War. Initially with Tow Law, he joined Wolves in May 1936 and had a spell with their nursery side Cradley Heath before moving to Dean Court with Jack Rowley in February 1937. He guested for Luton Town, York City, Crystal Palace and Fulham during wartime RAF service and scored five goals in 89 Third Division (South) games overall for Bournemouth. Joining Brighton August 1947, he briefly played for Weymouth before serving Poppies over 20 years in various capacities. He taught at several junior schools and died locally in July 2002.

HARRY REDKNAPP

Ex-England Youth winger Harry Redknapp was a player and manager at AFC Bournemouth. Previously with West Ham, he reunited with John Bond at Dean Court for £31,000 in August 1972 and netted five goals in 101 League games for Cherries prior to joining Brentford in September 1976. Later with Seattle Sounders, he rejoined Cherries as coach and became manager in November 1983, plotting the 1986-87 Third Division title triumph. He resigned in June 1992, since managing West Ham, Portsmouth (2002-03 First Division title) Southampton, Pompey again (2008 FA Cup), Spurs and QPR (2013-14 promotion).

JAMIE REDKNAPP

Midfielder Jamie Redknapp gained 17 England caps after leaving AFC Bournemouth. The youngest son of Harry Redknapp, he was a trainee at Dean Court and made his League debut as a 16 year old in Cherries' 4-1 win at Hull City five months before turning professional in June 1990. He played 13 League games prior to joining Liverpool for £350,000 in January 1991. Helping to win the League Cup in 1995, he was an FA Cup finalist in 1996 and became captain at Anfield, but injuries hindered his progress. He joined Spurs in April 2002 and linked up with his father at Southampton in January 2005. Now a Sky Sports football pundit.

JAMIE REEVE

Young striker Jamie Reeve appeared for AFC Bournemouth during the 1994-95 campaign. Signing professional for Cherries in July 1994, he was given his League debut in the following month's 2-1 defeat at home to Blackpool. He played against Chelsea in the 1994-95 League Cup second round, making seven Second Division appearances while at Dean Court prior to joining Hereford United in March 1995. Failing to start a match for them, he moved to Dorchester Town four months later, then had a spell with Bridport and was Portland United's leading marksman in successive seasons until a back injury curtailed his career.

DEREK REEVES

Experienced centre-forward Derek Reeves was a Bill McGarry signing for Cherries. Initially with Bournemouth Gasworks, he joined Southampton in December 1954 and was leading marksman four times, including a record 39 goals in their 1959-60 Third Division title triumph. He also starred in Saints'

1960-61 League Cup run with a record five goals in the fourth round win against Leeds United and moved to Dean Court for £8,000 in November 1962. Scoring eight times in 35 League games for Bournemouth, he joined Worcester City in June 1965, then worked for a Bournemouth building firm and died locally in May 1995.

KEVIN REEVES

Young striker Kevin Reeves was Cherries' top scorer in 1975-76. Born in Burley, he turned professional at Dean Court in July 1975 and netted 20 goals in 63 League outings before joining Norwich City for £50,000 in January 1977. The England international was sold to Manchester City for £1,000,000 in March 1980, scoring in the 1981 FA Cup final replay. Following John Bond to Burnley, his League career was ended at 26 by an arthritic hip. He coached under Bond at Burnley and Birmingham, then assisted Brian Flynn at Wrexham and Swansea, since being chief scout for Roberto Martinez at Swansea, Wigan and Everton.

DAVE REGIS

Striker Dave Regis had a loan spell at AFC Bournemouth early in the 1992-93 campaign. The younger brother of England international Cyrille Regis, he played for Dunstable, Fisher Athletic, Windsor & Eton and Barnet before joining Notts County in September 1990. He helped reach the top-flight in 1990-91 and joined Plymouth Argyle in November 1991. Loaned to Cherries in August 1992, he scored twice in six League outings while at Dean Court. Later with Stoke City, Birmingham City, Southend United, Barnsley and several other clubs, he has since been Charlton Athletic's Academy education and welfare officer.

MICKY REID

Inside-right Micky Reid appeared for Cherries during the 1948-49 season. Previously with hometown Wolves, he joined Bournemouth in February 1949 and scored on his League debut in that month's 2-1 victory at home to Watford. He netted twice in five League games while at Dean Court, moving to reigning champions Portsmouth in July 1950, then Watford in December 1952. Starring as Yeovil Town won the Southern League and Cup 'double' in 1954-55, he then played for Bedford, Poole Town, Hastings United and Guildford City. He later became a school teacher in Havant and died in Portsmouth in April 1975.

ARTHUR RHODES

Inside-right Arthur Rhodes scored on his home debut as Bournemouth hammered Southend United 7-1 on New Year's Day 1938. A former 'Buckley Babe' at Wolves, he joined Stockport County in July 1936 but failed to make an impact as they won the Third Division (North) title in 1936-37. He moved to Dean Court in June 1937 and netted three goals in eight League games for Cherries before joining Torquay United in exchange for Jack Jones in June 1938. Moving to Cardiff City in December 1938, shortly after impressing against them, he guested for Leeds United during the Second World War. He died in September 1998.

CARL RICHARDS

Former England Semi-Pro international striker Carl Richards was top scorer in AFC Bournemouth's 1986-87 Third Division title triumph. Initially with Dulwich Hamlet, he was leading marksman in Enfield's 1985-86 Conference title success and moved to Dean Court for £10,000 in July 1986. He partnered Trevor Aylott in Cherries' attack and netted 16 goals in 71 League games prior to joining Birmingham City for £70,000 in October 1988. Later playing for Peterborough United, Blackpool, Enfield again, Bromley and Tooting & Mitcham, he has since been a house husband with two children in Brockley, SE London.

GEORGE RICHARDSON

Wing-half George Richardson played for Bournemouth during the 1924-25 season. Initially with hometown Gainsborough Wednesday, he joined Lincoln City in February 1920 and helped to win the Midland League title in 1920-21. Sold to Sheffield United for £1,225 in December 1921, he had limited opportunities in the top-flight and joined Cherries in July 1924. Making nine Third Division (South) appearances while at Dean Court, he returned to Lincolnshire with Boston Town in June 1925. Settling in Boston, he became landlord of 'The Axe & Cleaver' pub, then 'The Hessle House' for 23 years until his death in November 1963.

JOCK RICHARDSON

Scottish full-back Jock Richardson briefly appeared for Bournemouth early in the 1934-35 campaign. He began with hometown Motherwell and had spells with Hamilton Academical and nursery side Northfleet United before joining Tottenham Hotspur in May 1925. Given his First Division debut at Newcastle in April 1927, he moved to Reading in June 1929 and missed just two matches as they were Third Division (South) runners-up in 1931-32. He joined Cherries in May 1934, making seven League appearances prior to joining Folkestone in July 1935. Settling in Glasgow, he scouted for Reading and died in January 1986.

BILLY RICHMOND

Scottish left-half Billy Richmond contested a first-team slot with Bill Moralee while at Dean Court. A former shipyard engineer, he had spells with Raith Rovers, Dundee United and Montrose before joining Carlisle United in July 1929. After trials with Southport and Ayr United, he moved to Bournemouth in October 1932 and made 27 League appearances prior to joining Walsall in June 1935. Missing just two matches in 1936-37, he later played for Clapton Orient and Guildford City, then back in Scotland with St Bernard's and Valentine Thistle. He settled back in his native Kirkcaldy and died in September 1973.

DEREK RICKARD

Striker Derek Rickard featured in AFC Bournemouth's 1974-75 relegation battle. He played for Torpoint and St Austell while a joiner at Devonport dockyard, moving to Plymouth Argyle in July 1969. Top scorer in 1971-72, he helped them to reach the League Cup semi-finals in 1973-74 and joined Cherries with Neil Hague for £15,000 in July 1974. He netted six goals in 32 League outings before joining Falmouth in June 1976, then Saltash United and later player-coach and chairman of Weston Mill Oak Villa. After being a newsagent in Weston Mill for 22 years, he became a driver for the Evening Herald newspaper in Plymouth.

LIAM RIDGEWELL

England U-21 central defender Liam Ridgewell had a loan spell at AFC Bournemouth during the 2002-03 promotion campaign. He turned professional with Aston Villa in July 2001 and featured in their 2002 FA Youth Cup final triumph. Loaned to Cherries in October 2002, he made his League debut in that month's 2-1 win over Hartlepool and played five Third Division games. Helping Villa to finish sixth in the Premier League in 2003-04, he was sold to Birmingham City for £2,000,000 in August 2007, featuring in their 2008-09 promotion success and 2011 League Cup final triumph. He joined West Brom in January 2012.

HUGHEN RILEY

Midfielder Hughen Riley was an experienced member of John Benson's squad at AFC Bournemouth. Initially with Rochdale, he helped them win promotion in 1968-69 and beat top-flight Coventry City in the 1970-71 FA Cup third round. He joined Crewe Alexandra in December 1971 and scored as they defeated top-flight Birmingham City in the 1974-75 League Cup second round. Moving via Bury to Cherries in April 1976, he netted seven goals in 72 League outings before joining David Best's Dorchester Town in July 1978, then reunited with Stuart Morgan at Weymouth. He has since been a licensee at various pubs.

JOE RILEY

Centre-forward Joe Riley was Cherries' leading marksman in two consecutive seasons. He played for Conisbrough Welfare, Denaby United and Goldthorpe United prior to joining Bristol Rovers in May 1931. Scoring a hat-trick on his League debut in their 4-1 win over Bournemouth eight months later, he moved to Bristol City in May 1933 and was top scorer as they won the Welsh Cup in 1933-34. He joined Cherries in June 1935 and netted 57 goals in 93 League outings before joining Notts County in exchange for Harry Mardon in December 1937. Later with Gloucester City, he became a Bristol City scout in Cheltenham.

ALEX RITCHIE

Scottish outside-right Alex Ritchie was Cherries' joint top scorer in 1934-35. He had spells at Fauldhouse United, Airdrie, Armadale, St Bernards, Raith Rovers, Peebles Rovers and Dunfermline Athletic prior to rejoining Raith in May 1926. Featuring in their 1926-27 promotion campaign, he joined Blackpool in July 1928 and helped win the Second Division title in 1929-30. He then played for Reading and Watford before joining Bournemouth in June 1934. Scoring 11 goals in 33 League games, he moved to Third Lanark in June 1935, then Hibernian and Albion Rovers. He scouted for Reading and died in Mossend in July 1954.

MATT RITCHIE

Scotland international winger Matt Ritchie was ever-present in Cherries' 2014-15 Championship title triumph. He began with Portsmouth and was loaned to Dagenham & Redbridge for the 2008-09 season, where voted 'Player of the Year'. Gaining top-flight experience, he had loan spells at Notts County and Swindon, rejoining Swindon in January 2011. He starred in their 2011-12 League One title success and joined Cherries for £400,000 in January 2013, helping clinch promotion. Given his full international debut against Northern Ireland in March 2015, he has scored 27 goals in 93 League games for Cherries by the end of the 2014-15 season.

BEN RIX

Midfielder Ben Rix played for AFC Bournemouth on loan during the 2005-06 season. A former Crewe Alexandra trainee, he turned professional in February 2001 and made his League debut in their 1-0 defeat at Coventry eight months later. He helped the Alex regain First Division status at the first attempt in 2002-03 but missed the entire 2004-05 campaign through injury. After a loan spell at Scarborough, he was loaned to Cherries in January 2006 and made 11 League appearances. His progress was hindered by further injury problems and he left Crewe in January 2009, then played for Cypriot side Nea Salamis and St Blazey.

LES ROBERTS

Much-travelled inside-right Les Roberts starred as Cherries took eventual winners Bolton Wanderers to an FA Cup fourth round replay in 1925-26. A former Aston Villa amateur, he joined Chesterfield in May 1922, then had spells with Sheffield Wednesday and Merthyr Town before moving to Bournemouth with Pat Clifford in December 1924. He scored 11 goals in 51 League games prior to joining Bolton in February 1926. Later with Swindon Town, Brentford, Manchester City, Exeter, Crystal Palace, Chester, Rotherham, Scunthorpe and New Brighton, he spent 18 years in local business and died in Christchurch in May 1980.

WALTER ROBERTS

Welsh left-half Walter Roberts played alongside Dai Woodward and Jim Stirling while at Dean Court. Signing professional for hometown Wrexham in August 1938, he served in the Royal Artillery during the Second World War and moved to Bournemouth in exchange for Fred Rowell in August 1948. He helped Cherries win the Combination Cup in 1949 and made 14 Third Division (South) appearances, joining Ellesmere Port in July 1950. Later with Winsford United and Blaenau Ffestiniog, he briefly returned to Wrexham as reserve coach, then spent 25 years as a shop assistant in Wrexham and died in March 2006.

ANTON ROBINSON

Former England Semi-Pro midfielder Anton Robinson starred in AFC Bournemouth's 2009-10 promotion success. He turned professional with Millwall in April 2004, then had spells with Eastleigh, Exeter City, Eastbourne Borough, Fisher Athletic and was Weymouth's captain before moving to Dean Court in February 2009. Helping Cherries to reach the League One play-offs in 2010-11, he netted ten goals in 106 League games before sold to Huddersfield Town for £250,000 in August 2011. He featured in their 2011-12 promotion success, then was loaned to Gillingham (2012-13 League Two title) and Coventry City.

FOSTER ROBINSON

Outside-left Foster Robinson featured prominently in Cherries' 1923-24 Football League debut campaign. Initially with Simonside, he joined Coventry City in July 1920 and was loaned to Nuneaton Town before making his League debut in their 4-0 defeat at Fulham in December 1922. He moved to Bournemouth in June 1923 and played in the club's first-ever Football League match at Swindon Town two months later, making 32 Third Division (South) appearances while at Dean Court. Briefly appearing for Luton Town during the 1925-26 season, he settled back in his native South Shields and died in December 1975.

SAM ROBINSON

Versatile centre-half Sam Robinson understudied Alex Forbes while at Dean Court. A former Luton Town amateur, he joined Bournemouth in July 1929 and made his League debut in the 0-0 draw at Watford seven months later. His solitary goal in 11 Third Division (South) games came in Cherries' 2-1 defeat at home to Brentford in March 1930 and he joined top-flight Derby County in May 1931. Moving via Mansfield Town to Clapton Orient in February 1934, he joined Guildford City six months later, featuring prominently as they won the Southern League title in 1937-38, then finished Southern League runners-up in 1938-39.

STEVE ROBINSON

Northern Ireland international midfielder Steve Robinson won five caps while at AFC Bournemouth. A former Tottenham Hotspur trainee, he turned professional in January 1993, making his Premier League debut at Blackburn Rovers nine months later. He was loaned to Leyton Orient before following Neil Young to Cherries in October 1994. Playing in the 1998 Auto Windscreens Shield final, he scored 51 goals in 240 League games prior to joining Preston for £375,000 in May 2000. He moved to Luton Town for £50,000 in July 2002 and helped them win the League One title in 2004-05 before hanging up his boots in July 2008.

JOCK ROBSON

Scottish goalkeeper Jock Robson starred as Cherries took Liverpool to an FA Cup third round replay in 1926-27. He impressed with hometown Vale of Leithen prior to joining Arsenal in November 1921 and was ever-present in the top-flight in 1923-24. Following Leslie Knighton to Bournemouth in August 1926, he contested the goalkeeping slot with Vic Crumley and made 32 League appearances before moving to Montrose in August 1928. He coached Leithen Rovers while a labourer for Innerleithen Borough Council, then spent 27 years as caretaker of Innerleithen Memorial Hall and died in Innerleithen in September 1995.

DANI RODRIGUES

Portugal U-21 winger Dani Rodrigues had two spells at AFC Bournemouth. Initially with Farense, he was loaned to Cherries in October 1998 and joined Southampton for £170,000 in February 1999. He briefly appeared in the Premier League, then was loaned to Bristol City and joined Walsall in August 2002. Later with Greek side Ionikos and Yeovil Town, he returned to Cherries in July 2004, netting six goals in 57 League games overall. He joined New Zealand Knights in June 2006, then Eastleigh and Dorchester before Cypriot clubs Digenis Morphou, Onisilos Satira, ASIL Lysi, Omonia Aradippou and Doxa Katokopia.

ARTHUR ROE

Experienced centre-half Arthur Roe helped Cherries take eventual winners Bolton Wanderers to an FA Cup fourth round replay in 1925-26. Starting with hometown South Normanton, he joined Luton Town in July 1914 and featured prominently as they finished fourth in the Third Division (South) in 1921-22. He joined Arsenal in April 1925 and briefly appeared in the top-flight before following Leslie Knighton to Dean Court in July 1925. Scoring five times in 50 Third Division (South) games for Bournemouth, he joined Mansfield Town in July 1927, then playing in the Midland League. He died in Ilkeston in February 1960.

FRANCK ROLLING

French central defender Franck Rolling scored in each leg of Cherries' 1997-98 Auto Windscreens Shield regional final victory over Walsall, but was an unused substitute in the Wembley final. Starting with Colmar, he had spells with Strasbourg, FC Pau and Ayr United prior to joining Leicester City for £100,000 in September 1995. He featured in their 1995-96 promotion campaign and moved to AFC Bournemouth in July 1997. Scoring four times in 30 League games, he joined Tony Pulis' Gillingham in September 1998, then appeared for Austrian side Vorwarts Steyr, Greek side Veria and French side Jura Sud Lavaris.

JACK ROSE

Outside-right Jack Rose briefly appeared for Cherries during the 1946-47 campaign. Initially with Devizes Town, he served in the Army and had a spell with Salisbury before joining Bournemouth in February 1946. He played in the following month's 2-1 victory at Bristol Rovers in the Third Division (South) Cup but his only League appearance was in Cherries' 1-0 defeat at home to Norwich City in December 1946. Moving to Trowbridge Town in August 1947, he later played for Devizes again and was a psychiatric nurse at Roundway Hospital in Devizes until retirement. He died in Devizes on his 83rd birthday in August 2003.

JAMES ROWE

Midfielder James Rowe was a young member of Sean O'Driscoll's squad at AFC Bournemouth. A former trainee at Dean Court, he was a regular in Cherries' youth and reserve sides before making his League debut as a substitute in the 2-2 draw at home to Bristol City in August 2004. He also appeared as a substitute in the following month's 2-1 defeat at Brentford, then overcame an ankle injury to make two further substitute appearances for Cherries in 2005-06. After loan spells at Lymington & New Milton and Bashley, he joined Dorchester Town in June 2006, then Poole Town and Merley before moving to Christchurch in June 2015.

FRED ROWELL

Inside-left Fred Rowell appeared in Cherries' 1946 Third Division (South) Cup final triumph. Signing professional for Bournemouth in September 1941, he scored twice on his League debut in the 6-1 victory at Norwich City on Boxing Day 1946 and featured in Cherries' 1947-48 promotion near-miss. He netted 11 goals in 31 League games before swapped for Wrexham's Walter Roberts in July 1948. Joining Aldershot in August 1950, he later played for Weymouth and Portland United, then was Bournemouth Gasworks' trainer. He was clerk of works in the housing department of Poole Corporation and died in March 1988.

KEITH ROWLAND

Versatile left-back Keith Rowland gained 19 Northern Ireland caps after leaving AFC Bournemouth. He turned professional at Dean Court in October 1989 and made his League debut in Cherries' 2-1 defeat at home to Darlington in August 1991. Featuring in the 1991-92 FA Cup third round replay win at Newcastle United, he scored twice in 72 League games before following Harry Redknapp to West Ham for £110,000 in August 1993. He joined QPR as part of the Trevor Sinclair deal in January 1998, then had spells with Chesterfield, Barnet, Dublin City, Redbridge and Welling before coaching at Aveley and Braintree.

EDDIE ROWLES

Striker Eddie Rowles featured in Cherries' 1970-71 promotion campaign. A former apprentice at Dean Court, he made his League debut in the 4-0 defeat at Bury six months before turning professional in March 1968 and helped Bournemouth beat top-flight Sheffield Wednesday in the 1969-70 League Cup second round. He scored 12 goals in 67 League games before being swapped for York City's Ian Davidson in July 1971. Moving to Torquay United in June 1973, he was top scorer in 1973-74, then played for Darlington and Colchester United. He has settled in Colchester and became a self-employed painter and decorator.

JACK ROWLEY

Ace marksman Jack Rowley was capped six times by England after leaving Dean Court. He turned professional with Wolves in November 1935 and joined Bournemouth in February 1937, netting 12 goals in 22 League games before sold to Manchester United for £3,000 in October 1937. Helping them regain top-flight status, he scored twice in their 1948 FA Cup final success and was top scorer six times including their 1951-52 League Championship triumph. Later Plymouth Argyle's player-boss, he managed Oldham Athletic, Ajax, Wrexham and Bradford PA. He ran a sub post office in Shaw and died in June 1998.

JOHN RUDGE

Striker John Rudge was an early John Benson signing for AFC Bournemouth. Initially with Huddersfield Town, he joined Carlisle United in December 1966 and moved via Torquay United to Bristol Rovers in exchange for Robin Stubbs in February 1972. He featured in their 1973-74 promotion campaign and reunited with John Benson at Dean Court for £6,000 in

March 1975. Scoring twice in 21 League games for Cherries, he rejoined Torquay as assistant-boss in May 1977. He became Port Vale's manager in December 1983, plotting three promotion successes during a 15 year reign, then was Stoke City's director of football.

ALAN RULE

Versatile right-half Alan Rule played alongside Joe Brown and Harry Hughes while at Dean Court. He had spells with Pirelli General, Thornycrofts, Basingstoke Town and Winchester City before joining Chelsea in November 1952. He helped their reserves win the Football Combination title in 1954-55, moving to Norwich City in September 1956. Freddie Cox signed him in June 1957 and he played 25 League games for Cherries, becoming youth team coach for a season after a knee injury ended his career in June 1959. He later worked for Thorns Lighting, Vosper Thornycrofts, Safeways and Circle K in the Southampton area.

PETER RUSHWORTH

Right-half Peter Rushworth was a member of Jack Bruton's squad at Dean Court. Initially with Cheltenham Town, where his father Keith gave long service, he joined Leicester City in November 1951. He joined Bournemouth in June 1953 and scored once in 88 League games prior to joining Salisbury with Ian Allen in July 1957. Starring in their 1957-58 and 1960-61 Western League title triumphs, he coached Poppies, Poole Town and Christchurch. He was a design draughtsman at BAC (Hurn), then spent 20 years as a PE teacher at Homefield School together with ex-Cherries Sid Miles and Eric Wilkinson until July 1992. He died in November 2014.

COLIN RUSSELL

Striker Colin Russell played alongside Colin Clarke in AFC Bournemouth's attack. Signing professional for Liverpool in April 1978, he had few top-flight opportunities and joined Huddersfield Town for £15,000 in September 1982. He starred in their 1982-83 promotion success, moving to Dean Court for £15,000 in August 1984. Playing at Manchester United in the 1984-85 FA Cup third round, he netted 14 goals in 68 League games for Cherries before joining Doncaster Rovers in July 1986, then Scarborough, Wigan Athletic, Colne Dynamoes, Bangor City, Morecambe, Droylsden and Warrington, settling on Merseyside.

JACK RUSSELL

Flying outside-left Jack Russell was Cherries' leading marksman in two consecutive seasons. He played for Northfield, Bournville and Bromsgrove Rovers before joining Birmingham in February 1924. Gaining top-flight experience, he moved to Bristol Rovers in June 1927, then helped Worcester City to twice win the Birmingham League title. He joined Bournemouth in May 1930 and netted 42 goals in 138 League games prior to joining Luton Town in June 1934. Later with Norwich City and Worcester again, he was Shirley Town's player-manager, then had a spell with Solihull Town. He died in Bromsgrove in December 1995.

KEVIN RUSSELL

Ex-England Youth striker Kevin Russell was a Tony Pulis signing for AFC Bournemouth. He helped Portsmouth win promotion in 1986-87 and was Wrexham's top scorer before joining Leicester City for £175,000 in June 1989. Sold to Stoke City for £95,000 in July 1992, he helped win the Second Division title in 1992-93, then had a spell with Burnley, moving to Cherries for £125,000 in March 1994. He scored once in 30 League games prior to joining Notts County for £60,000 in February 1995, then was Wrexham's assistant-boss before assisting Darren Ferguson at Peterborough United, Preston and Peterborough again.

LEE RUSSELL

Central defender Lee Russell had a loan spell at AFC Bournemouth during the 1994-95 season. A former Portsmouth trainee, he turned professional in July 1988 and made his League debut in their 1-1 draw with Crystal Palace two months later, helping reach the FA Cup semi-finals in 1991-92 and First Division play-offs in 1992-93. He was loaned to Cherries in September 1994 and made three League appearances while at Dean Court. Joining Torquay United in March 1999, he became captain and helped preserve Football League status in 2000-01. Later with Forest Green Rovers and Weymouth, he is an electrician in Torquay.

GARY RUSSO

Teenage full-back Gary Russo made his solitary League appearance in AFC Bournemouth's 1-1 draw at Hartlepool in August 1975, the club's first match back in the Fourth Division. A former Ipswich Town apprentice, he turned professional in August 1974 but failed to make an impact in the top-flight. He joined Cherries in July 1975 and featured in the following month's League Cup first round first-leg defeat at Plymouth Argyle. Moving to Maidstone United in September 1975, he later played for Edmonton Black Gold, Chelmsford City, Sutton United and Basildon, selling cars at the Essex Ford dealership in Basildon.

JOHN RUTTER

Young full-back John Rutter helped AFC Bournemouth win the Football Combination title in 1973-74. Signing professional for Wolves in September 1970, he was unable to secure a first-team slot and moved to Dean Court in August 1973. He made four League appearances for Cherries prior to joining Exeter City in July 1974. Moving to Stockport County in August 1976, he was virtually ever-present during ten years at Edgeley Park, playing over 400 League games. He worked for a property company, then rejoined Stockport as commercial manager and has since been an area manager for Egan Reid office supplies in Bredbury.

JOHN SAINTY

Versatile striker John Sainty was AFC Bournemouth's leading marksman in 1973-74. Initially with Spurs, the England Schoolboy international joined Reading in August 1967 and scored twice on his League debut at home to Stockport County. He moved to Dean Court for £5,000 in February 1970 and starred in Cherries' 1970-71 promotion success, netting 21 goals in 118 League outings before joining Aldershot in August 1974. Reuniting with John Bond as a coach at Norwich City and Manchester City, he managed Chester and later assisted Dave Jones at Stockport County before following him to Southampton, becoming a scout.

JOE SANAGHAN

Fearless left-back Joe Sanaghan featured prominently in Cherries' 1947-48 promotion near-miss. Starting with Bradford PA, he moved to Dean Court in June 1937 and helped Bournemouth win the Third Division (South) Cup in 1946. He formed an ever-present defensive quartet with Ken Bird, Fred Marsden and Fred Wilson in 1946-47. Appearing in the big FA Cup third round ties against Derby, Wolves and Manchester United, he played 170 League games prior to joining Stockport County in August 1949. Featuring in their 1949-50 FA Cup run, he was a licensee in Stockport, then returned to Ireland and died in November 1951.

ALI SANTOS

Young striker Ali Santos briefly appeared for AFC Bournemouth during the 1995-96 season. Christened Yazalde, he was born in Jersey and played for leading side Jersey Scottish prior to joining Cherries in November 1995 after writing to the club asking for a trial. He made his first-team debut in that month's Auto Windscreens Shield second round defeat at Bristol Rovers and also featured as a substitute for Cherries in three League matches early in the New Year, at home to Shrewsbury and both games against Bristol City. Returning to Jersey Scottish in July 1996, he helped them win the title on numerous occasions.

RICKY SAPPLETON

Jamaica Youth striker Ricky Sappleton played on loan for AFC Bournemouth at the start of the 2008-09 season. A former QPR trainee, he turned professional with Leicester City in August 2007 and made his League debut in their 2-1 defeat at home to Southampton four months later. He was loaned to Cherries in August 2008 and his only goal in three League Two games came in his debut in a 1-1 draw at Aldershot. Following loan spells at Oxford United and AFC Telford United, he joined Macclesfield initially on loan in August 2009. He moved to Bishop's Stortford in July 2012 and has since played for Billericay Town.

BOBBY SAUNDERS

Young winger Bobby Saunders understudied Ray Bumstead while at Dean Court. Born locally, he was Cherries' first apprentice and turned professional in June 1963. He made his League debut as substitute in Cherries' 3-0 reverse at Hull City in October 1965 and also featured in that season's defeats at Scunthorpe and Mansfield. Joining Poole Town in October 1966, he moved to Salisbury in July 1967, helping finish Western League runners-up in 1967-68. He emigrated to Australia in 1971 and played for Hakoah and Waverley City, spending 25 years working for Oce printers. Now retired, he lives in Berwick Victoria.

BOBBY SAVAGE

Midfielder Bobby Savage starred in AFC Bournemouth's 1984 Associate Members Cup final triumph. Initially with Liverpool, he had spells with Wrexham and Stoke City before joining Cherries for £15,000 in December 1983. He inspired the 1983-84 FA Cup third round win over holders Manchester United and overcame a broken leg to feature in the 1986-87 Third Division title campaign. Scoring 18 times in 82 League games, he moved to Bradford City for £35,000 in December 1986. Later with Bolton Wanderers, helping win promotion in 1987-88 and the Sherpa Van Trophy in 1989, he coaches football on Merseyside.

EDGAR SAXTON

Hard-tackling right-back Edgar Saxton was an influential figure during Cherries early Football League days. Starting with Carlton Victoria, he joined Barnsley in May 1917 but failed to secure a regular first-team slot and moved to Dean Court in July 1921. He helped Boscombe to finish Southern League runners-up in 1922-23, making 77 Third Division (South) appearances for Cherries before becoming assistant-trainer in July 1928, then head trainer until the Second World War. Later a sales rep for Hunt & Co engineers, he resided locally until returning to his native Carlton in ill health and died in March 1966.

MARK SCHIAVI

England Youth midfielder Mark Schiavi was a young member of Harry Redknapp's squad at Dean Court. Signing professional for West Ham in November 1981, he failed to make an impact and joined Cherries on loan in September 1983, then returned on a permanent basis in July 1984. He made 29 Third Division appearances overall before moving to Northampton Town in July 1985, then played for Cambridge United, Kettering Town, Enfield, Brixworth, Irthingborough Diamonds, Bourne Town and Warboys. Settling in Rippingale, he was a computer programmer for Hotpoint before running a computer consultancy firm.

HARRY SCOTT

Inside-forward Harry Scott partnered record goalscorer Ron Eyre in Cherries' attack. A former miner at Stainforth Colliery, he impressed alongside his younger brother Jack (later with Saints) at Pilkington Recs before joining Bournemouth in June 1929. He scored on his League debut in the 3-0 win over Exeter three months later and netted 35 goals in 81 Third Division (South) games, moving to Swindon Town in June 1932. Later with Doncaster Rovers and Pilkington Recs again, he settled in Edenthorpe and spent 30 years as a pipe fitter for the Pilkington division of Rockware Glass in Doncaster and died in February 1989.

JOEY SCOTT

Striker Joey Scott scored twice in Cherries' 7-1 victory over Doncaster Rovers in February 1979. A former Plymouth Argyle amateur, he starred as Falmouth Town won the Western League title in four successive seasons and moved to Dean Court for £1,000 in June 1978. He netted four goals in 21 Fourth Division games for AFC Bournemouth before following Trevor Finnigan to Yeovil Town for £5,500 in December 1979. Later with Hungerford Town, Barnstaple Town and Derek Rickard's Weston Mill Oak Villa, he was foreman of the painters back at Plymouth dockyard for 11 years, then became a social worker in Plymouth.

KEITH SCOTT

Loan striker Keith Scott scored once in eight League games for AFC Bournemouth during the 1995-96 season. Initially with Leicester United, he moved via Lincoln City to Wycombe Wanderers in March 1991 and starred as they won the Conference title in 1992-93 and FA Trophy twice. Joining Swindon Town in November 1993, he played for Stoke City and Norwich City before returning to Wycombe in March 1997. Later at Reading, Colchester, Dover, Scarborough, Leigh RMI and Dagenham & Redbridge, he managed Leighton Town, Windsor & Eton and Windsor. He is a sales manager for Advanced Interior Solutions.

PETER SCOTT

Experienced midfielder Peter Scott was an early Tony Pulis signing for AFC Bournemouth. Signing professional for Fulham in October 1981, he was a member of their 1981-82 promotion squad and helped reach the Third Division play-offs in 1988-89. He moved to Cherries in August 1992 but injury problems restricted him to nine League appearances. Briefly with Burnham, he joined Barnet in November 1993 and was captain. He played for Hayes and Aylesbury United before his lengthy association with Beaconsfield SYCOB. Later Burnham's assistant-boss, he has since been head coach at Amersham & Wycombe College.

TONY SCOTT

Ex-England Youth winger Tony Scott starred in Cherries' 1970-71 promotion success. Initially with West Ham, he joined Aston Villa for £25,000 in October 1965 and moved to Torquay United in September 1967. He linked up with

John Bond again at Bournemouth for £4,000 in July 1970, creating numerous chances for Ted MacDougall and Phil Boyer. Featuring in the record 11-0 FA Cup win over Margate in 1971-72, he netted six goals in 61 League games prior to joining Exeter City in June 1972, then held various coaching posts including a spell as Manchester City's youth coach under John Bond before emigrating to Australia.

TONY SCULLY

Republic of Ireland U-21 winger Tony Scully had a loan spell at AFC Bournemouth during the 1994-95 campaign. He turned professional with Crystal Palace in December 1993 but had few first-team chances and was loaned to Cherries in October 1994, making ten Second Division appearances while at Dean Court. Sold to Manchester City for £80,000 in August 1997, he joined QPR for £155,000 in March 1998, then had spells playing for Cambridge United, Southend United, Peterborough United, Dagenham & Redbridge, Barnet, Tamworth, Notts County and Crawley Town. He has since become a postman in Cambridge.

DANNY SEABORNE

Loan defender Danny Seaborne helped AFC Bournemouth to win promotion in 2012-13. He turned professional with Exeter City in July 2005, skippering their 2008 Conference play-off final triumph and helping them win promotion again the following season. Sold to Southampton in January 2010, he again featured in two consecutive promotion campaigns. He had a loan spell at Charlton Athletic before loaned to Cherries in January 2013, making 13 successive League appearances while at Dean Court. Moving to Yeovil Town in July 2013, he had a spell with Coventry prior to joining Partick Thistle in August 2014.

TONY SEALY

Loan striker Tony Sealy helped AFC Bournemouth clinch the Third Division title in 1986-87. Initially with Southampton, he played in the 1979 League Cup final shortly before moving to Crystal Palace. He helped win the Second Division title in 1978-79, then repeated the feat at QPR in 1982-83. Later with Fulham and Leicester City, he was loaned to Cherries in March 1987 and scored twice in 13 League games. He had spells at Sporting Lisbon and Sporting Braga, also winning promotion with Bristol Rovers in 1989-90 and Brentford in 1991-92, before Hong Kong sides Michelotti, Eastern and Hong Kong, where since coaching.

WILLIE SELLARS

Scottish goalkeeper Willie Sellars contested a first-team slot with Len Brooks while at Dean Court. Previously with Celtic's nursery side St Anthony's, he joined Bournemouth in July 1937 and was given his League debut in the 2-1 defeat at home to Swindon Town nine months later. He played for Cherries at top-flight Leeds United in the FA Cup third round shortly before loaned to Wolves in February 1939 after Ken Bird made the opposite move. Featuring in Cherries' 10-0 win over Northampton in September 1939, he made 23 Third Division (South) appearances before the Second World War, settling back in Scotland.

TERRY SHANAHAN

Versatile striker Terry Shanahan played for AFC Bournemouth during the 1977-78 season. A former Spurs apprentice, he joined Ipswich Town in July 1969 and gained top-flight experience before moving to Halifax Town in November 1971. He was leading scorer in 1973-74, then had spells at Chesterfield and Millwall, starring in their 1976-77 League Cup run. Moving to Dean Court in July 1977, he scored once in 18 League games for Cherries prior to joining Aldershot in July 1978. He managed Swanage T&H, then coached under Harry Redknapp at AFC Bournemouth and West Ham before running County News in Winchester.

CHRIS SHAW

Midfielder Chris Shaw was a young member of Harry Redknapp's squad at AFC Bournemouth. Born locally, he was an apprentice at Dean Court and made his League debut in Cherries' 2-2 draw at home to Wigan Athletic a month before turning professional in June 1983. He played against Everton in the 1985-86 League Cup second round second-leg and regularly featured as a substitute, netting twice in 25 League games before joining Bath City in July 1986. Moving to Salisbury in July 1987, he was 'Player of the Year' in 1989-90 and joined Weymouth in August 1991, then Salisbury, Poole Town and Salisbury again.

FRED SHAW

Inside-right Fred Shaw appeared for Bournemouth during the 1938-39 season. Starting with Annesley Colliery, he moved via Darlaston to Birmingham in September 1932 and gained top-flight experience prior to joining Notts County in December 1934. He was leading marksman that season and helped them finish Third Division (South) runners-up in 1936-37, then had a spell at Mansfield Town before moving to Dean Court in June 1938. His solitary goal in ten Third Division (South) games came in Cherries' 4-0 victory at home to Bristol City four months later. Later with Ollerton Colliery, he died in Worksop in March 1994.

DAVID SHEARER

Scottish striker David Shearer briefly partnered Trevor Aylott in AFC Bournemouth's attack. Initially with Inverness Clachnacuddin, he joined Middlesbrough in January 1978 and scored twice on his First Division debut, securing a regular top-flight slot after a loan spell at Wigan Athletic. He moved to Grimsby Town in August 1983, then Gillingham in August 1984. Harry Redknapp paid £15,000 for him in October 1987 and he scored three goals in 11 League games for Cherries before joining Scunthorpe United in February 1988. Later with Darlington and Billingham Synthonia, he was a labourer, then a house-husband in Fort William.

PETER SHEARER

England Semi-Pro international midfielder Peter Shearer had a spell as AFC Bournemouth's captain. Starting with Birmingham City, he made his League debut three months before turning professional in February 1985, then had spells with Nuneaton Borough and Cheltenham Town, moving to Cherries for £18,000 in March 1989. He scored ten goals in 85 League games prior to rejoining Birmingham for £75,000 in January 1994. Featuring in their 1994-95 Second Division title and Auto Windscreens Shield 'double' triumph, his career was ended by injury. He has since coached at Birmingham City's Academy.

JOE SHEERIN

Young striker Joe Sheerin played for AFC Bournemouth at the end of the 1999-2000 season. A former Chelsea trainee, he made his Premier League debut as a late substitute in their 1-0 win at Wimbledon three months before turning professional in July 1997. He joined Cherries in February 2000 and his solitary goal in six League games came on his home debut in a 3-0 victory over Oldham Athletic two months later. After suffering injury problems, he moved to Kingstonian in October 2000, then newly-formed AFC Wimbledon in August 2002. He later played for Croydon Athletic and Leatherhead before injury curtailed his career.

CHARLIE SHERINGHAM

Striker Charlie Sheringham appeared for AFC Bournemouth during the 2011-12 campaign. The son of England international Teddy Sheringham, he helped Ipswich Town to win the FA Youth Cup in 2005. He joined Crystal Palace in August 2006 but failed to make an impact, then had spells with Cambridge City, Welling United, Bishop's Stortford, Histon and Dartford before moving to Dean Court in October 2011. His solitary goal in six League games clinched Cherries' 1-1 draw at Brentford two months later. He was loaned back to Dartford prior to joining AFC Wimbledon in June 2013, then Ebbsfleet United in June 2014.

FRED SHERMAN

Outside-right Fred Sherman contested a first-team slot with Len Williams while at Dean Court. He had spells with Cheshunt and Hampstead Town before moving to Tottenham Hotspur in June 1930. Failing to make an impact at White Hart Lane, he joined Bournemouth in November 1930 and was given his League debut in that month's 2-1 defeat at home to Brighton. He missed just five of the remaining matches that season, playing on the opposite flank to Jack Russell, but then lost his place and netted four goals in 25 Third Division (South) games before released in May 1932. He died in Bournemouth in April 1985.

DOMINIC SHIMMIN

Central defender Dominic Shimmin had a loan spell at AFC Bournemouth in 2007-08. A former Arsenal trainee, he turned professional with QPR in March 2005 and made his League debut in their 3-0 defeat at Coventry City five months later. He was unlucky with injuries and failed to secure a regular first-team slot at Loftus Road. Loaned to Cherries in November 2007, he featured in the following month's League One defeats at Yeovil Town and Tranmere Rovers. He briefly moved to Crawley Town in February 2008, then appeared in Scottish football with Morton and Dundee before finishing his career with Dover Athletic.

DEREK SHOWERS

Ex-Welsh international striker Derek Showers was AFC Bournemouth's leading marksman in 1977-78. Initially with Cardiff City, he was a member of their 1975-76 promotion and Welsh Cup 'double' squad. He moved to Dean Court in July 1977 and netted 19 goals in 60 League games for Cherries prior to joining Portsmouth in February 1979. Moving to Hereford United in December 1980, he was a Welsh Cup finalist in 1981, then played for Swanage T&H, Dorchester Town, AFC Lymington, Barry Town and Brecon before managing Treharris. He has settled in Merthyr Tydfil, working as a postman and then a driver.

ERIC SIBLEY

Young full-back Eric Sibley quickly impressed with Cherries in the 1937-38 campaign. Born locally, he turned professional with Tottenham Hotspur in May 1934 but failed to make an impact and moved to Dean Court in August 1937. He made seven Third Division (South) appearances for Bournemouth before joining Blackpool in October 1937 and helped them finish fifth in the top-flight in 1946-47. Later with Grimsby Town, Chester and Lytham's player-manager, he was employed in the drawing office at Hawker aircraft in Blackpool, then worked for a paint firm back in Bournemouth. He died in Bournemouth in May 1996.

BRIAN SIDDALL

Versatile forward Brian Siddall scored in Cherries' record 7-0 League win over Swindon in September 1956. Starting with Witton Albion, he joined Wolves in July 1947, then played for Witton again and Northwich Victoria before moving to Stoke City in February 1951. Joining Bournemouth in January 1954, he netted 14 goals in 86 League games prior to joining Ipswich Town in May 1957 and was a member of their 1960-61 Second Division title squad. He became Haverhill Rovers' player-boss, then had a spell at Clacton. Later working at Felixstowe docks until retirement, he died in Castle Douglas in August 2007.

LES SILLE

Outside-left Les Sille briefly appeared for Cherries during the 1946-47 campaign. A former Tranmere Rovers amateur, he moved to Bournemouth in March 1947 and his solitary League appearance was in the following month's 1-0 defeat at home to Watford. He also played as an amateur for Ipswich Town, Crystal Palace and Tranmere during RAF service. Joining Marine in March 1949, he helped win the Liverpool Amateur Cup in 1953 and moved to New Brighton with Harry Connor in July 1957, then played for Blaenau Ffestiniog. He spent 40 years in British Rail management and died in Liverpool in April 2007.

FRANK SIMEK

United States Youth defender Frank Simek had a loan spell at AFC Bournemouth during the 2004-05 season. A former Arsenal trainee, he turned professional in July 2002 and featured in their 2003-04 League Cup third round victory over Wolves. He was loaned to QPR, then Cherries in March 2005, playing eight League games while at Dean Court. Joining Sheffield Wednesday in August 2005, he gained five full caps but suffered a serious ankle injury. He featured in Carlisle United's 2011 Johnstone's Paint Trophy final triumph and has since appeared for Vietnamese sides Song Lam Nighe An and Xi Mang Hai Phong.

MEL SIMMONDS

Ex-England Schoolboy midfielder Mel Simmonds featured in Cherries' 1969-70 relegation battle. A former Manchester United apprentice, he shared digs with George Best at Mrs Fullaway's in Chorlton-cum-Hardy but grew homesick and joined Reading in January 1969. He moved to Dean Court in July 1969 and made six Third Division appearances for Bournemouth including the 8-1 defeat at Bradford City in January 1970 prior to joining Guildford City in January 1971, then played for Salisbury, Thatcham Town, Hungerford Town and Thatcham again. Settling in Tilehurst, he spent over 35 years as a postman until May 2007.

DAVE SIMMONS

Loan striker Dave Simmons netted three goals in seven League games for Cherries midway through the 1968-69 season. Initially with Arsenal, he scored twice in their 1966 FA Youth Cup final triumph and joined Aston Villa in February 1969. He moved to Colchester United in December 1970, netting in their epic 1970-71 FA Cup fifth round win over Leeds United and 1971 Watney Cup final triumph. Joining Cambridge United in March 1973, he helped to clinch promotion, then played for Brentford, Bishop's Stortford and Cambridge City. He became an insurance salesman in Cambridge and died in July 2007.

ALBERT SIMPSON

Inside-forward Albert Simpson featured in Cherries' first-ever Football League match at Swindon Town in August 1923. Born in Salford, he began with Manchester City and made his First Division debut in their 3-1 defeat at Birmingham in April 1922. He failed to make any further appearances in the top-flight and moved to Bournemouth in July 1923. Scoring in both matches against Northampton in February 1924, he netted three goals in 12 Third Division (South) games while at Dean Court prior to joining Peterborough & Fletton United in June 1925. He later settled back in the Bournemouth area and died in January 1963.

JIMMY SINGER

Inside-left Jimmy Singer was Cherries' top scorer in 1962-63. Signing professional for Newport County in May 1956, he made his League debut against Brentford in March 1958 and moved to Birmingham City in September 1960, featuring in the 1961 Fairs Cup final. He followed Brian Farmer to Dean Court for £7,000 in September 1962, netting 22 goals in 59 Third Division games for Bournemouth before rejoining Newport County in July 1964, where injury ended his playing career. After running a fish and chip shop in Caerleon, he moved to Guernsey and ran a restaurant/night-club in St Peter Port. He died in July 2010.

JUSTIN SKINNER

Young left-back Justin Skinner had a loan spell at AFC Bournemouth at the end of the 1993-94 campaign. A former Wimbledon trainee, he turned professional in July 1991 and made his Premier League debut in their 3-2 victory at Liverpool in September 1992. He was loaned to Cherries in March 1994, playing in the final 16 Second Division games of the season including a 2-1 win at home to champions Reading. After a similar loan spell at Wycombe Wanderers, he joined Aylesbury United in August 1996, then Gravesend & Northfleet in July 1998. He was their 'Player of the Year' in 2001-02 and moved to Margate in May 2006.

NEIL SLATTER

Welsh international full-back Neil Slatter played on loan for AFC Bournemouth during the 1989-90 relegation battle. A former Bristol Rovers apprentice, he was given his League debut as a 16 year-old in their 1-1 draw at home to Shrewsbury Town in April 1981 and turned professional in May 1982. He joined newly promoted Oxford United for £80,000 in July 1985, featuring in their 1987-88 League Cup run. Loaned to struggling Cherries in March 1990, he made six Second Division appearances while at Dean Court. He later played for Gloucester City and became a police constable back in his native Cardiff.

JOHN SMEULDERS

Ex-England Youth goalkeeper John Smeulders had three spells at AFC Bournemouth. Initially with Orient, he moved to Dean Court in July 1979, then played for Trowbridge and Weymouth, rejoining Cherries in January 1984. He kept seven consecutive clean sheets during the 1984-85 campaign, following Stuart Morgan to Torquay United in July 1986. Returning as non-contract cover for Gerry Peyton in August 1987, he made 98 League appearances overall for Cherries, then had spells with Brentford, Weymouth and Farnborough Town until a knee injury. He became a driver for Allied Bakeries, settling in Corfe Mullen.

ADAM SMITH

England U-21 right-back Adam Smith helped AFC Bournemouth to win the Championship title in 2014-15. He turned professional with Tottenham Hotspur in May 2009 and was loaned to Wycombe Wanderers and Torquay United before joining Cherries on an extended loan in September 2010, scoring a late equaliser in the thrilling 3-3 draw at Peterborough United seven months later. Also loaned to MK Dons, Leeds United and Derby County, he made his long-awaited Premier League in Spurs' 2-0 victory over Fulham in May 2012. He returned to Dean Court in January 2014, scoring once in 68 League games by the end of 2014-15.

BERTIE SMITH

Centre-half Bertie Smith was an experienced member of Cherries' 1928-29 FA Cup run squad. Starting with Nunhead, he joined Huddersfield Town in April 1922 and understudied England star Tom Wilson as they won the League Championship in three successive years. He moved to Bradford City in September 1926, then had spells with Rhyl and Bangor City before joining Bournemouth in July 1928. Making 28 League appearances, he joined Cherries' coaching staff for the 1929-30 season, then played for Streatham Town back in south London. He later became a Surrey FA coach and died in Wandsworth in July 1957.

BRIAN SMITH

Ex-England Youth midfielder Brian Smith featured in AFC Bournemouth's 1981-82 promotion campaign. Signing professional for Bolton Wanderers in September 1973, he helped reach the League Cup semi-finals in

1976-77, moving via Tulsa Roughnecks to Blackpool in August 1979. He joined Cherries in December 1980 and scored twice in 40 Fourth Division games before moving to Bury in March 1982, then played for Parley Sports and Salisbury. Settling in Atherton, he had a mobile video round, then his Fizeek sportswear company. He also coached Atherton Collieries, Daisy Hill and Ashton Town and died in August 2013.

CHARLIE SMITH

Influential left-half Charlie Smith was ever-present as Cherries took Liverpool to an FA Cup third round replay in 1926-27. Initially with Spen Black & White in his native Newcastle, he joined Bolton Wanderers in May 1921 and made his First Division debut in their 1-0 defeat at home to Burnley in February 1922. He failed to secure a regular slot in the top-flight and moved to Dean Court in an exchange deal involving Vince Matthews in January 1923. Helping Cherries take his former club Bolton to an FA Cup fourth round replay in 1925-26, he scored nine goals in 173 League outings before injury ended his career in May 1929.

DANNY SMITH

Central defender Danny Smith was a young member of Sean O'Driscoll's squad at AFC Bournemouth. A former trainee at Dean Court, he turned professional in April 2000 and was given his League debut in that month's 1-0 defeat at Stoke City. He regularly featured as a substitute, playing 18 Second Division games before moving to Winchester City in August 2002. Appearing in their 2004 FA Vase final triumph, he joined Eastleigh in July 2004 and was a promotion winner in 2004-05. He moved to Bashley in December 2007, then played for Bognor Regis prior to rejoining Eastleigh and has since been with Gosport Borough.

DAVID SMITH

Loan winger David Smith made his solitary League appearance for Cherries in the 3-0 defeat at Port Vale in January 1993. Signing professional for Coventry City in July 1986, the England U-21 international held a regular place in the top-flight before being swapped for Birmingham City's David Rennie in March 1993. He joined West Brom in January 1994 and followed Alan Buckley to Grimsby Town in January 1998, helping to beat Cherries in the 1998 Auto Windscreens Shield final and also regain First Division status at the first attempt that season. After a spell at Swansea City, he became Grimsby's commercial manager.

GEORGE SMITH

Tigerish full-back George Smith played for Cherries during the 1934-35 season. Initially with Connah's Quay & Shotton, he joined Bristol City in May 1928, then had spells with Thames, Bradford City and Newport County, moving to Dean Court in June 1934. He made 16 Third Division (South) appearances for Bournemouth prior to joining Bath City in July 1935 and followed Ted Davis to Colchester United in October 1937, helping them to win the Southern League title in 1938-39. Later with Clacton Town, he worked for the Colchester Lathe company, then settled back in Bristol and died in December 1990.

JACK SMITH

Ex-England international inside-right Jack Smith played alongside Joe Riley in Cherries' attack. He had spells with Whitburn and North Shields Athletic before joining South Shields in June 1919. Top scorer three times, he was ever-present in 1925-26 and moved to Portsmouth in December 1927. He was an FA Cup finalist in 1929 and 1934, twice topping their goalscoring charts prior to joining Bournemouth in May 1935. Scoring twice in 41 Third Division (South) games, he moved to Clapton Orient in October 1936 but injury ended his playing career soon after. He settled in Stockton after the war and died in January 1977.

RONNIE SMITH

Young winger Ronnie Smith was a member of Don Welsh's squad at Dean Court. A former Stoke City amateur, he joined Liverpool in December 1957 and followed Don Welsh to Bournemouth in May 1959. He netted six goals in 36 League outings before joining Crewe Alexandra in July 1961, helping them win promotion in 1962-63. Moving via Port Vale to Southport in July 1965, he was a promotion winner again in 1966-67, then played for Altrincham, Netherfield and Formby while employed at Liverpool docks. He has settled in Formby, assisting Alan Kershaw at Everton's Football in the Community residential courses.

WILLIE SMITH

Scottish right-half Willie Smith was an influential figure as Cherries finished sixth in the Third Division (South) in 1936-37. Born in Cellardyke, he played for Anstruther Amateurs, St Monans Swifts and St Andrews Athletic before joining Bournemouth on the recommendation of Billy Birrell's father who was a local baker. He made his League debut in Cherries' 2-1 defeat at Cardiff City in October 1934 and netted six goals in 154 Third Division (South) games. A wartime guest for Dunfermline, he then played for Dundee United. He was chief draughtsman at the British Aluminium works in Burntisland for 30 years.

FRANCK SONGO'O

Cameroon international winger Franck Songo'o was Kevin Bond's first loan signing for Cherries. A son of Cameroon star Jacques Songo'o, he played youth football for Deportivo de La Coruna and Barcelona before joining Portsmouth for £250,000 in August 2005. He had limited top-flight chances and was loaned to AFC Bournemouth in October 206, making four League appearances. Also loaned to Preston, Crystal Palace and Sheffield Wednesday, he moved to Real Zaragoza in July 2008 and helped win promotion in 2008-09. He has since played for Real Sociedad, Albacete, Portland Timbers, Glyfada and PAS Giannina.

TOMMY SOUTHREN

Flying winger Tommy Southren was an early Don Welsh signing for Cherries. Born in Sunderland, he grew up in Welwyn Garden City and impressed with Peartree Old Boys prior to joining West Ham in December 1949, helping to win the Combination 'double' in 1953-54. He joined Aston Villa for £12,000 in December 1954, moving to Bournemouth for £4,000 in October 1958 and netting 11 goals in 64 Third Division outings until a knee injury ended his playing career in May 1960. Settling in Welwyn Garden City, he spent 30 years as a fitter with Nabisco (Shredded Wheat) until retiring and died in May 2004.

NIGEL SPACKMAN

Young midfielder Nigel Spackman starred in AFC Bournemouth's 1981-82 promotion success. Previously with Andover, he joined Cherries in May 1980 and scored ten goals in 119 League games before moving to Chelsea for £40,000 in June 1983. He helped win the Second Division title in 1983-84 and joined Liverpool for £400,000 in February 1987. A League Championship winner and FA Cup finalist in 1987-88, he then played for QPR, Glasgow Rangers and Chelsea again. He briefly managed Sheffield United, Barnsley and Millwall, since working in the media and becoming a senior coach at the Glenn Hoddle Academy in Spain.

RON SPELMAN

Winger Ron Spelman featured in Cherries' 1961-62 promotion near-miss. He turned professional with Norwich City in July 1956 but had few opportunities and joined Northampton Town in November 1960. Helping them win promotion that season, he moved to Bournemouth in exchange for Arnold Woollard in March 1962. He netted four goals in 28 League games before following Bill McGarry to Watford in September 1963, then played for Oxford United and Wisbech Town. After 12 years as a heating engineer, he ran the 'Little John' pub in Norwich, then was a driver for Fyffes until May 1992. He died in June 2006.

JOHN SPICER

Versatile England Youth midfielder John Spicer helped AFC Bournemouth reach the FA Cup fourth round in 2004-05. A former Arsenal trainee, he turned professional in July 2001 but his only first-team outing for the Gunners was in their 2003-04 League Cup third round victory over Rotherham. He joined Cherries for £10,000 in September 2004 and netted six goals in 43 League games while at Dean Court. Following Wade Elliott and Garreth O'Connor to Burnley for £35,000 in August 2005, he reunited with Sean O'Driscoll at Doncaster Rovers in July 2008. He then played for Notts County, joining Southend United in August 2012.

MICHAEL STANDING

Former England Youth midfielder Michael Standing briefly appeared for AFC Bournemouth in 2006-07. He turned professional with Aston Villa in March 1998 but failed to make an impact and joined Bradford City in March 2002. Moving to Walsall in May 2004, he had brief spells with Chesterfield and QPR before joining Cherries in March 2007. His solitary League appearance was as a substitute in that month's 3-1 defeat at Northampton Town. He joined Oxford United in July 2007, then played for Grays Athletic, Lewes and hometown Shoreham. Now an agent for his former team-mate and long-term friend Gareth Barry.

TOMMY STANDLEY

Versatile left-half Tommy Standley was an influential figure in Cherries' 1961-62 promotion near-miss. Initially with Basildon United, he joined QPR in May 1957 and moved to Dean Court in exchange for Tommy Anderson in November 1958. He starred as Bournemouth beat top-flight Cardiff City in the 1961-62 League Cup third round, netting five goals in 159 League games before quitting football in May 1965 to become a chaser for Harris Legus furniture manufacturers. Settling in Great Cornard, he was a machine mechanic for Gainsborough Knitting Mills until closure, then a printer for Lucas until retiring in July 1997.

JUNIOR STANISLAS

England U-21 winger Junior Stanislas featured in AFC Bournemouth's 2014-15 Championship title campaign. A former west ham trainee, he turned professional in July 2007 and was loaned to Southend United in 2008-09, scoring twice on his debut against Luton Town in the FA Cup second round and helping take Chelsea to a third round replay. he gained top-flight experience with the Hammers and moved to Burnley in August 2011. Reunited with Eddie Howe at Dean Court in June 2014, his solitary goal in 13 Championship games last season clinched Cherries' 1-0 victory over Brentford on his home debut.

WALLY STANNERS

Scottish goalkeeper Wally Stanners understudied Ken Bird while at Dean Court. Initially with hometown Carriden Hearts, he had spells with Bonnyrigg Rose and Bo'ness United prior to joining Bournemouth in July 1947. He made his League debut in the 2-1 win at Bristol Rovers in April 1948, also playing in the next two matches, beating Northampton Town 6-3 and losing 3-1 to Norwich City, as Harry Lowe's side finished Third Division (South) runners-up. Moving to Rochdale in August 1949, his career was ended by a broken leg soon after. He settled in Rochdale and worked as a joiner, then a gear cutter until retirement.

BRIAN STATHAM

England U-21 defender Brian Statham made two League appearances while on loan at AFC Bournemouth in November 1991. Born in Zimbabwe, he grew up in Essex and turned professional with Spurs in July 1987. He appeared in the top-flight but was hampered by injuries and also loaned to Reading before joining Brentford in January 1992. Helping Phil Holder's side to clinch the Third Division title that season, he reunited with Tony Pulis at Gillingham in August 1997, then played for Chesham United, Chelmsford City, Welling United and East Thurrock. He has since managed Heybridge Swifts and Billericay Town.

MAREK STECH

Czech Republic U-21 goalkeeper Marek Stech had a loan spell with AFC Bournemouth in 2009-10. He played youth football for Sparta Prague and joined West Ham in July 2008. Given his League debut while on loan to Wycombe Wanderers, he joined Cherries on an emergency loan when the club had no fit keepers and made his solitary League appearance in the 5-0 defeat at Morecambe in December 2009. He also had loan spells at Yeovil Town and Leyton Orient before rejoining Yeovil in July 2012-13. Ever-present in their 2012-13 promotion success, he returned to Sparta Prague in July 2014 and is now a full international.

BILLY STEELE

Young Scottish midfielder Billy Steele had a loan spell at AFC Bournemouth during the 1975-76 season. He turned professional with Norwich City in June 1973 and John Bond gave him his First Division debut at home to rivals Ipswich Town six months later. Helping the Canaries to regain top-flight status at the first attempt in 1974-75, he reunited with John Benson on loan at Cherries in January 1976 and scored twice in seven League outings while at Dean Court. His career was ended by a knee injury in April 1977 and he worked in a sports shop in Norwich, then was a publican. He now lives in Burlington, Ontario, Canada.

MARK STEIN

Ex-England Youth striker Mark Stein was twice AFC Bournemouth's leading marksman. Initially at Luton Town, he appeared alongside his brother Brian in their 1988 League Cup final success, then played for QPR and Oxford United. He helped Stoke City to win the Second Division title in 1992-93, moving to Chelsea for £1,400,000 in October 1993. Joining Cherries in March 1998, he appeared in that year's Auto Windscreens Shield final and netted 30 goals in 90 League games before rejoining Luton in July 2000. He later played for Dagenham & Redbridge and Waltham Forest, becoming physio at Barnet, then Crawley.

ARNOLD STEPHENS

Young winger Arnold Stephens featured in Cherries' Golden Jubilee match at home to Nottingham Forest in November 1949. Signing professional for Wolves in April 1945, 'Steve' failed to secure a first-team slot and joined Bournemouth in December 1948, making his League debut in the 2-0 defeat at Swansea on New Year's Day 1949. He was struck down by illness in the summer of 1950 but defied medical advice to regain his first-team place in 1953-54. Helping Cherries to beat Southampton in the FA Cup first round replay, he scored 12 goals in 70 League games but returned to hospital in April 1955 and died the following month.

GEORGE STEVENS

George Stevens was one of seven different players who appeared at outside-left for Bournemouth during the 1932-33 campaign. Previously with Chelsea, he failed to secure a first-team slot behind George Pearson at Stamford Bridge and joined Cherries in August 1932. His solitary Third Division (South) appearance was in the 2-2 draw at home to Watford on Christmas Eve 1932. He had a brief trial with Clapton Orient before moving to Ashford Town in August 1934, then joined Ballymena United and played in Irish football until the Second World War. Later settling back in London, he died in Walthamstow in November 1982.

GARETH STEWART

Ex-England Youth goalkeeper Gareth Stewart starred as AFC Bournemouth narrowly failed to qualify for the Second Division play-offs in 2000-01. He turned professional with Blackburn Rovers in February 1997 and moved to Dean Court in July 1999, making his League debut in Cherries' 3-1 defeat at Wigan four months later. Missing just one match in 2001-02, he was sidelined by injury and understudied Neil Moss until regaining his place in 2005-06. He made 164 League appearances for Cherries prior to joining Dorchester Town in July 2008, then Welling United, becoming Yeovil Town's player/goalkeeper coach.

JON STEWART

Tall goalkeeper Jon Stewart understudied Shwan Jalal during the 2010-11 season. A former Swindon Town scholar, he had a spell with Weymouth before joining Portsmouth in July 2008. He failed to secure a first-team slot and moved to Dean Court in July 2010. Making his League debut as substitute in Cherries' 2-2 draw at Leyton Orient four months later, he also played in the following two League matches at home to Yeovil and Hartlepool. He was sacked by the club for misconduct in April 2011 and reunited with Eddie Howe at Burnley. Loaned to Alfreton, he joined Worksop in October 2013, since returning to Alfreton.

NELSON STIFFLE

Small, skilful outside-right Nelson Stiffle helped Cherries reach the FA Cup sixth round in 1956-57. Born in India, he came to England as a 21 year-old and had spells with Ashton United, Chester, Altrincham and Chesterfield before moving to Dean Court in May 1955. He featured in the epic FA Cup wins over Wolves and Spurs, netting seven goals in 35 League games for Bournemouth prior to joining Exeter City in March 1958. Later with Coventry City, he emigrated to Australia in July 1961 and played for Bankstown in New South Wales. He then coached various clubs and resided in Brisbane until his death in April 2005.

JIM STIRLING

Tough-tackling centre-half Jim Stirling succeeded Fred Wilson in the heart of Cherries' defence. He played for Coltness United and was serving with Johnny Mackenzie in the Scots Guards at Victoria Barracks when Harry Lowe signed him in July 1947. Scoring once in 73 League games for Bournemouth, he was sold to Birmingham City for £10,500 in June 1950. He joined Southend United six months later and helped them beat Liverpool in the 1956-57 FA Cup third round, then was ever-present in 1957-58. Later playing for Poole Town, he was a newsagent in Charminster until December 1995 and died locally in November 2006.

BRIAN STOCK

Welsh U-21 midfielder Brian Stock featured in AFC Bournemouth's 2002-03 Third Division play-off final success. He turned professional at Dean Court in January 2000 and scored the first-ever goal at Cherries' new stadium in the 3-0 victory over Wrexham in November 2001. Netting 16 times in 145 League outings before joining Preston for £125,000 in January 2006, he reunited with Sean O'Driscoll at Doncaster Rovers for a similar fee in September 2006, helping win the Johnstone's Paint Trophy in 2007 and promotion in 2007-08. The Welsh international moved to Burnley in August 2012, then Havant & Waterlooville.

JAYDEN STOCKLEY

Striker Jayden Stockley was the second youngest player to appear in Cherries' first-team when he made his debut in the 2-1 Johnstone's Paint Trophy defeat at Northampton in October 2009. The club had to ask his headmaster permission to take him out of Lytchett Minster School. Given his League debut on his 16th birthday in Cherries' 2-1 defeat at home to Chesterfield four days later, he turned professional at Dean Court in November 2009. He has made 16 League appearances for Cherries and been loaned to Dorchester, Accrington Stanley, Woking, Leyton Orient, Torquay, Cambridge United, Luton Town and Portsmouth.

DAVID STOCKS

Versatile defender David Stocks was twice ever-present for Cherries. Initially with Charlton Athletic, he joined Gillingham with Ralph Miller in May 1965 and followed Freddie Cox to Dean Court in exchange for Charlie Crickmore in June 1966. He starred as Bournemouth took Liverpool to an FA Cup third round replay in 1967-68 and won promotion in 1970-71, scoring twice in 220 League games before joining Torquay United in January 1972. Ever-present in 1974-75, he later played for Parley Sports and Wimborne Town. He worked with Hambro Life Assurance, Coleman Group and his Stocks Financial Management.

FRANK STRINGFELLOW

Inside-forward Frank Stringfellow scored as Cherries took eventual winners Bolton Wanderers to an FA Cup fourth round replay in 1925-26. Initially with Ilkeston, he joined Sheffield Wednesday in December 1908 and followed Bob Brown to Portsmouth in July 1911. Ever-present in their 1919-20 Southern League title triumph, he moved via Hearts to Poole, reuniting with Harry Kinghorn at Bournemouth in July 1925. He helped take Liverpool to an FA Cup third round replay in 1926-27, netting 30 goals in 117 League games. Moving to Scunthorpe in September 1929, then Cowes, he died in Portsmouth in December 1948.

STEVE STRONG

Versatile striker Steve Strong was a young member of Mel Machin's squad at AFC Bournemouth. A former trainee at Dean Court, he also played in defence for the reserves and made his League debut as a substitute in Cherries' 3-0 victory at home to Shrewsbury Town in May 1995. His only other Second Division appearance for AFC Bournemouth was in the 3-1 defeat at York City six months before joining Bashley in September 1996. He played for Marley in Australia, then Lymington & New Milton and Salisbury City, appearing at Sheffield Wednesday in the 2003-04 FA Cup first round, while working as a bed salesman.

DEREK STROUD

Young outside-right Derek Stroud played on the opposite flank to Tommy Tippett and Peter Harrison while at Dean Court. Initially with hometown Wimborne, he moved via Poole Town to Bournemouth in August 1950 and scored the winner on his home debut against Northampton Town four months later. He netted 17 goals in 78 Third Division (South) games before joining Grimsby Town in June 1953. Reuniting with Ken Bird at Dorchester Town in July 1955, he later played for Portland United and Ringwood. He spent 38 years as a despatch manager for Keith Spicer Ltd, residing in Wimborne until his death in August 2015.

DAN STRUGNELL

Teenage defender Dan Strugnell briefly appeared for AFC Bournemouth during the 2011-12 campaign. Born locally, he captained Cherries' youth team before turning professional at Dean Court in May 2011. Following a loan spell at Wimborne Town, together with fellow AFC Bournemouth youngster Alex Parsons, he made his solitary League appearance as a substitute in Cherries' 1-0 defeat at Rochdale in February 2012. He was loaned to Bashley during the closing weeks of that season and joined Havant & Waterlooville initially on loan in November 2012, with the move becoming permanent in May 2013.

BRUCE STUCKEY

Experienced winger Bruce Stuckey had a loan spell at AFC Bournemouth during the 1976-77 campaign. Starting with Exeter City, he moved to Sunderland in November 1967 and appeared in the top-flight before joining hometown Torquay United in February 1971. He reunited with Charlie Hurley at Reading in November 1973, helping them win promotion in 1975-76. Following a loan spell back at Torquay, he was loaned to Cherries in March 1977 and made five consecutive Fourth Division appearances while at Dean Court. He has settled back in Torquay, working as a drayman and also coaching at Torquay United.

BLAIR STURROCK

Scottish striker Blair Sturrock had a loan spell at AFC Bournemouth in 2008-09. Initially with Dundee United, he followed his father Paul to Plymouth Argyle in October 2001. He helped them to win the Third Division title in 2001-02 and Second Division title in 2003-04. After spells at Kidderminster and Rochdale, he reunited with his father at Swindon in December 2006 and helped clinch promotion.

He joined Cherries on loan in September 2008 and played four League games. Moving via Mansfield to his father's Southend in July 2010, he has since been with Bishop's Stortford, Basildon and Canadian side Victoria Highlanders.

CHRIS SULLEY

Popular left-back Chris Sulley was ever-present for AFC Bournemouth in three consecutive seasons. Initially with Chelsea, he moved to Dean Court in March 1981 and starred in Cherries' 1981-82 promotion success. He helped beat Manchester United in the 1983-84 FA Cup third round and win the Associate Members Cup, netting three goals in 206 League games before joining Dundee United in June 1986. Later with Blackburn Rovers, featuring in their 1987 Full Members Cup final triumph, he then played for Port Vale and Preston. He has been head of youth at Preston, Blackburn, Bolton Wanderers and Leeds United.

LUKE SUMMERFIELD

Teenage midfielder Luke Summerfield had a loan spell at AFC Bournemouth at the end of the 2006-07 season. The son of former Plymouth player and assistant-manager Kevin Summerfield, he was an Argyle trainee and made his League debut three months before turning professional in August 2005. He was loaned to Cherries in March 2007 and his solitary goal in eight League games came in the 2-1 defeat at Port Vale two months later. Also loaned to Leyton Orient, he joined Cheltenham Town in August 2011 and featured in the 2012 League Two play-off final, since playing for Shrewsbury Town and York City.

ALAN SUMMERHILL

Young defender Alan Summerhill featured in Cherries' 1969-70 League Cup second round replay win over top-flight Sheffield Wednesday. A former apprentice at Dean Court, he turned professional in July 1968 and helped Bournemouth reach the FA Youth Cup semi-finals in 1968-69. He was given his League debut in the 1-1 draw at Brighton in August 1969 and made 28 League appearances before moving to Crewe Alexandra in September 1970, then Wimbledon, Guildford City and Liss. Later a publican, he became a warehouse supervisor in Winsford, then a social worker for Cheshire County Council, living in Worleston.

ANDREW SURMAN

Former England U-21 midfielder Andrew Surman starred in AFC Bournemouth's 2014-15 Championship title triumph. Born in Johannesburg, he graduated from Saints' Academy and turned professional in August 2003. He was loaned to Walsall in January 2005, scoring the winner on his full League debut at Bristol City the following month. Joining Cherries on loan in August 2005, he was recalled by new Saints manager George Burley, helping reach the Championship play-offs in 2006-07. He moved via Wolves to Norwich City and was a promotion winner in 2010-11, rejoining Cherries initially on loan in August 2013.

JACK SURTEES

Inside-forward Jack Surtees played alongside Jack Russell in Cherries' attack. The younger brother of Aston Villa's Albert Surtees, he began with Percy Main Amateurs and joined Middlesbrough in March 1930, gaining top-flight experience. He moved via Portsmouth to Bournemouth in June 1933 and scored four times in 21 League outings prior to joining Northampton Town in May 1934. Moving to

Sheffield Wednesday seven months later, he featured alongside England international Ellis Rimmer in their 1935 FA Cup final triumph. He later appeared for Nottingham Forest and died in North Shields in July 1992.

MICHAEL SYMES

Striker Michael Symes had two spells with AFC Bournemouth. Initially with Everton, he played in the 2002 FA Youth Cup final and moved to Bradford City in July 2004. He joined Shrewsbury Town in August 2006 and appeared in the 2007 League Two play-off final. Loaned to Cherries in November 2008, he moved to Accrington in July 2009 and was top scorer in 2009-10. He rejoined Cherries in June 2010 and helped reach the League One play-offs in 2010-11. Scoring 11 goals in 42 League games overall, he was loaned to Rochdale before joining Leyton Orient with Mathieu Baudry in June 2012, then Burton Albion.

ERNIE TAGG

Versatile right-half Ernie Tagg starred in Cherries' 1947-48 promotion near-miss. Signing professional for hometown Crewe Alexandra in October 1937, he moved via Wolves to Bournemouth in May 1939 and starred in the 1946 Third Division (South) Cup final triumph. He netted eight goals in 80 League games before joining Carlisle United in November 1948. Returning to Crewe as part-time trainer while working as a milkman, he became manager in November 1964 and plotted their 1967-68 promotion success. Briefly club secretary, he was a director for seven years, then a life member until his death in November 2006.

JIMMY TAIT

Scottish inside-forward Jimmy Tait featured in Cherries' 1923-24 Football League debut campaign. He had spells with Petershill and Bo'ness before moving to Hearts in November 1920. Briefly appearing in the Scottish First Division, he was loaned to Broxburn prior to joining Bournemouth in October 1923. He made his League debut in the following month's 1-1 draw at Southend. Despite scoring three goals as Cherries won their final two matches of the season against Charlton, he was unable to prevent the club having to seek re-election, netting four times in 12 Third Division (South) games before returning to Scotland.

TOMMY TAIT

Ex-England Schoolboy centre-forward Tommy Tait briefly appeared for Cherries early in the 1934-35 campaign. A former Sunderland amateur, he had spells with Middlesbrough and Southport before joining Manchester City in March 1928. Top scorer as they finished third in the top-flight in 1929-30, he moved via Bolton Wanderers to Luton Town in June 1931 and was twice leading marksman. He joined Cherries in June 1934, scoring five goals in 12 League games before joining Reading in November 1934, then Torquay United. Later working for ICI in Northwich, then as a mail supervisor, he died in Northwich in April 1976.

WAYNE TALKES

Young midfielder Wayne Talkes appeared for AFC Bournemouth during the 1974-75 season. A former Southampton apprentice, he turned professional in July 1969 and made his First Division debut in their 1-0 defeat at West Ham in May 1972. He had few top-flight chances and was loaned to Doncaster Rovers before joining Cherries in July 1974. Playing five League games until an ankle injury, he played for AFC Totton, then was coach/manager of Brockenhurst, Basingstoke, Eastleigh and AC Delco. He spent 20 years in sales with Eden Vale food group, then was an account manager with Palmer & Harvey and WS Retail.

CHRIS TARDIF

Goalkeeper Chris Tardif played on loan at AFC Bournemouth during the 2002-03 promotion campaign. Born in Guernsey, he turned professional with Portsmouth in July 1998 and was given his League debut in their 2-1 defeat at home to Bolton Wanderers in February 2001. He was loaned to Cherries in August 2002 and made nine League appearances. Reuniting with Graham Rix at Oxford United in July 2004, he joined Basingstoke Town in December 2007, then played for Maidenhead United, Farnborough Town and Bognor Regis. He returned to his home island in August 2010 and has appeared for St Martin's AC and Guernsey.

HAROLD TARRANT

Young outside-right Harold Tarrant was a fringe member of Charlie Bell's squad that finished sixth in the Third Division (South) in 1936-37. Born locally, a cousin of Reg Trim, he played for New Milton before joining Cherries in October 1936 and made his solitary League appearance in the 4-1 defeat at Bristol City in January 1937. He joined Poole Town in August 1937 and was an upholsterer with Rogers in Boscombe, then ran his own upholstery business in Pokesdown. A Cherries matchday steward for 20 years, he died locally in January 2002. His son Roger and grandsons Shaun and Kieran are Cherries season-ticket holders.

EDEN TAYLOR

Forward Eden Taylor briefly played for Bournemouth during the 1937-38 campaign. A former 'Buckley Babe' at Wolves, he failed to make an impact at Molineux and followed the well-worn trail to Dean Court in June 1937. He was given his League debut in Cherries' 2-0 victory at Gillingham five months later and scored twice in four Third Division (South) games before joining Ipswich Town in February 1938. Moving to Portsmouth in August 1938, he gained top-flight experience with that season's FA Cup winners and joined Watford in June 1939. The war ended his career and he died in Bournemouth in January 1975.

FRANK TAYLOR

Inside-right Frank Taylor scored as Cherries took Liverpool to an FA Cup third round replay in 1926-27. He helped Sunbeam Motor Works win the Staffs Junior Cup shortly before joining Port Vale in July 1921. Moving to Newport County in July 1923, he made his League debut in their 2-1 defeat at Gillingham three months later and joined Bournemouth in June 1926, netting 21 goals in 61 Third Division (South) outings before moving to Gillingham in September 1928. He featured prominently as Shrewsbury Town reached the Welsh Cup final in 1931. Settling back in his native Wolverhampton, he died in September 1973.

LYLE TAYLOR

Striker Lyle Taylor helped AFC Bournemouth qualify for the League One play-offs in 2010-11. Initially with Staines Town, he had a spell with Millwall before being leading marksman for Concord Rangers in 2009-10. He joined Cherries in August 2010 and made his League debut in that month's 3-3 draw at home to Notts County. Making 29 League appearances, he was loaned to Lewes, Hereford and Woking prior to joining Falkirk in July 2012. He has since played for Sheffield United, Partick Thistle, Scunthorpe United and Partick again, scoring on his international debut for Montserrat against Curacao in March 2015.

RODNEY TAYLOR

Versatile left-half Rodney Taylor was a member of Freddie Cox's squad at Dean Court. Initially with Portsmouth, he skippered them to the FA Youth Cup semi-finals in 1961-62 and followed Freddie Cox to Gillingham in July 1963. He was a fringe member of their 1963-64 Fourth Division title squad and reunited with Cox at Bournemouth in February 1966, making 30 League appearances before joining Poole Town in August 1967. Later playing for Andover and Ringwood Town, he ran a building firm with Tony Priscott until August 1982, then had a nursing home and returned to the building trade, settling in Moor Crichel.

TOMMY TAYLOR

Inside-forward Tommy Taylor was Cherries' joint leading marksman in 1966-67. A former Spurs junior, he turned professional with Portsmouth in April 1964 and joined Gillingham in May 1965. He moved to Dean Court with David Stocks in June 1966, netting eight goals in 26 League games for Bournemouth before joining Bath City in May 1968. Later with Poole Town, Salisbury, Minehead, Poole again, Swanage T&H and Flight Refuelling, he managed Bournemouth Poppies (twice) and Wimborne Town. He worked in the aircraft industry, becoming logistics quality supervisor for FR Aviation (Cobham Group) at Hurn Airport.

SHAUN TEALE

Ex-England Semi-Pro central defender Shaun Teale was twice AFC Bournemouth's 'Player of the Year'. A former Everton apprentice, he had spells at Burscough, Ellesmere Port, Southport, Northwich Victoria and Weymouth prior to joining Cherries for £50,000 in January 1989. He was ever-present in 1990-91, netting four goals in 100 League games before sold to Aston Villa for £300,000 in July 1991. Starring as they won the League Cup in 1994, he then played for Tranmere, Motherwell, Carlisle and Southport. He was player-boss of Burscough (2003 FA Trophy triumph), Northwich and Chorley while a publican in Burscough.

PAUL TEATHER

England Youth midfielder Paul Teather had a loan spell at AFC Bournemouth during the 1997-98 season. A former Manchester United trainee, he turned professional in August 1994 but failed to make an impact at Old Trafford and was loaned to Cherries in December 1997. He made his League debut in that month's 1-0 defeat at home to Watford and played ten Second Division games while at Dean Court. His progress was hampered by injuries and he was released by Manchester United in March 2001, then played for Northwich Victoria, Armthorpe Welfare and Alfreton Town. He has since become Sheffield United's physio.

PAUL TELFER

Former Scotland international midfielder Paul Telfer played for AFC Bournemouth in 2007-08. He turned professional with Luton Town in November 1988 and was ever-present in 1994-95. Sold to Coventry City for £1,500,000 in July 1995, he followed Gordon Strachan to Southampton in November 2001. He was an FA Cup finalist in 2003 and linked up with Strachan again at Celtic in July 2005, helping to twice win the Scottish League title. Moving to Cherries in July 2007, he made 18 League appearances until hanging up his boots in December 2007. He revived his career with Leeds United and Slough Town before coaching.

JO TESSEM

Ex-Norwegian international midfielder Jo Tessem appeared for AFC Bournemouth in 2007-08. He played for Orland BK, Lyn Oslo (promotion in 1996) and Molde in his native country while a working part-time as police officer before joining Southampton in November 1999. An FA Cup finalist in 2003, he was loaned to Lyn Oslo and Millwall, rejoining Lyn Oslo in May 2005. He moved to Cherries in January 2008, making 11 League appearances in a stirring but vain battle against relegation before sidelined by injury. Briefly playing for Eastleigh, Lyn Oslo again, Totton & Eling and AFC Totton, he has coached at Totton College.

ALBERT THAIN

Experienced inside-forward Albert Thain appeared for Cherries in 1931-32. Initially with Metropolitan Railway Works, he was a prolific goalscorer with Southall before turning professional with Chelsea in April 1922. He made his First Division debut in their 2-0 defeat at Oldham Athletic five months later and secured a regular first-team slot in 1925-26, starring in successive promotion near-misses as well as their 1926-27 FA Cup run. Helping to regain top-flight status in 1929-30, he joined Bournemouth in June 1931, netting six goals in 20 League games until injury ended his career. He died in Beverley in December 1979.

BARRIE THOMAS

Welsh midfielder Barrie Thomas briefly appeared for AFC Bournemouth during the 1979-80 campaign. He made his League debut as a 17 year-old for Swansea City against Blackburn Rovers in April 1972 and also played for hometown Merthyr Tydfil before studying a history degree at Oxford University. Captaining their football team, gaining his Blue against Cambridge University in 1974, he coached football in Jamaica, then joined Cherries in August 1979, playing three League games before breaking a leg. He had spells with Dorchester and Poole, then worked locally for Lloyds Bank and became HR director with Logica CMG.

DAN THOMAS

Teenage goalkeeper Dan Thomas played for AFC Bournemouth during the 2009-10 promotion campaign. He was a trainee at Brockenhurst College and made his first-team debut in Cherries' 2-1 Johnstone's Paint Trophy defeat at Northampton Town in October 2009. Given his League debut as substitute for the injured Shwan Jalal in the 1-0 victory over Shrewsbury Town two months later, he made two further League appearances. He was loaned to Dorchester Town, Welling United and AFC Totton before joining Havant & Waterlooville in March 2012. Hollowing a spell with Poole Town, he joined Aldershot in August 2014.

DANNY THOMAS

Flying left winger Danny Thomas featured in AFC Bournemouth's 2002-03 Third Division play-off final triumph. A former Nottingham Forest trainee, he joined Leicester City in May 1998 and moved to Cherries in February 2002. He regularly featured as a substitute and scored twice in 59 League games before joining Boston United in March 2004. Moving to Shrewsbury Town in November 2006, he was briefly at Hereford United prior to joining Macclesfield in July 2007. He was 'Player of the Year' in 2007-08, then played for Kettering, Tamworth and helped FH win the Icelandic title in 2012 before working for an estate agency.

JACK THOMAS

Young goalkeeper Jack Thomas understudied Tommy Godwin while at Dean Court. Born in Parkstone, he represented Combined Services and turned professional with Cherries in May 1958. He made his League debut in the 0-0 draw at home to Notts County in April 1959, also playing in the final three matches of that season as Cherries remained unbeaten against Stockport, Mansfield and Newport. Joining King's Lynn in July 1959, he was briefly with Poole Town before giving Parley Sports lengthy service, then played for Christchurch and Ringwood. He spent 21 years with Hamworthy Engineering and settled locally.

REES THOMAS

Former Welsh Schoolboy full-back Rees Thomas played alongside Mike Lyons in Cherries' defence. He began with Cardiff City and was loaned to Torquay United before joining Brighton in September 1956. Featuring in their 1957-58 Third Division (South) title campaign, he moved to Bournemouth in January 1958 and played 48 League games before following Freddie Cox to Portsmouth in July 1959. He joined Aldershot in July 1961, then helped Hereford United win promotion in 1964-65 and became a postman. Settling back in his native Aberdare, he was unable to keep steady employment due to back trouble.

WES THOMAS

Striker Wes Thomas was AFC Bournemouth's leading marksman in 2011-12. A former QPR scholar, he was top scorer for Waltham Forest in 2005-06 and Thurrock in 2006-07. He moved via Fisher Athletic to Dagenham & Redbridge in September 2008 and helped win promotion in 2009-10. Joining Cheltenham Town in July 2010, he was top scorer in 2010-11 and briefly at Crawley Town before moving to Cherries initially on loan in September 2011. He netted 11 goals in 52 League games and was loaned to Portsmouth, Blackpool and Birmingham City. Moving to Rotherham in January 2014, he then rejoined Birmingham.

BILL THOMPSON

Scottish left-back Bill Thompson was a member of Jack Bruton's squad at Dean Court. Initially with Carnoustie, he joined Portsmouth in March 1946 and helped retain the League Championship in 1949-50. He moved to Bournemouth in January 1953, making 45 League appearances prior to joining Guildford City in July 1954. Later player-boss, he plotted their 1955-56 Southern League title triumph, then managed Exeter City and Worcester City. He coached Pompey, Sparta Rotterdam (1966 Dutch Cup success) and Ismaili (1967 Egyptian League title), coaching back in Portsmouth until his death on Boxing Day 1988.

CYRIL THOMPSON

Inside-forward Cyril Thompson briefly appeared for Bournemouth during the closing weeks of the 1935-36 campaign. Previously with Crittall Athletic (now Braintree Town), he moved to Dean Court in December 1935 and made his League debut in Cherries' 2-0 victory at home to Newport County in March 1936. His solitary goal in five Third Division (South) games clinched that month's 1-1 draw at home to Torquay United. He was a prisoner of war, then played for Southend United, Derby County, Brighton, Watford and Folkestone Town. Later an electrical foreman for British Rail, he died in Folkestone in April 1972.

IAN THOMPSON

Striker Ian Thompson scored in AFC Bournemouth's 1983-84 FA Cup third round win at home to holders Manchester United. Initially with Welling United, he had spells at BAT, Andover and Poole Town before joining Salisbury in August 1981. He was twice top scorer and moved to Cherries for £16,000 in July 1982. Also featuring in the 1984 Associate Members Cup final triumph, he netted 30 goals in 121 League games prior to rejoining Salisbury in August 1986 after a pelvic injury. Later with Newport County, Merthyr Tydfil, Haverfordwest and Inter-Cardiff, he became deputy head of Morriston Comprehensive School.

MAX THOMPSON

Central defender Max Thompson played for AFC Bournemouth during the 1983-84 season. Signing professional for Liverpool in January 1974, he had limited top-flight chances and moved to Blackpool in December 1977. He reunited with John Toshack at Swansea City in August 1981, helping them finish sixth in the top-flight and win the Welsh Cup in 1981-82. Joining Cherries in August 1983, he made nine League appearances while at Dean Court, then had spells with Baltimore Blast, Newport County, Caernarfon Town and Southport. He was physio at Knowsley, Liverpool and Southport, since becoming an ambulance driver.

PETER THOMPSON

Ex-England Amateur centre-forward Peter Thompson featured in Cherries' 1961-62 promotion near-miss. Initially with Blackhall CW, he joined Wrexham in November 1955 and scored twice on his League debut against Crewe a month later, moving via Hartlepool United to Derby County in November 1958. Leading scorer in 1959-60, he joined Bournemouth in January 1962, netting 14 goals in 39 League games before rejoining Hartlepool in September 1963, then had spells with Boston United and Scarborough. He lectured Secondary Teacher Training at Sunderland Polytechnic, then ran the Seagull Inn in his native Blackhall.

DAN THOMSON

Scottish outside-left Dan Thomson helped Cherries take Liverpool to an FA Cup third round replay in 1926-27. He had spells with Aberdeen and St Johnstone before joining Bristol City in July 1925, making his League debut in their 1-0 win over Exeter City seven months later. Moving to Bournemouth in June 1926, he created numerous chances for Ron Eyre and scored in the 6-2 victory at home to Plymouth Argyle on New Year's Day 1927. He netted twice in 20 Third Division (South) games prior to joining Football League new-boys Torquay United in June 1927, then played for Walsall before returning to Scotland.

JAKE THOMSON

Ex-England Youth winger Jake Thomson had a loan spell at AFC Bournemouth in 2008-09. He turned professional with Southampton in May 2006 and made his League debut in their 2-1 defeat at Cardiff City in August 2008. Loaned to Cherries in January 2009, his solitary goal in six League games came in that month's 3-1 win at home to Wycombe. Born in Southsea of a Trinidadian father, he made his international debut for Trinidad & Tobago against Egypt in September 2009. He joined Exeter City in June 2010, since playing for Cheltenham, Kettering, Forest Green Rovers, Newport County, Lincoln City and Salisbury.

WILF THRELFALL

Outside-left Wilf Threlfall had a trial spell at Bournemouth during the 1927-28 season. He impressed with hometown Morecambe, helping win the Lancashire Cup in 1926, then had a spell with Sunderland before joining Birmingham in July 1927. Given his League debut in the following month's 1-0 defeat at Spurs, he moved to Dean Court in January 1928 and made three consecutive Third Division (South) appearances for Cherries. He returned to Morecambe in March 1928, then played for Lancaster Town, Morecambe again, Rossendale United and Morecambe Victoria. Settling in Morecambe, he died in February 1988.

RON TILSED

England Youth goalkeeper Ron Tilsed appeared in Cherries' then record 8-1 defeat at Bradford City in January 1970. A former apprentice at Dean Court, his only other League appearance for Bournemouth was in the previous week's 4-1 reverse at Halifax, following Roger Jones' sale to Blackburn Rovers. He was loaned to Leicester City, Wolves and Shrewsbury Town before joining Chesterfield in February 1972, then had a spell at Arsenal, moving to Portsmouth in March

1973 and later Hereford United, He worked for TNT couriers in Australia, then ran the 'Bear Cross' pub near Wimborne and settled back in Sydney.

JASON TINDALL

Central defender Jason Tindall was a versatile member of AFC Bournemouth's 2002-03 promotion squad. Signing professional for Charlton Athletic in July 1996, he helped their reserves win the Combination title in 1997-98 and moved to Dean Court in July 1998. He scored a penalty on his full League debut and skippered Cherries' reserves to Combination Cup final glory in 2000. Unlucky with injuries, he netted six goals in 171 League games before joining Weymouth in June 2006, becoming their player-boss. He became Cherries' assistant-manager in January 2009, following Eddie Howe to Burnley, then back to Dean Court.

TOMMY TIPPETT

Outside-left Tommy Tippett was a member of Jack Bruton's squad at Dean Court. The son of the former West Ham winger of the same name, he guested for West Ham, Southend United and Plymouth Argyle during wartime service in the Royal Navy before turning professional with Southend in May 1946. He joined Bournemouth in September 1951 and netted ten goals in 37 Third Division (South) games before moving to Dartford in July 1953. Later playing for Gravesend & Northfleet, Canterbury City and Jimmy Blair's Ramsgate, he spent 40 years as a self-employed electrician in Romford and died in March 2005.

GRAEME TOMLINSON

Young striker Graeme Tomlinson had a loan spell at AFC Bournemouth during the 1997-98 campaign. A former Bradford City trainee, he joined Manchester United for £100,000 in July 1994 and was loaned to Luton Town but sidelined for a year with a broken leg. He joined Cherries on loan in August 1997 and his solitary goal in seven League games came in that month's 2-0 victory at home to Blackpool. Also loaned to Millwall before joining Macclesfield Town in July 1998, he then had spells with Exeter City, Stevenage Borough, Kingstonian, Bedford Town, St Albans, Billericay, Stotfold and Dunstable, working as a DJ.

DAVID TOWN

Striker David Town was a young member of Mel Machin's squad at AFC Bournemouth. Born locally, he was still a trainee at Dean Court when given his League debut in Cherries' 2-1 win at home to Reading in May 1994. He was loaned to Dorchester Town and regularly featured as a substitute, scoring twice in 56 League games before joining Rushden & Diamonds for £30,000 in June 1999. Featuring in their 1999-2000 FA Cup run, he moved to Boston United in March 2001 and helped win the Conference title in 2001-02, then had spells with Havant & Waterlooville, Eastleigh, Dorchester again, Bashley and Wimborne Town.

NEIL TOWNSEND

Ex-England Youth central defender Neil Townsend played alongside John Impey for AFC Bournemouth. Initially with Northampton Town, he failed to secure a regular first-team slot, moving via Bedford Town to Southend United in July 1973. He helped them reach the FA Cup fifth round in 1975-76 and win promotion in 1977-78. Joining Weymouth in November 1978, he moved to Cherries for £15,000 in July 1979 and scored twice in 34 League games until an Achilles tendon injury ended his career in May 1981.

He settled back in Northampton and ran Kingfisher Health Studio, then Derngate Gym before working for Securicor.

RAY TRAIN

Loan midfielder Ray Train helped AFC Bournemouth beat holders Manchester United in the 1983-84 FA Cup third round. Initially with Walsall, he joined Carlisle United in December 1971 and helped reach the top-flight in 1973-74. He moved via Sunderland to Bolton Wanderers in March 1977 and was a promotion winner again in 1977-78, then repeated the feat with Watford in 1978-79. Loaned to Cherries from Oxford United in November 1983, he made seven League appearances. Later with Northampton Town, Tranmere Rovers and Walsall again, he was later coach and chief scout during 13 years with Middlesbrough.

BOB TREVISONE

Goalkeeper Bob Trevisone briefly played for Bournemouth during the 1933-34 campaign. Christened Luigi Roberto, he was born locally, the youngest son of Italian musician Alfonso Trevisone who was a leading member of Bournemouth Symphony Orchestra for 42 years. He appeared for Bournemouth Gasworks before moving to Dean Court and understudied Billy Gold and Joe Coen, making his only Third Division (South) appearance for struggling Cherries in the 4-1 defeat at home to Southend United in February 1934. Later playing for Poole Town in the Western League, he settled in Parkstone and died in February 1969.

REG TRIM

Young full-back Reg Trim was one of Cherries' finest discoveries during the inter-war era. A former England Schoolboy captain, he turned professional at Dean Court in April 1931 and made 20 League appearances for Bournemouth before sold to Arsenal for £1,000 in April 1933. He understudied England international Eddie Hapgood as they won the League Championship in three successive seasons, moving to Nottingham Forest in July 1937. An RAF squadron leader during the war, he played for Swindon Town, then was Orient's trainer. He later worked for Bournemouth Water Company and died in June 1997.

MATT TUBBS

England Semi-Pro striker Matt Tubbs featured in AFC Bournemouth's 2012-13 promotion campaign. A former Cherries trainee, he played for Dorchester before joining Salisbury in October 2003. He starred as they twice won promotion and was loaned back to Cherries prior to joining Crawley Town in July 2010. Leading scorer as they won the Conference title in 2010-11, he also appeared in their 2011-12 promotion campaign and rejoined Cherries in January 2012. Scoring eight times in 46 League games overall, he was loaned to Rotherham United, Crawley and AFC Wimbledon before joining Portsmouth in January 2015.

BILL TUNNICLIFFE

Outside-left Bill Tunnicliffe played for Cherries either side of the Second World War. Starting with Port Vale, he moved to Dean Court in July 1938 and featured in Bournemouth's 10-0 win over Northampton in September 1939. He netted seven goals in 49 Third Division (South) games prior to joining Wrexham in June 1947. Top scorer in 1947-48, he was twice ever-present and a Welsh Cup finalist in 1950. Moving to Bradford City in January 1953, he then played for Stafford Rangers and Congleton Town before managing local side Queen Street Boys in his native Potteries. He died in Newcastle-under-Lyme in March 1997.

BILLY TUNSTALL

Centre-forward Billy Tunstall contested a first-team slot with Stewart Littlewood during the 1933-34 campaign. Initially with St Helen's Town, he moved via Prescot Cables to Aston Villa in May 1928 but failed to make an impact. Moving to Dean Court in June 1933, he scored on his League debut in Cherries' 4-1 defeat at Crystal Palace three months later. His only other goal in eight Third Division (South) games clinched the 3-2 victory at home to QPR in October 1933. Unable to prevent Bournemouth having to seek re-election that season, he had another spell at St Helens. He died in his native St Helens in January 1983.

HARRY TURNER

Strongly-built wing-half Harry Turner understudied Cliff Halliwell during the 1930-31 season. Born in Desborough, he was a key figure in Market Harborough Town's 1929-30 Birmingham Combination title triumph and moved to Dean Court in June 1930. He impressed in the reserves before being given his League debut in Cherries' 2-1 victory at home to eventual champions Notts County seven months later. Playing nine Third Division (South) games, including the 5-2 victory at Bristol Rovers in February 1931, he was released by Billy Birrell at the end of that season. He died in Southampton in January 1987.

JACK TURNER

Full-back Jack Turner missed just three matches for Bournemouth during the 1934-35 campaign. A former 'Buckley Babe' at Wolves, he had a spell with West Brom before moving to Dean Court in June 1934. He made his League debut in Cherries' 6-1 defeat at Newport County on the opening day and his solitary goal in 40 Third Division (South) appearances clinched the 1-0 victory at home to Brighton in March 1935. Displaced by George Bellis and Tom King the following season, he joined Chester in August 1935 and later played for Bristol City before the outbreak of war. He died in Wolverhampton in January 1985.

DICKIE TWISS

Versatile wing-half Dickie Twiss understudied Bill Moralee while at Dean Court. He began with Chorley, then had a spell with top-flight Wolves but failed to secure a first-team slot at Molineux and joined Port Vale in August 1933, making his League debut in their 2-1 defeat at Hull City eight months later. Moving to Bournemouth in June 1934, he played four Third Division (South) games for Cherries over two seasons, then appeared for Stubshaw Cross Rovers. He later worked as a coal dealer in his native Ashton-in-Makerfield until he and his younger daughter Dorothy were tragically killed in a car crash in January 1970.

BILL TYLER

Wing-half Bill Tyler had a trial spell with Cherries early in the 1927-28 campaign. A former Army PT instructor, he played for New Cross in his native Manchester before joining Manchester United in May 1922. He then had spells with Southport and Bradford City, moving to Bournemouth in August 1927 and making his only League appearance in the 1-1 draw at home to Torquay two months later. Joining Grimsby Town in October 1927, then Hurst, Accrington Stanley and Ashton National., he was a plankeeper for the Highways Department and became head gateman at Old Trafford. He died in Manchester in March 1974.

JOE TYRRELL

Inside-forward Joe Tyrrell scored Cherries' winner on his debut against Watford in August 1957. Signing professional for Aston Villa in May 1950, he netted twice on his home League debut against West Brom in April 1954 but his progress in the top-flight was hampered by a knee injury. He joined Millwall in March 1956 and featured in their 1956-57 FA Cup run. Moving to Bournemouth in June 1957, he made just one further Third Division (South) appearance while at Dean Court prior to joining Folkestone Town in August 1959. Helping to win promotion in 1959-60, he later managed a cash 'n' carry store, settling in Folkestone.

JAMIE VICTORY

Young left-back Jamie Victory appeared for AFC Bournemouth during the 1995-96 season. Signing professional for West Ham in July 1994, he failed to make an impact and joined Cherries in July 1995. His solitary goal in 16 League games clinched the 1-0 victory at home to Brentford four months later. He moved to Cheltenham Town in July 1996 and gained England Semi-Pro honours. Starring in their rise under Steve Cotterill, he helped win the FA Trophy in 1998, Conference title in 1998-99 and promotion in 2001-02 and 2005-06. He hung up his boots in May 2007 and now works at a hospital in Cheltenham.

BJARNI VIDARSON

Iceland U-21 midfielder Bjarni Vidarson had a loan spell with AFC Bournemouth in 2006-07. From a football family, he began with FH Hafnarfjordur and turned professional with Everton in March 2006, moving to Dean Court on loan in February 2007 after impressing in a friendly against Cherries. He made his League debut in that month's 5-0 win at home to Leyton Orient and his only goal in six League games clinched the 2-1 win over Oldham. Moving to FC Twente initially on loan in January 2008, making his full international debut a month later, he has since been with Roeselare, KV Mechelen, Silkeborg and FH again.

JAMIE VINCENT

Attacking left-back Jamie Vincent played for AFC Bournemouth in the 1998 Auto Windscreens Shield final. He turned professional with Crystal Palace in July 1993 and helped qualify for the First Division play-offs in 1995-96. Moving to Dean Court for £25,000 in August 1996, after a loan spell, he starred as Cherries twice narrowly missed the play-offs. He netted five goals in 113 Second Division games before sold to Huddersfield for £550,000 in March 1999, where 'Player of the Year' in 2000, then appeared for Portsmouth, Derby County, Millwall, Yeovil Town, Swindon Town, Walsall, Aldershot and Didcot Town.

BILL VOISEY

Experienced half-back Bill Voisey featured in Bournemouth's 1923-24 Football League debut campaign. He developed in local soccer on the Isle of Dogs prior to joining Millwall in July 1908 and was a sergeant in the Royal Artillery during the Great War. Playing for England in the Victory international against Wales in October 1919, he scored Millwall's first-ever goal in the Football League and moved to Cherries in July 1923. He netted twice in 26 League games prior to joining Leytonstone as coach in July 1924, then was trainer at Fulham and Millwall where later manager and scout. He died in Worcester in October 1964.

SAM VOKES

Welsh U-21 striker Sam Vokes has gained full international recognition since leaving AFC Bournemouth. A former trainee, born in Lymington, he was given his League debut in Cherries' 2-0 victory at home to Nottingham Forest a month before turning professional in January 2007. He was joint top scorer in 2007-08 and netted 16 goals in 54 League games before sold to Wolves for £250,000 in May 2008. Helping win the Championship title in 2008-09, he was loaned to several clubs prior to joining Burnley in July 2012. He was ever-present in 2012-13, then starred alongside Danny Ings in the Clarets' 2013-14 promotion success.

SCOTT WAGSTAFF

Teenage winger Scott Wagstaff had a loan spell with AFC Bournemouth at the start of the 2008-09 campaign. He turned professional with Charlton Athletic in January 2008 and made his League debut in their 3-0 defeat at Barnsley three months later. Voted the Addicks' Young Player of the Year in 2007-08, he was loaned to Cherries in August 2008 and made five League Two appearances while at Dean Court. He helped Charlton win the League One title in 2012-13 and had loan spells at Northwich Victoria and Leyton Orient before joining Bristol City in July 2013, featuring in their 2014-15 League One title campaign.

JOSH WAKEFIELD

Attacking midfielder Josh Wakefield was a fringe member of AFC Bournemouth's 2014-15 Championship title squad. A former trainee at Dean Court, he had loan spells with Wimborne Town and Hamworthy United before turning professional with Cherries in April 2012. He was given his League debut in that month's 1-1 draw at Scunthorpe United and made two further League appearances for Cherries. He has since been loaned to Dagenham & Redbridge, Dorchester Town, Welling United, Torquay United, Bristol Rovers (helping the Pirates to regain Football League status at the first attempt in 2014-15), and Yeovil Town in August 2015.

BOB WALKER (1)

Versatile defender Bob Walker was a member of Freddie Cox's squad at Dean Court. Initially with Gateshead, he joined Brighton in May 1962, making his League debut at Halifax Town four months later, then had spells with Ashford Town, Hartlepool and Margate before moving to Bournemouth in August 1965. He provided reliable defensive cover and made ten Third Division appearances prior to joining Colchester United in July 1967. Later with Dover, Salisbury and Poole Town, he was a fund-raiser and groundsman for Cherries before being course manager at Queens Park Golf Club and Dudsbury Golf Club.

BOB WALKER (2)

Scottish centre-forward Bob Walker scored twice on his League debut in Cherries' 3-2 defeat at home to Walsall in January 1947. Initially with hometown Aberdeen, the Second World War interrupted his career and he moved to Dean Court in November 1946. His only other Third Division (South) appearance for Bournemouth was in the 2-2 draw at home to Aldershot two months later and he followed Bill Tunnicliffe to Wrexham in June 1947. He also struggled to make an impact with them, joining Kidderminster Harriers as they returned to the Southern League. Later settling back in Aberdeen, he died in September 1991.

BOB WALKER (3)

Left-back Bob Walker understudied former Scotland international Jimmy Blair. He impressed with Cowes before moving to Dean Court in July 1926 and was given his League debut in Cherries' 2-1 defeat at home to Swindon two months later. Making 21 Third Division (South) appearances before leaving in May 1929, he became a local electrical contractor. Stepfather of comedian Tony Hancock, he later ran Durlston Court Hotel with his wife Lily, then the Green Dragon pub in Sambourne. He settled back in Bournemouth and managed the Talbot Hotel, then the Harbour Heights Hotel until committing suicide in November 1959.

HARRY WALKER

Inside-right Harry Walker briefly appeared in Cherries' 1923-24 Football League debut campaign. He impressed with Clay Cross before joining Derby County in May 1910 and made his League debut in their 3-0 defeat at Clapton Orient in September 1911, helping to win the Second Division title in 1911-12 and 1914-15. Moving to Notts County in June 1920, he had spells with Fulham and Aberdare prior to joining Bournemouth in March 1924. His only League appearance was in place of Albert Simpson in that month's 4-0 defeat at Plymouth Argyle and he joined Chesterfield in June 1924. He died in Doncaster in April 1934.

JOSH WALKER

England Youth midfielder Josh Walker had a loan spells with AFC Bournemouth at the end of the 2006-07 campaign. A former Middlesbrough trainee, he helped them win the FA Youth Cup in 2004 and turned professional two months before making his Premier League debut in their 1-0 win at Fulham in May 2006. He was loaned to Cherries in March 2007 and made six League One appearances. Captaining England in the U-20 World Cup in 2009, he was also loaned to Northampton, Rotherham and Aberdeen before joining Watford in August 2010. He has since played for Scunthorpe, Gateshead and Indian champions Bengaluru.

TREVOR WALLBRIDGE

Teenage striker Trevor Wallbridge briefly played for AFC Bournemouth during the 1977-78 campaign. Born in Southampton, he was a prolific goalscorer for Lyndhurst, then AFC Totton in the Hampshire League before John Benson signed him in January 1978. His only Fourth Division appearance for Cherries was as substitute for Trevor Finnigan in the following month's 0-0 draw at Halifax Town and he returned to Hampshire League football with Swaythling (now Eastleigh) in July 1978. He settled in Stoke-on-Trent, his wife's hometown, employed as a financial consultant with Royal London, then UK Personal Finance.

ELLIOTT WARD

Central defender Elliott Ward was an experienced member of AFC Bournemouth's 2014-15 Championship title squad. He began with West Ham and featured in their 2005 Championship play-off final triumph. Loaned to Bristol Rovers and Plymouth, he was sold to Coventry City for £1,000,000 in July 2006 and had loan spells with Doncaster and Preston before moving to Norwich City in May 2010. He helped them regain top-flight status in 2010-11, then had two loan spells with Nottingham Forest prior to joining Cherries in June 2013. Making 25 League appearances, he was sidelined with a long-term knee injury. He was loaned to Huddersfield Town in September 2015.

JOEL WARD

Young defender Joel Ward had a season-long loan at AFC Bournemouth in 2008-09. A former Portsmouth trainee, he turned professional with the FA Cup winners in July 2008 and was quickly loaned to Cherries by Harry Redknapp, making his League debut in the following month's 1-1 draw at Aldershot. He overcame an ankle injury to score his only goal in 21 League Two games in the 4-0 victory at Morecambe on the final day of the season. Gaining Premier League experience with Pompey, he was sold to Crystal Palace for £400,000 in May 2012, featuring prominently in the 2013 Championship play-off final triumph.

CHRISTER WARREN

Versatile left-sided player Christer Warren appeared for AFC Bournemouth in the 1998 Auto Windscreens Shield final. Initially with Cheltenham Town, he scored against Cherries in the 1992-93 FA Cup second round. He joined Southampton for £60,000 in March 1995 and was loaned to Brighton and Fulham before moving to Cherries for £50,000 in October 1997. Scoring 13 goals in 103 League games, he joined QPR in June 2000, then Bristol Rovers, Eastleigh, Winchester and Lymington & New Milton. He was Wimborne Town's player-boss until November 2008, then played in France before joining Christchurch in June 2015.

ALEX WATSON

Ex-England Youth central defender Alex Watson was ever-present for AFC Bournemouth in 1992-93. The younger brother of Everton stalwart Dave Watson, he turned professional with Liverpool in May 1985 and featured in their 1988 Charity Shield triumph. He joined Cherries for £100,000 in January 1991, as Jamie Redknapp moved in the opposite direction, netting five goals in 151 League outings before sold to Torquay United for £50,000 in November 1995. Starring as they reached the Third Division play-off final in 1997-98, he joined Exeter City in July 2001, then had spells with Taunton and Clevedon before coaching.

GORDON WATSON

Former England U-21 striker Gordon Watson appeared for AFC Bournemouth during the 1999-2000 season. Initially with Charlton Athletic, he moved to Sheffield Wednesday in February 1991 and helped clinch promotion. He joined Southampton for £1,200,000 in March 1995 but suffered a badly broken leg after joining Bradford City for £550,000 in January 1997. Resurrecting his career with Cherries in August 1999, he played six League games. He helped Hartlepool United win promotion in 2002-03 and became a director of Kicker Indoor Sports in Eastleigh, also renovating property and scouting for Nigel Pearson.

MARK WATSON

Striker Mark Watson played for AFC Bournemouth during the 1996-97 campaign. He impressed with Sutton United prior to joining West Ham in May 1995 and was loaned to Leyton Orient, Cambridge United and Shrewsbury Town. He moved to Dean Court in exchange for Steve Jones in May 1996 and scored twice in 15 League outings for Cherries. Joining Welling United in July 1997, he was top scorer as Sutton United won the Isthmian League title and Surrey Senior Cup 'double' in 1998-99, then played for Woking, Chesham United, Aldershot, Lewes, Bromley, Metropolitan Police, Worthing, Kingstonian and Margate.

BILLY WAUGH

Scottish winger Billy Waugh was a member of Jack Bruton's squad at Dean Court. Initially with Bathgate Thistle, he joined Luton Town in September 1944 and scored in their first post-war League match. He helped the Hatters to reach the FA Cup fifth round three times, moving via QPR to Bournemouth in July 1953. Netting three goals in 18 League outings for Cherries, he joined Chelmsford City in July 1954, then had spells playing for Bedford Town, Ashford Town and March Town. Settling in Luton, he spent 30 years as secretary for Electrolux Sports and became president of Langford. He died in Felixstowe in March 2009.

DAVID WEBB

David Webb managed AFC Bournemouth's 1981-82 promotion success. Starting with Leyton Orient, the central defender moved to Southampton in March 1966 and helped clinch promotion. He joined Chelsea in February 1968, starring as they won the FA Cup in 1970 and ECWC in 1971. Later with QPR, Leicester City and Derby County, he became Cherries' player-coach in May 1980. He made 11 League appearances and was manager for two years until December 1982. Later managing Torquay United, Southend United (three times), Chelsea, Brentford and Yeovil Town, he has since run a property company in Dorset.

GEORGE WEBB

Teenage midfielder George Webb briefly appeared in AFC Bournemouth's 2009-10 promotion campaign. Born locally, he was a trainee at Dean Court and had a loan spell at Dorchester Town before making his League debut as a late substitute in the 4-0 win at Morecambe in May 2009. He also featured as a substitute in the 2-0 victory at Darlington four months later and the Johnstone's Paint Trophy matches against Yeovil Town and Northampton Town. Moving to Gosport Borough in October 2009, he then appeared for Bournemouth Poppies, Hamworthy United and Poppies again, joining Wimborne Town in May 2011.

WILLIE WEBB

Scottish forward Willie Webb was a member of Billy Birrell's squad at Dean Court. Born in Glasgow of English parents, he played for Cambuslang Rangers before joining Leicester City in September 1925. He was injured on his First Division debut at Bolton Wanderers five months later and joined St Johnstone in July 1927. Moving to Bournemouth in May 1930, he netted six goals in 57 League games prior to joining Ramsgate Press Wanderers in July 1933, then appeared for Guildford City before returning to Glasgow with Third Lanark. He then had spells with Bo'ness and Hinckley United, settling in Leicestershire.

ERNIE WEBSTER

Right-half Ernie Webster understudied Cliff Halliwell during the 1931-32 campaign. He failed to secure a first-team slot during spells with Bolton Wanderers, Reading and Brighton before moving to Dean Court in July 1931. Given his League debut in Bournemouth's 2-0 defeat at home to Gillingham three months later, he retained his place for the next four matches including a 3-0 victory at home to Cardiff City. His sixth and final League appearance for Cherries was in the 1-1 draw at Crystal Palace in January 1932. He joined Ramsgate Press Wanderers in July 1932 and resided in Ramsgate until his death in January 1989.

GRAHAM WEEKS

Young midfielder Graham Weeks appeared for AFC Bournemouth during the 1978-79 season. Signing professional for Exeter City in March 1976, he made his League debut in their 3-1 defeat at Colchester six months later and featured in their 1976-77 promotion success. He moved to Cherries in May 1978 and made three League appearances prior to joining Taunton Town in July 1979, then had spells with Exmouth Town and Bideford before returning to Exmouth and helping twice win the Western League title. Later player-boss of Dawlish, Exmouth and Crediton, he still lives in Exeter and works for British Telecom.

RAY WEIGH

Versatile outside-left Ray Weigh scored in Cherries' Golden Jubilee match against Nottingham Forest in November 1949. He was an Army Cup finalist with the Royal Engineers stationed in Liss and joined Bournemouth in March 1949. Scoring on his League debut at Ipswich five months later, he netted eight goals in 28 League games, joining Stockport in July 1951. Later with Shrewsbury, Aldershot, Dorchester and Christchurch, he was a salesman for Brooke Bond Tea, then caretaker at Beaufort School and ran a car hire business. He died locally in June 2015. His nephews Tony and Gren Millington were both goalkeepers.

CHRIS WELLER

Inside-forward Chris Weller had two spells at Dean Court. Previously an amateur with Reading, he joined Bournemouth in August 1959 and featured in the 1961-62 promotion near-miss, moving to Bristol Rovers in June 1965. He rejoined Cherries in January 1966 and netted 26 goals in 111 League games overall before joining Yeovil Town in June 1967. Starring in their 1970-71 Southern League title triumph, he later played for Salisbury, Poole and Ringwood. He was then manager/coach of Holt United, Shaftesbury, Holt again, Wimborne, Brockenhurst and Bournemouth Poppies while a self-employed plumber and heating engineer.

DAVE WELLS

Northern Ireland Youth goalkeeper Dave Wells understudied Neil Moss, Ian Andrews and Jimmy Glass while at AFC Bournemouth. He was a trainee at Dean Court and Mel Machin gave him his only League appearance as a 16 year-old substitute for Neil Moss in Cherries' 3-1 defeat at home to Wrexham in December 1994. Loaned to Cheltenham and Salisbury, he joined Barry Town in July 1998 and helped win the League of Wales title in 1998-99. He moved to Dorchester Town in August 2000, since playing for Cliftonville, Portadown, Newry, Dungannon Swifts and Cliftonville again back in Northern Ireland.

ALAN WELSH

Scottish striker Alan Welsh was a Trevor Hartley signing for AFC Bournemouth. Initially with Bonnyrigg Rose, he moved via Millwall to Torquay United in November 1967. He was top scorer in 1971-72, then repeated the feat with Plymouth Argyle in 1972-73 and helped reach the League Cup semi-finals in 1973-74. Joining Cherries for £25,000 in February 1974, he netted three goals in 35 League games, returning to Millwall in August 1975, then Maidstone United and Cape Town City. He helped his brother-in-law Billy Neil in Millwall's commercial department, then worked in the print trade and building trade in London.

IKE WHELPTON

Goalkeeper Ike Whelpton featured in Cherries' first home League match against Swindon in September 1923, his only appearance for the club. Christened James Isaac, he began with Mexborough Town, then had spells at Lincoln City and Castleford prior to joining Huddersfield Town in October 1911. He then played for Guildford United, Castleford, Mexborough again, Grimsby Town and had further spells at Castleford and Guildford before moving to Bournemouth in August 1923. Understudying Alec Heron at Dean Court, he was a journalist, then scouted for Leicester and Birmingham. He died in Sheffield in February 1944.

ALFIE WHITE

Inside-forward Alfie White helped Cherries to reach the FA Cup fourth round in 1931-32. Starting with hometown Spennymoor United, he joined Derby County in November 1927 and understudied England stars Harry Bedford and Jack Bowers as they finished League Championship runners-up in 1929-30. He moved to Bournemouth in October 1931, scoring 35 goals in 125 Third Division (South) games before joining Wrexham in May 1936. Returning to Spennymoor in July 1937, he was twice leading marksman before the Second World War, then a storeman for Siemens until his death in Spennymoor in May 1970.

JIMMY WHITE

Ex-England Youth central defender Jimmy White was ever-present for Cherries in 1967-68. Locally born, he became Bournemouth's youngest League debutant at 15 years 321 days in the 3-1 win at home to Port Vale in April 1958. He followed Freddie Cox to Portsmouth that summer, then to Gillingham in June 1963 and back to Cherries in July 1966. Scoring seven goals in 177 League games overall, he joined Cambridge United in December 1970, then was manager/coach of King's Lynn, Cambridge City, Chatteris and Histon. He settled in Over, becoming an operating theatre assistant at Addenbrooke's Hospital in Cambridge.

KEVIN WHITE

Young midfielder Kevin White helped Cherries take Liverpool to an FA Cup third round replay in 1967-68. Signing professional at Dean Court in August 1966, he was given his League debut by Freddie Cox in Bournemouth's 1-0 win at Scunthorpe United a month later. He scored four times in 48 Third Division games before being displaced by new signings such as Lou Peters and John Meredith, moving to Bath City in June 1971, then hometown Poole, Salisbury, Parley Sports and New Milton. Settling in Parkstone, he became a self-employed plumber and heating engineer, then worked for John Hickman (Heating) Ltd.

TONY WHITE

Young defender Tony White briefly played for AFC Bournemouth during the 1985-86 campaign. Initially with Dorchester Town, he moved to Dean Court in July 1985, making his solitary League appearance in Cherries' 4-1 defeat at Rotherham in April 1986. He rejoined Dorchester, helping win promotion in 1986-87 and reach the Southern League Cup final in 1992. Given a testimonial match against AFC Bournemouth in October 1995, he joined Havant Town in July 1996, then had spells with Newport IW, Wimborne and Poole Borough. He has since been a director of Falcon information technology and services in Dorchester.

JACK WHITEHOUSE

Experienced inside-forward Jack Whitehouse played alongside Ron Eyre in Bournemouth's attack. Initially with Smethwick Hall, he moved via Redditch to Birmingham in August 1916 and starred in their 1920-21 Second Division title triumph. He joined Derby County in May 1923 and helped regain top-flight status in 1925-26. Sold to League Champions elect Sheffield Wednesday for £5,000 in February 1929, he joined Cherries in August 1930. He netted 17 goals in 105 League games, moving to Folkestone in May 1933, then was Worcester City's player-boss. Later scouting for Derby, he died in Halesowen in January 1948.

BOB WHITELAW

Scottish wing-half Bob Whitelaw contested a first-team slot with Bill Moralee during the 1932-33 season. He began with Larkhill Thistle and moved to Celtic in July 1926, playing in their 1931 tour of the United States. Loaned to Albion Rovers, he joined Cherries in June 1932, scoring twice in ten League games prior to joining Glentoran in July 1933. He then had spells with Queen of the South, Celtic again, Cowdenbeath, Albion Rovers, Southampton and Kidderminster Harriers. An interpreter in Army intelligence during the war, he was landlord of the 'Corn Exchange' in Kidderminster for many years and died in January 1965.

KEN WHITESIDE

Centre-forward Ken Whiteside made his only League appearance for Cherries in the 1-0 defeat at Ipswich Town in October 1955. A former Everton amateur, he played alongside his older brother Charlie for British Enka and moved via Preston to Chesterfield in May 1953. He joined York City in May 1954 but failed to secure a place in their side that reached the FA Cup run semi-finals in 1954-55 and joined Bournemouth in July 1955. Understudy to Ollie Norris while at Dean Court, he moved to Skelmersdale United in July 1956, then worked for Dunlop and Cargil Oil at Liverpool docks. He became the starter at Formby Golf Club.

MARK WHITLOCK

Central defender Mark Whitlock featured prominently in AFC Bournemouth's 1986-87 Third Division title triumph. Signing professional for Southampton in March 1979, he helped finish League Championship runners-up in 1983-84 and joined Cherries with David Puckett as part of the Colin Clarke deal in July 1986. He helped beat Saints in the 1987-88 League Cup second round and scored once in 99 League games while at Dean Court. Reuniting with Ian Branfoot at Reading in December 1988, he then played for Aldershot and Aerostructures. He has settled in Southampton, since working as a security officer and an HGV driver.

ERNIE WHITTAM

Inside-right Ernie Whittam was a member of Charlie Bell's squad at Dean Court. He turned professional with Huddersfield Town in November 1928 and gained top-flight experience before joining Chester in May 1933. Featuring in their 1934-35 promotion near-miss, he had spells with Mansfield Town and Wolves, moving to Bournemouth in May 1936. He formed an effective right-wing triangle with Willie Smith and Bob Redfern, netting 28 goals in 107 Third Division (South) games prior to joining Reading in June 1939. Blind in one eye, he settled back in Huddersfield and suffered an early death from cancer in July 1951.

ALAN WHITTLE

Former England U-23 striker Alan Whittle appeared for AFC Bournemouth during the 1980-81 season. Starting with Everton, he made his First Division debut in their 6-2 win at West Brom in March 1968 and helped clinch the League Championship in 1969-70. He joined Crystal Palace for £100,000 in December 1972, moving to Orient in September 1976, then Iranian side Persepolis and Orient again. David Webb signed him in January 1981 and he made nine League appearances, then played for Preston Macedonia, Gravesend & Northfleet and Corinthian Casuals. He settled on the Wirral and organises soccer camps.

RHOYS WIGGINS

Welsh U-21 left-back Rhoys Wiggins helped AFC Bournemouth to clinch promotion in 2009-10. He turned professional with Crystal Palace in July 2006 and was given his League debut in their 2-1 defeat at home to Nottingham Forest in October 2008. Loaned to Cherries in January 2009, he helped to preserve Football League status. He joined Norwich City in July 2009 and rejoined Cherries initially on loan in January 2010. Helping to qualify for the League One play-offs in 2010-11, he scored twice in 67 League games overall before joining Charlton Athletic in June 2011. He starred in their 2011-12 League One title triumph.

DAVE WILKINSON

Inside-forward Dave Wilkinson was a member of Jack Bruton's squad at Dean Court. He appeared for Distillery and North Shields during RAF service and moved to Blackburn Rovers in July 1948, making his League debut in their 2-0 defeat at Luton two months later. Following Bruton to Cherries in June 1950, he netted three goals in eight League games before joining Berwick Rangers in June 1952, then played for Ashington, Horden CW and Ryhope CW. He was foreman at Thorn TV factory, then a driver at Vane Tempest Colliery in Seaham. Settling in Ryhope, he captained Houghton le Spring and Seaham Golf Clubs.

ERIC WILKINSON

Inside-forward Eric Wilkinson played for Cherries during the 1955-56 campaign. Signing professional for Bradford City in January 1951, he joined Sheffield United in August 1953 but also failed to secure a first-team slot with the Blades and moved to Bournemouth in July 1955. He made four League appearances prior to joining Hastings United in July 1956, then played for Weymouth and Dorchester Town. After teaching geography at Homefield School for 40 years, he became estates manager at their Winkton site and died in October 2002. His cousin Howard Wilkinson managed Sheffield Wednesday and Leeds United.

DAVID WILLIAMS

Former Welsh international midfielder David Williams appeared as a substitute in AFC Bournemouth's 2-1 defeat at home to Bolton Wanderers in April 1993. Initially with Clifton Athletic, he joined Bristol Rovers in August 1975 and turned professional after completing a teacher-training course. He was player-boss at 28, joining Norwich City in July 1985 and helping win the Second Division title in 1985-86. Reuniting with Tony Pulis as Cherries' assistant-boss from August 1992 until January 1994, he then coached at Everton, Leeds United, Manchester United and Norwich again before assisting Brian Flynn at Wales and Doncaster.

EMLYN WILLIAMS

Welsh centre-forward Emlyn Williams understudied club record goalscorer Ron Eyre during the 1931-32 season. He was a prolific scorer with Aberdare Athletic in their final Football League campaign and joined Clapton Orient in May 1928. Following spells with 1929-30 FA Cup semi-finalists Hull City and back in South Wales with Merthyr Town, he moved to Dean Court in December 1931. His two goals in six Third Division (South) games clinched Cherries' 1-1 draws at Crystal Palace and at home to Northampton Town. He joined Ramsgate Press Wanderers in July 1932. Settling back in Merthyr, he died in April 1983.

GARETH WILLIAMS (1)

Welsh U-21 striker Gareth Williams had a loan spell at AFC Bournemouth during the 2003-04 campaign. A former Crystal Palace scholar, he turned professional in July 2002 but had few first-team opportunities. He was loaned to Colchester United and Cambridge United before joining Cherries on loan in February 2004, making his only League appearance as a substitute in that month's 3-0 defeat at Brighton. Rejoining Colchester in September 2004, he helped win promotion in 2005-06. He was loaned to Blackpool, since playing for

Weymouth, Bromley, Croydon Athletic, Ebbsfleet United, Bromley again and Cray Wanderers.

GARETH WILLIAMS (2)

Much-travelled winger Gareth Williams had a trial spell at AFC Bournemouth during the 1994-95 season. Born in Cowes, he impressed with Gosport Borough prior to joining Aston Villa in January 1988 and moved to Barnsley for £200,000 in August 1991. Reuniting with Mel Machin at Cherries in September 1994, he appeared as a substitute in that month's 1-1 draw with Chester. He quickly joined Northampton Town and moved to Scarborough in August 1996. Joining Hull City in November 1998, he then played for Scarborough again, Ilkeston Town, Gainsborough Trinity and Matlock Town, becoming player-manager.

JOHN WILLIAMS

Central defender John Williams was an influential figure in AFC Bournemouth's 1986-87 Third Division title triumph. Initially with Tranmere Rovers, 'Willo' joined Port Vale in July 1985 and starred in their 1985-86 promotion success. He moved to Cherries for £30,000 in December 1986, helping take Manchester United to an FA Cup fifth round replay in 1988-89. Scoring nine goals in 117 League games, he joined Cardiff City for £15,000 in December 1991. He coached at Cherries from July 1993 until February 2000, then was a publican and coached at Homefield School. Now a Cherries match summariser for Radio Solent.

KEITH WILLIAMS

Versatile midfielder Keith Williams starred in AFC Bournemouth's 1981-82 promotion success. Initially with Aston Villa, he failed to make an impact and joined Northampton Town in February 1977. He was their 'Player of the Year' in 1980-81. Moving to Cherries in August 1981, he became player-coach, scoring once in 102 League games. Briefly with Bath City, he reunited with Roger Brown at Colchester United in December 1987, then had spells at Swanage T&H, Salisbury, Poole Town, Bournemouth Poppies and Ringwood before managing Poppies, becoming a despatch manager for Bezier Corporate Print in Poole.

LEN WILLIAMS

Young Welsh winger Len Williams created numerous goalscoring chances for Ron Eyre. He joined Cherries from Wrexham amateur football in December 1929 and netted 15 times in 90 League games before moving to Portsmouth in an exchange deal involving Jack Friar and Jack Surtees in August 1933. Joining Aldershot in August 1934, he was top scorer in 1935-36, then had spells with Charlton Athletic, Aldershot again and Worcester City. He coached Poole Town while working as an insurance agent, then ran Sterte sub Post Office for 21 years until May 1973 and resided in Poole until his death in June 1990.

BEN WILLIAMSON

Striker Ben Williamson briefly featured as AFC Bournemouth qualified for the League One play-offs in 2010-11. A former Millwall youth player, he studied Maths and Business Studies at Brighton University and played for Worthing before joining the Glenn Hoddle Academy in Spain, appearing for their partner club Jerez Industrial. Moving to Cherries in January 2011, an ankle injury restricted him to four League appearances. He joined Hyde in June 2011 but spent the 2011-12 season on loan to Port Vale before a permanent transfer, helping them to win promotion in 2012-13. He moved to Gillingham in June 2015.

CALLUM WILSON

England U-21 striker Callum Wilson was leading scorer in AFC Bournemouth's 2014-15 Championship title triumph. A former trainee with Coventry City, he made his League debut in their 2-0 defeat at home to QPR in December 2010 and secured a regular first-team slot with his hometown club after loan spells at Kettering Town and Tamworth. He was top scorer and 'Player of the Year' in 2013-14, moving to Dean Court in July 2014. Scoring twice on his Cherries debut in the 4-0 victory at Huddersfield Town on the opening day, he netted 20 goals in 45 Championship games as Eddie Howe's side reached the top-flight.

CHARLIE WILSON

Experienced right-back Charlie Wilson played for Cherries during the 1933-34 campaign. He captained Grimsby Schoolboys and played for Cleethorpes Town before turning professional with Grimsby Town in May 1923. Starring in their 1925-26 Third Division (North) title triumph and 1928-29 promotion success, he was ever-present in the top-flight in 1929-30 and joined Bournemouth in August 1933. He made 11 Third Division (South) appearances before joining Grantham in August 1934, then played for Peterborough United. Later a grocer in his native Cleethorpes, he died shortly after his 90th birthday in February 1994.

FRED WILSON (1)

Inside-right Fred Wilson briefly appeared for Bournemouth early in the 1933-34 season. Initially with Bowness Rovers near his native Windermere, he turned professional with Bolton Wanderers and made his First Division debut in their 4-2 defeat at home to Sheffield Wednesday in January 1932. He scored in that season's 8-1 win over Liverpool, moving to Cherries in August 1933. His only goal in three League games came in the following month's 3-1 defeat at home to Cardiff. He joined Barnsley in January 1934, then played for Lancaster Town, where top scorer in 1935-36. Settling in Lancaster, he died in December 1982.

FRED WILSON (2)

Commanding centre-half Fred Wilson was a key figure in Cherries' 1947-48 promotion near-miss. Starting with Wolves, he moved to Bournemouth in May 1937 and made his League debut in the 0-0 draw at home to Clapton Orient in March 1939, the first appearance of the famed defensive quartet with Ken Bird, Fred Marsden and Joe Sanaghan. He helped win the Third Division (South) Cup in 1946 and was ever-present in 1946-47, making 98 League appearances before joining Weymouth in July 1951. Later a partner of Bailey & Wilson bookmakers, then a security guard at BDH Chemicals in Poole, he died in December 1993.

GEORGE WILSON

Irish goalkeeper George Wilson was a key figure as Cherries took eventual winners Bolton Wanderers to an FA Cup fourth round replay in 1925-26. Initially with Dublin Amateurs, he had spells with Bohemians, Holyhead and Clapton Orient before joining Bournemouth in June 1924. He made his League debut in the 3-1 defeat at Millwall two months later, playing 81 Third Division (South) games while at Dean Court prior to joining Witton Albion in August 1926. Later with Connah's Quay, New Brighton, Notts County, Mold Town, Llanelli, Waterford, Bray Unknowns, Belfast Celtic and Larne, he eventually settled back in Dublin.

MARC WILSON

Republic of Ireland U-21 defender Marc Wilson had two loan spells at AFC Bournemouth. He turned professional with Portsmouth in July 2005 and made his League debut on loan to Yeovil Town in March 2006. Loaned to Cherries in January 2007, he returned on loan in September 2007 and netted three goals in 26 League games overall. He was also loaned to Luton Town and unlucky not to play for Pompey in the 2010 FA Cup final due to injury. Moving to Tony Pulis' Stoke City in an exchange deal involving Liam Lawrence and Dave Kitson, he was an FA Cup finalist in 2011 and has gained full international honours.

JOHN WINGATE

Versatile midfielder John Wingate was a member of Trevor Hartley's squad at AFC Bournemouth. A former Exeter City junior, he had spells with Torquay United, Newton Abbot Spurs, Budleigh Salterton, Dawlish Town and Plymouth Argyle prior to rejoining Exeter City in February 1969. He moved to Dean Court in exchange for John Rutter in July 1974 and netted three goals in 33 League games for Cherries, returning to Exeter in July 1975. Later with Bideford and Falmouth, he became a partner in his family's Cornish Candy confectionery business, then a tennis coach at East Devon Tennis Centre in Exmouth.

HARRY WINGHAM

Right-back Harry Wingham featured in Cherries' first-ever Football League match at Swindon in August 1923. Born in Selsey, he played for Woolston and Thorneycrofts before moving to Dean Court in August 1921. He formed an effective partnership with James Lamb as Cherries finished Southern League runners-up in 1922-23, making 18 Third Division (South) appearances before joining Clapton Orient in May 1924. Moving to Norwich City in July 1925, he later played for Salisbury and became a committee member at Cowes, residing in Cowes until his death in April 1969. His son Ashley appeared for Newport (IW).

JIMMY WOOD

Flying outside-right Jimmy Wood appeared for Cherries during the 1926-27 campaign. Starting with Crompton Albion in the Oldham Amateur League, he impressed with Hyde United, joining Bournemouth in August 1926. He made his League debut in the following month's 2-0 defeat at Swindon Town, with his solitary goal in seven League games coming in Cherries' 6-2 victory at home to QPR. Returning to Hyde, he moved to West Ham in July 1929 and gained top-flight experience. He was an FA Cup semi-finalist in 1933 and joined Crystal Palace in June 1935. Settling in his native Oldham, he died in December 1947.

PAUL WOOD

Winger Paul Wood scored in Cherries' 1991-92 FA Cup third round replay victory at Newcastle United. Initially with Portsmouth, he helped them regain top-flight status in 1986-87, then was a promotion winner again with Brighton in 1987-88 and Sheffield United in 1989-90. He joined AFC Bournemouth for £40,000 in October 1991 after a loan spell, netting 18 goals in 99 League games before returning to Portsmouth for £40,000 in February 1994. Later with Hong Kong side Happy Valley, Andover and Havant & Waterlooville, where 'Player of the Year' in 2001-02, he has since worked as a local painter and decorator.

CHARLIE WOODS

Young inside-right Charlie Woods partnered Jimmy Singer and Denis Coughlin in Cherries' attack. Starting with Cleator Moor Celtic, he joined Newcastle United in May 1959 and scored on his First Division debut. He moved to Bournemouth in November 1962, netting 26 goals in 70 League games prior to joining Crystal Palace in November 1964. Reunited with Bill McGarry at Ipswich Town in July 1966, he joined Watford in June 1970, then was youth coach at Blackburn Rovers and Ipswich. He was later chief scout at Ipswich until May 1998, then Tottenham Hotspur, reuniting with Bobby Robson at Newcastle United.

DAI WOODWARD

Welsh wing-half Dai Woodward gave Cherries fine service in various capacities over 25 years at Dean Court. Real name Laurie, he began with Wolves and was loaned to Walsall, helping reach the FA Cup fifth round in 1938-39. He followed several other 'Buckley Babes' to Bournemouth in May 1939 and helped win the Third Division (South) Cup in 1946, then narrowly miss promotion in 1947-48. Scoring seven goals in 275 League games, he remained on Cherries' coaching staff until June 1964 and had a testimonial match against Arsenal. He was a painter and decorator until July 1988 and died locally in December 1997.

ARNOLD WOOLLARD

Cultured left-back Arnold Woollard helped Cherries reach the FA Cup sixth round in 1956-57. Born in Bermuda, he played for Hamilton and Bermuda AA prior to joining Northampton Town in August 1949. He had a spell with Peterborough United, starring in their 1952-53 FA Cup run, before joining Newcastle United for £5,000 in December 1952. Moving to Bournemouth for £2,000 in June 1956, he played 161 League games, rejoining Northampton in exchange for Ron Spelman in March 1962. He worked for the Bank of Butterfield back in Bermuda and returned to England in 1988, settling near Newport Pagnell.

DAVE WOOZLEY

Young central defender Dave Woozley had a loan spell at AFC Bournemouth during the 2000-01 season He turned professional with Crystal Palace in November 1997 and was loaned to Cherries in September 2000, making six Second Division appearances while at Dean Court. Joining Torquay United in March 2002, after a loan spell, he featured in their 2003-04 promotion campaign, then played for Oxford United, Yeovil Town, Crawley Town and Farnborough Town. He was a promotion winner with Windsor & Eton in 2009-10 and Slough Town in 2013-14, since appearing for Binfield and working in the fire service.

REG WRIGHT

Left-back Reg Wright played alongside Jack Hayward in Cherries' defence. Signing professional for Sheffield Wednesday in July 1921, he had spells with Worksop Town and Blackpool before moving to Bournemouth in June 1928. He made 31 Third Division (South) appearances, reuniting with Teddy Davison at Chesterfield in June 1931. Later with Frickley Colliery, Worksop, Buxton and Mosborough Trinity, he linked up with Davison again as Sheffield United's trainer in July 1936. He was Wednesday's trainer-coach, then assisted Davison at Chesterfield. Settling in Chesterfield, he died in January 1973.

ANDY YOUNG

Experienced centre-half Andy Young briefly appeared for Bournemouth during the 1927-28 campaign. Initially a forward with Blyth Spartans, he joined Aston Villa in November 1919 and contested a first-team slot with Billy Kirton, Harry Hampton and Billy Walker. He moved to Arsenal in March 1922 and switched to a defensive role, helping their reserve team to twice win the London Combination title. Reunited with Leslie Knighton at Dean Court in June 1927, he played two Third Division (South) games for Cherries before joining Kidderminster Harriers in July 1928. He settled in Birmingham and died in February 1975.

BOB YOUNG

Reliable left-back Bob Young understudied Joe Sanaghan as Cherries finished Third Division (South) runners-up in 1947-48. Born locally, the elder brother of Ron Young, he turned professional at Dean Court in January 1946 and made his solitary League appearance for Bournemouth in the 5-0 victory at home to Newport County in September 1947. He moved to Crewe Alexandra in June 1948 and secured a regular first-team slot at Gresty Road. Joining Corby Town in July 1952, managed by former Cherries winger Wally Akers, his career was curtailed by a knee injury soon afterwards and he emigrated to Australia.

NEIL YOUNG

Long-serving right-back Neil Young featured in AFC Bournemouth's 2002-03 Third Division play-off final triumph. The elder brother of England international Luke Young, he turned professional with Spurs in August 1991 but failed to secure a first-team slot and moved to Dean Court in October 1994. He starred in Cherries' 1994-95 relegation escape and appeared in the 1998 Auto Windscreens Shield final. Sidelined by a knee problem, he had a loan spell at Jason Tindall's Weymouth and netted four goals in 429 League games before leaving in May 2008. He joined Cumbernauld United and became a youth coach in Adelaide.

RON YOUNG

Right-half Ron Young helped Cherries finish third in the Third Division (South) in 1948-49. Born locally, he was an amateur with Southampton before turning professional at Dean Court in June 1948. He made his League debut in Bournemouth's 5-0 victory at home to Torquay United six months later, when Doug McGibbon scored four goals. Contesting a first-team slot with Dai Woodward, he made 18 League appearances prior to joining Chelmsford City in July 1950. Later with Dorchester Town and Poole Town, he was an area manager for a dental supply company and remained local until his death in March 1991.

STEPHANE ZUBAR

Guadeloupe international defender Stephane Zubar was a fringe member of AFC Bournemouth's 2012-13 promotion squad. The younger brother of former Wolves player Ronald Zubar, he began with Caen and had loan spells with Par and Brussels before helping Vaslui to reach the 2010 Rumanian Cup final. Moving to Plymouth Argyle in November 2010, he joined Cherries in September 2011 and made his international debut in the 2011 CONCACAF Gold Cup. He remains a fringe member of Eddie Howe's squad and has made 24 League appearances for AFC Bournemouth, since loaned to Bury, Port Vale and York City.